A History of Chinese Martial Arts

Chinese martial arts have a long, meaningful history and deep cultural roots. They blend the physical components of combat with strategy, philosophy and tradition, distinguishing them from Western sports.

A History of Chinese Martial Arts is the most authoritative study ever written on this topic, featuring contributions from leading Chinese scholars and practitioners. The book provides a comprehensive overview of all types of Chinese martial arts, from the Pre-Qin Period (before 221 BC) right up to the present day in the People's Republic of China, with each chapter covering a different period in Chinese history. Including numerous illustrations of artefacts, weaponry and historical drawings and documents, this book offers unparalleled insight into the origins, development and contemporary significance of martial arts in China.

This is a fascinating read for researchers and students working in sports history, Chinese sport and Chinese Studies.

Fuhua Huang is Professor of Sport History at Jiangxi Normal University, China.

Fan Hong is Professor in Asian Studies at Bangor University, UK and Academic Editor of *The International Journal of the History of Sport*.

Routledge Research in Sports History

The *Routledge Research in Sports History* series presents leading research in the development and historical significance of modern sport through a collection of historiographical, regional and thematic studies which span a variety of periods, sports and geographical areas. Showcasing ground-breaking, cross-disciplinary work from established and emerging sport historians, the series provides a crucial contribution to the wider study of sport and society.

Available in this series:

7 **Taekwondo**
  From a Martial Art to a Martial Sport
  Udo Moenig

8 **The Black Press and Black Baseball, 1915–1955**
  A Devil's Bargain
  Brian Carroll

9 **Football and Literature in South America**
  David Wood

10 **Cricket: A Political History of the Global Game, 1945–2017**
  Stephen Wagg

11 **Wrestling in Britain**
  Sporting Entertainments, Celebrity and Audiences
  Benjamin Litherland

12 **A History of Chinese Martial Arts**
  Translated and edited by Fuhua Huang and Fan Hong

www.routledge.com/sport/series/RRSH

Chinese Fund for the Humanities and Social Sciences

A History of Chinese Martial Arts

Research Institute of Martial Arts, Ministry of Sport of China

Translated and edited by
Fuhua Huang and Fan Hong

LONDON AND NEW YORK

First published in English 2019
by Routledge
2 Park Square, Milton Park, Abingdon, Oxon OX14 4RN

and by Routledge
711 Third Avenue, New York, NY 10017

Routledge is an imprint of the Taylor & Francis Group, an informa business

© 2019 selection and editorial matter, Fuhua Huang and Fan Hong; individual chapters, the contributors

The right of Fuhua Huang and Fan Hong to be identified as the authors of the editorial matter, and of the authors for their individual chapters, has been asserted in accordance with sections 77 and 78 of the Copyright, Designs and Patents Act 1988.

All rights reserved. No part of this book may be reprinted or reproduced or utilized in any form or by any electronic, mechanical, or other means, now known or hereafter invented, including photocopying and recording, or in any information storage or retrieval system, without permission in writing from the publishers.

Trademark notice: Product or corporate names may be trademarks or registered trademarks, and are used only for identification and explanation without intent to infringe.

Published in Mandarin by People's Sports Press 1997

British Library Cataloguing-in-Publication Data
A catalogue record for this book is available from the British Library

Library of Congress Cataloging-in-Publication Data
A catalog record has been requested for this book

ISBN: 978-1-138-64558-5 (hbk)
ISBN: 978-1-315-62807-3 (ebk)

Typeset in Goudy
by Wearset Ltd, Boldon, Tyne and Wear

Contents

List of illustrations		vi
List of contributors		ix
Foreword to the first edition		xi
Preface		xiii
Acknowledgements		xv
List of abbreviations		xvi
1	Martial arts in the pre-Qin period (before 221 BC)	1
2	Martial arts in the Qin and Han dynasties and Three Kingdoms period (221 BC–280)	45
3	Martial arts in the Jin and the Southern and Northern dynasties (265–589)	66
4	Martial arts in the Sui, Tang, and Five Dynasties and Ten Kingdoms period (581–979)	82
5	Martial arts in the Song dynasty (960–1279)	107
6	Martial arts in the Liao, Jin, Western Xia, and Yuan dynasties (916–1368)	126
7	Martial arts in the Ming dynasty (1368–1644)	139
8	Martial arts in the Qing dynasty (1644–1911)	160
9	Martial arts in the Republic of China (1912–1949)	176
10	Martial arts in the People's Republic of China (1949–)	189
	Index	211

Illustrations

Figures

1.1	An image of martial dance in a primitive rock painting in Cangyuan County, Yunnan Province	4
1.2	A wooden spearhead from the Neolithic Age, excavated in the Hemudu ruins in Yuyao, Zhejiang Province	6
1.3	An image of a seven-hole broadsword from the Neolithic Age, excavated in Nanjing, Jiangsu Province	6
1.4	An image of a stone axe on a painted pottery vat from the Neolithic Age, excavated in Linru, Henan Province	7
1.5	Bronze dagger-axes with crooked blades from the Shang dynasty, Liaoning Provincial Museum	10
1.6	Bronze dagger-axes from the Western Zhou dynasty, Tianjin Museum	11
1.7	A mid-Shang dynasty bronze halberd, excavated in Taixi Village in Gaocheng, Hebei Province	12
1.8	A halberd with three bronze spearheads from the Warring States period, excavated in Sui County, Hubei Province	13
1.9	A bronze lance from the Warring States period, excavated in Sui County, Hubei Province	14
1.10	A restored image of a crossbow from the Warring States period, excavated in Changsha, Hunan Province	16
1.11	Jing Ke's assassination attempt on Emperor Yingzheng of Qin, a stone inscription in Wushi Temple in Jiaxiang, Shandong Province	26
1.12	A sword of a king named Fuchai of the State of Wu in Warring States, Hubei Provincial Museum	27
1.13	Various bronze dagger-axes of the Ba and Shu peoples in the Warring States period	36
1.14	A bronze broadax from the Warring States period, excavated in Qinhuangdao, Hebei Province	37
1.15	Rock paintings of martial dance from Guangxi Province painted between the Warring States period and the Qin and Han dynasties	38

1.16	A bronze plate from the Han dynasty, excavated in Yunnan Province	39
2.1	An image of Han dynasty swordplay	50
2.2	An image of two men fighting from the Han dynasty, excavated in Tanghe, Henan Province	50
2.3	Halberd vs. sword fights from the Han dynasty, excavated in Tongshan County, Jiangsu Province	51
2.4	An image of strength training from the Han dynasty excavated in Xuzhou, Jiangsu Province	53
2.5	A Jiaodi mural excavated in Mi County, Henan Province	53
2.6	An image of silk painting of Jiaodi from the Western Han dynasty excavated in Lingyi, Shandong Province	55
2.7	A wooden comb with lacquer painting of Jiaodi from the Qin dynasty excavated in Phoenix Mountain in Jiangling County, Hubei Province	55
2.8	Bronze swords in the Terracotta Warriors vaults	57
2.9	An image of sitting on the ground to draw a crossbow from the Han dynasty, excavated in Yinan County, Shandong Province	61
3.1	A Dunhuang mural of fighting between heavy cavalry and infantry during the Western Wei dynasty, number 285 mural in Dunhuang, Gansu Province	67
3.2	Two iron ring-headed sabres in Nanyang, Henan Province	68
3.3	A mural of horseback archery from the Sui dynasty excavated in Ji'an, Jilin Province	69
3.4	A Jiaodi mural from the Northern Zhou, number 290 mural in Dunhuang, Gansu Province	71
4.1	A Buddhist silk painting from the Tang dynasty excavated in Mogao Grottoes	88
4.2	A Dunhuang mural of archery during the Tang dynasty, number 346 mural in Dunhuang, Gansu Province	90
4.3	A silk flower with shooting pattern from the Tang dynasty excavated in Turpan, Xinjiang	91
4.4	Various iron arrowheads from the Sui and Tang dynasties	93
4.5	A brick painting of soldiers walking with spears and shields from the Sui dynasty, excavated in Lu'an, Anhui province	95
4.6	An image of officials standing with walking sabre from the tomb of the Tang dynasty excavated in Xianyang, Shaanxi Province	98
4.7	A Dunhuang mural of martial skills practicing during the Tang dynasty, number 217 mural in Dunhuang, Gansu Province	101
5.1	Bows from the Song dynasty	111
5.2	Chuang Crossbow with three bows	112

5.3	Sabres from the Song dynasty	113
5.4	Various spears used by infantry and cavalry	114
5.5	Miscellaneous weapons (part) in the Song dynasty	116
6.1	Battle picture of the Yuan army	129
6.2	Archery picture of Emperor Shizu of Yuan and his followers, National Palace Museum	129
7.1	Shaolin Cudgel Skills from the Ming dynasty	144
7.2	Practicing sabres displayed by Cheng Zongyou in the Ming dynasty	149
7.3	Thirty-two Forms of Quan Treatise (part) from the Ming dynasty	153
8.1	Miscellaneous weapons one in the Qing dynasty (part one)	161
8.2	Miscellaneous weapons in the Qing dynasty (part two)	162

Table

| 10.1 | Competitions of martial arts forms at the national level between 1953 and 1997 | 200 |

Contributors

Consultant

Xu Cai, Former President of the Chinese Martial Arts Association

Zhang Wenguang, Professor of Martial Arts at Beijing Sport University, China

Zhou Xikuan, Professor of Sport History of Chengdu Institute of Physical Education, China

Editor-in-chief

Zhang Yaoting, Dean of the Research Institute of Martial Arts, the Ministry of Sport of China

Deputy editors-in-chief

Zhang Shan, Deputy Dean of the Research Institute of Martial Arts, the Ministry of Sport of China

Cai Longyun, Former Vice President of the Chinese Martial Arts Association

Chang Cang, Editor-in-Chief of the journal of the *Chinese Martial Arts* since 1982

Kuang Wennan, Professor of Sport History of the Chengdu Institute of Physical Education, China

Xi Yuntai, Professor of Martial Arts of the Chengdu Institute of Physical Education, China

Xia Bohua, Director of the Research Department of the Research Institute of Martial Arts, the Ministry of Sport of China

Wang Yulong, Deputy Director of the Research Department of the Research Institute of Martial Arts, the Ministry of Sport of China

Editorial committee

Ma Mingda, Professor of Cultural History of Ji'nan University, China

Xi Yuntai, Professor of Martial Arts of the Chengdu Institute of Physical Education, China

Wang Yulong, Deputy Director of the Research Department of the Research Institute of Martial Arts, the Ministry of Sport of China

Liu Wanchun, Member of the Chinese Martial Arts Association

Yang Shaoyu, Professor of Gymnastics of the Capital Normal University, China

Kuang Wennan, Professor of Sport History of the Chengdu Institute of Physical Education, China

Zhang Shan, Deputy Dean of the Research Institute of Martial Arts, the Ministry of Sport of China

Zhang Xuanhui, Associate Professor of Martial Arts of the Chengdu Institute of Physical Education, China

Zhang Yaoting, Dean of the Research Institute of Martial Arts, the Ministry of Sport of China

Lin Boyuan, Professor of Martial Arts of Beijing Sport University, China

Chang Cang, Editor-in-Chief of the journal of *Chinese Martial Arts* since 1982

Hao Xinlian, Member of the Chinese Martial Arts Association

Xia Bohua, Director of the Research Department of the Research Institute of Martial Arts, the Ministry of Sport of China

Kang Gewu, Secretary-general of the Research Institute of Martial Arts, the Ministry of Sport of China

Cheng Dali, Associate Professor of the Chengdu Institute of Physical Education, China

Cai Longyun, Former Vice President of the Chinese Martial Arts Association

Foreword to the first edition

Martial arts are a form of preeminent traditional culture of the Chinese nation. Since ancient times, they have been recognized as the quintessence or treasure of Chinese culture and the martial spirit of the Chinese nation. Why? Because they have a long history and profound connotations. Martial arts have played an indispensable role in the survival and growth of the Chinese nation throughout history. They still maintain multiple functions, such as enhancing physical fitness, self-defence, and self-cultivation, as well as entertainment.

Inquiries concerning the long history and profound meaning of Chinese martial arts may arise. The aim of *A History of Chinese Martial Arts* is to answer these questions in a comprehensive way. In so doing, the editorial committee has been committed to employing various historical sources and referring to the remarkable works published previously.

In brief, Chinese martial arts originated from our ancestors' fighting experience with nature and with other tribes, and evolved, coexisted, and became embedded with the development of Chinese philosophy, military science, education, medicine, aesthetics, and other health sciences, and have a long history and profound connotations.

It has not been easy to produce this book. Although it has taken over two years, with contributions from a number of scholars and veteran practitioners, the book is not an ideal work in its current form. But the committee has tried its best.

Overseen by Xu Cai and Zhang Yaoting of the Research Institute of Martial Arts (RIMA), Xia Bohua and Wang Yulong of the RIMA Research Department were responsible for working out the objectives, outline, styles, and sources of the book. The proposal was completed with the participation of Ma Mingda, Xi Yuntai, Liu Wanchun, Kuang Wennan, Yang Shaoyu, Lin Boyuan, Hao Xinlian and Kang Gewu. The book was authored by Professor Kuang Wennan (Chapters 1, 3, and 6), Associate Professor Cheng Dali (Chapters 2 and 4), Associate Professor Zhang Xuanhui (Chapter 5), Professor Xi Yuntai (Chapter 7), Associate Research Fellow Kang Gewu (Chapters 8 and 9), and Research Fellow Hao Xinlian (Chapter 10).

More than 30 martial arts experts and practitioners were invited to Beijing to give their suggestions during a forum convened by Zhang Yaoting. Overseen by

Zhang Shan, the chapters were compiled and edited by Kuang Wennan, Chang Cang, and Hao Xinlian in Chengdu, Sichuan Province. The manuscript was reviewed by Zhang Shan, Xia Bohua, and Wang Yulong and revised by Chang Cang accordingly. The final manuscript was reviewed by Zhang Yaoting. The illustrations were selected by Dr. Cui Lequan of China Sports Museum and Zhang Xiaoqin of the RIMA. In addition, the committee received great assistance from Zhai Jinsheng, Lei Daxie, Liu Tongwei, Liu Taifu, Pan Yijing and Han Jianming.

Historiography is a huge project. Writing the history of Chinese martial arts is like boating in the ocean. Therefore, the book inevitably contains mistakes and bias. The committee welcomes comments, criticism and suggestions from both Chinese and non-Chinese scholars in the field of martial arts and historical studies.

Editorial Committee
December 1994

Preface

After a couple of years of effort from the Research Institute of Martial Arts (RIMA) under the Ministry of Sport of China (MSC), A History of Chinese Martial Arts is now on the way to be published. Editor-in-chief Zhang Yaoting invited me to write a preface for the book, and I am very happy to take this opportunity to say a few words.

I am keen on martial arts and indebted to them. I began to practice martial arts in childhood, but didn't have a master to teach me. I learned the simplified Taijiquan and swordsmanship while studying at Tsinghua University, and I have been practicing since then. It has become a very good form of physical exercise for me, and I feel energetic and indefatigable at work, though I am over 50 years old now. I have expressed my own positive opinions on Chinese martial arts on different occasions. Chinese martial arts have a very long history and a rich variety of forms. Martial arts are a splendid traditional sport embedded with the growth of the Chinese nation. They have played different roles in different historical phases. In the primitive age, martial arts originated, developed, and turned into an indispensable means for Chinese people to survive in fighting with nature and other tribes. Before the advent of firearms, martial arts were the paramount weapon for the Chinese people to resist invasion and consolidate state sovereignty. Nowadays, martial arts have inevitably been replaced by high-tech weapons in the military domain. However, martial arts remain popular among normal people for fitness, self-defence, and self-cultivation.

Chinese martial arts have survived and thrived in competitive natural and social environments for thousands of years and they have demonstrated their unique value. Martial arts are not merely forms of fighting skill, but forms of excellent traditional Chinese culture. They are not only closely related to humanities and social sciences, such as Chinese literature, history, and philosophy, but also to natural sciences and folk remedies, such as human kinetics and Chinese medicine.

In general, the term 'martial arts' carries more profound connotations than does 'sport' (a term introduced from Western countries). Chinese martial arts are also distinct from Western sports. Western sports stress external body movements, drawing heavily on knowledge of medicine and anatomy. However,

Chinese martial arts advocate the integration of internal breath exercise, to achieve 'Oneness of Heaven and Men' alongside external body movements. Therefore, martial arts are an advanced scientific sporting form. In this sense, we can say that martial arts originated in China but belong to the world, and martial arts are a kind of sport but more than a game.

Chinese government has always cherished the development of martial arts. A number of state leaders of the past generation, such as Mao Zedong, Zhu De, Liu Shaoqi, Chen Yi, and He Long, have left important instructions for the inheritance and development of Chinese martial arts, and President Deng Xiaoping famously inscribed a banner for Japanese friends, reading 'Taijiquan is Great!'. In the early 1980s, the MSC employed more than 8,000 people and spent three years and a large sum of money to classify the existing martial arts throughout the country. Li Menghua, former director of the MSC, said, 'we must try to put all our effort to develop martial arts.' The 8th National Games in 1997 included 28 sports – 27 Olympic sports, and martial arts.

I am confident that Chinese martial arts will grow further in popularity with the implementation of the *Sport for All Plan* of China, and will be accepted by the world. One can say that martial arts are a great act of devotion for the healthy and happy life of all mankind, dedicated by the Chinese nation.

We should be aware that the study of martial arts is no more straightforward than that of other sports. I hope that Chinese martial arts continue to proliferate. I believe that they will take a leap, both technically and theoretically, with the hard work of practitioners and participants.

The publication of *A History of Chinese Martial Arts* is the start of this progress. Let Chinese martial arts take another step forward in serving all the people of China and the world! We would be pleased and proud to see it happening.

Wu Shaozu
Minister of Sport of China

Acknowledgements

This book is an unusual product. The original book was published in Chinese in 1996 and its originality and rich historical sources were very well received by people in China and Asian countries. After more than 20 years of its original publication, with the encouragement and financial support of the Chinese Fund for the Humanities and Social Sciences, we now translate and edit the book into English and introduce it to the English speaking world. We hope it will help people who are interested in Chinese martial arts to understand its origin and development from the ancient time to the present. We hope it will serve as a reference book to provide researchers original sources to advance their research on Chinese culture, history, and martial arts.

We would like to take this opportunity to thank the Chinese Fund for the Humanities and Social Sciences for its financial support; the People's Sports Press for authorizing us to translate and edit the Chinese version of the book into English; Routledge for giving us the opportunity to publish the book, especially, Jonathan Manley, Simon Whitmore, Cecily Davey and Rebecca Connor, for their patience and professional assistance.

We are deeply beholden to a number of people who have been involved in producing this book at different stages. Special thanks go to Prof. Cui Lequan (General Administration of Sport), Prof. Luo Shiming (Soochow University), Prof. Tan Hua (South China Normal University), Prof. Zheng Guohua (Shanghai University of Sport), Prof. He Qun (China Foreign Affairs University) and colleagues and students at Jiangxi Normal University: Dr. Zhang Huijie, Prof. Luo Lin, Prof. Dai Yongguan, Associate Prof. Cao Yingchun, Yu Ao'nan, Xiao Wenyan, Liu Xiaofang, Zhou Fengchun and Dr. Liu Chuqun.

Fuhua Huang and Fan Hong
May 2018

Abbreviations

ACSF	All-China Sports Federation
CCP	Chinese Communist Party
CMAA	Chinese Martial Arts Association
GACM	General Administration of Chinese Medicine
MAMC	Martial Arts Management Center
MEC	Ministry of Education of China
MSC	Ministry of Sport of China
NGO	Non-governmental Organization
NPC	National People's Congress
PRC	People's Republic of China
RIMA	Research Institute of Martial Arts

Chapter 1

Martial arts in the pre-Qin period (before 221 BC)

Chinese martial arts have a long history. As early as the pre-Qin period, martial arts had developed into a clear form based on their primitive origin. This period spans from the uncivilized primitive age to the Xia dynasty (c.2070–1600 BC), through the Shang dynasty (c.1600–1046 BC) and the Zhou dynasty (c.1046–221 BC), until the end of the Spring and Autumn (c.770–476 BC) and Warring States (c.475–221 BC) periods; that is, before the unification of the Qin dynasty (221–207 BC) and the Han dynasty (202 BC–AD 220). Chinese martial arts are integral to the treasury of Eastern culture. They originated and developed closely alongside Chinese civilization and constitute a significant part of the cultural history of China.

The origin of Chinese martial arts

Primitive society in China began with the appearance of Sinanthropus approximately 600,000–70,000 years ago, and ran through the unclearly recorded era of the Huangdi, Yandi, Yaodi and Shundi to the Xia dynasty. During this long period, martial arts started to sprout and develop with the beginning of human civilization. Tactical fighting is the most fundamental feature of martial arts. Therefore, the study of the origin of martial arts entails beginning with an exploration of the emergence of these tactical fighting arts.

Tactical fighting arts emerged in the struggles for survival

In primitive society, people inhabited a vast wilderness. *Hanfeizi* notes that there were far more beasts than human beings.[1] The fossils also show that there were a large number of beasts with incisors, in particular the ferocious sabre-toothed tiger. *Huainanzi* writes that in ancient times, predatory beasts ate people and violent birds were able to carry off the old and the weak.[2] *Classic of Mountains and Seas* records that wild boar and serpents were both perilous to mankind.[3] In the struggle for survival, the primary fight was with wild beasts. It was in these ruthless fights that tactical fighting arts took shape.

There were two major approaches in these tactical fighting arts: using bare hands, and using tools. As far back as the Paleolithic Age, essential unarmed fighting skills, such as running, jumping, dodging, rolling, punching and kicking, had been naturally and gradually developed in fights against animals. However, using tools was a more effective way to enable mankind to defeat beasts in the struggle for survival. A great deal of primitive stoneware, including stone hammers, stone knives, stone needle-nosed chisels and boneware, has been found in Sinanthropus deposits that are more than 600,000 years old, with some of the blades still sharp. Cudgels and stoneware were the most widely used instruments, but wooden weapons such as cudgels and spears tend to decay over time, so they may not have survived the centuries. These armed and unarmed fights inevitably resulted in the accumulation of fighting experience, though such experience remained fairly undeveloped. As tens of thousands of years went by, skills such as striking and stabbing, movement, and gestures of attacking and defending were eventually formed. In mastering these skills and movements, people gradually developed self-awareness in applying them. In this way, tactical fighting arts and the awareness of martial arts emerged. This struggle for survival was the origin of martial arts.

Primitive warfare triggered the emergence of martial arts

While the struggle for survival between mankind and beasts undoubtedly led to the emergence of tactical fighting arts, fighting between men was a catalyst for the emergence of martial arts in a more direct way. There have been inter-tribal fights for food and land and inter-personal fights for spouses for time immemorial. *Annals of Master Lv* notes that before Chiyou was born, people fought each other with tree trunks and branches, and that these fights commenced long ago, with any notion of banning these fights seemingly impractical.[4] This reveals that before the outbreak of large-scale inter-tribal warfare, people had already been fighting for leadership.

At the end of primitive society, warfare began to occur between clans, and the emergence of organized inter-tribal battles accelerated the formation of martial arts. Ancient books record wars such as these between Huangdi and Yandi and between Huangdi and Chiyou, and that Yudi conquered the Jiuli people and the Sanmiao people. These wars strongly facilitated the production of weapons and the origin and development of tactical fighting arts. Among numerous legends, Chiyou, a descendant of Yandi, was the most famous 'Man of War' and there are many legends about preliminary martial arts in relation to him. According to *Records of the Grand Historian*, Huangdi defeated Yandi through three great battles in the vicinity of Banquan.[5] Chiyou disobeyed Huangdi and launched an armed rebellion. Huangdi then sent all his dukes and armies to fight against Chiyou in the vicinity of Zhuolu, and eventually killed Chiyou. Chiyou was so intrepid that victory over him was only achieved at great cost. In ancient legends, people tend to attribute the invention of weapons to

Chiyou. *Book of Origins* records that Chiyou invented the Five Weapons, namely the dagger-axe, lance, halberd, short spear and long spear.[6] This indicates that warfare promoted the invention and development of weapons.

Chiyou was not only an inventor of weapons, but also a notable barehanded fighter. *Arowana Apocrypha* describes him as bronze-headed and with an iron forehead.[7] *Accounts of Marvels* says his ears were like swords and halberds, and his head protruded with horns.[8] In fighting with Huangdi, Chiyou rushed towards his enemies with his horned head, leaving his opponents helpless. This also suggests that primitive warfare to a great extent drove the origin and development of barehanded fighting skills such as catching, holding, tumbling, and striking.

The emerging sense of fighting and competition among people was another important landmark in the initial development of martial arts. *Annals of Master Yan* says that all objects with blood and breath have a sense of competition.[9] *Huainanzi* adds that all human beings are born with this sense.[10] These ancient works demonstrate the belief that competing and fighting is an embodiment of manliness.

Warfare in primitive society further reinforced this. There is a widely transmitted myth praising the martial spirit of primitive people: Xingtian, a descendant of Yandi, vied with Huangdi for leadership and power, and as a result was beheaded by Huangdi and sent to be buried on Changyang Mountain. However, he continued performing the Ganqi Dance,[11] with his nipples becoming eyes while his belly button became a mouth.[12] This myth states that Xingtian did not wish to stop fighting even after being beheaded. Therefore, Tao Yuanming (c.365–427) highly eulogized him in his *Thirteen Poems on the Classic of Mountains and Seas*, saying that Xingtian's Ganqi Dance immortalized his intense martial spirit.[13]

To meet the needs of primitive wars, people were required to undertake military manoeuvres in order to familiarize themselves with movements of striking and stabbing, as well as wearing any battle garments necessary on the battlefield. Consequently, martial dances (or war dances) were born. In the primitive age, martial dances were also martial arts, during which performers held a variety of weapons to practice various movements and gestures of striking and stabbing. Mere decades ago, martial dances could still be found in some still-primitive Chinese minority communities. These dances were not only rehearsals of the movements of striking and stabbing, but also functioned to propagate military power through martial performance. It is recorded in *Huainanzi* that Shundi defeated the rebellious Sanmiao people three times, but they did not surrender. Shundi then led his warriors to perform the Ganqi Dance in front of the Sanmiao. The dance exhibited the Shun army's great power and superb martial arts, and finally overwhelmed the stunned and frightened Sanmiao.[14]

In the ancient rock paintings still found all over the country, some images of preliminary martial arts can be found. For example, a rock painting in Cangyuan County in Yunnan Province shows warriors standing smartly in a horizontal

4 Pre-Qin period

Figure 1.1 An image of martial dance in a primitive rock painting in Cangyuan County, Yunnan Province.

line with short dagger-axes in their right hands. Some hold a square shield in one hand and a weapon with two wide ends and slim shaft in the other, their bent legs in a horse-stance squat style. Figure 1.1 provides vivid evidence of early martial arts.

Primitive religion, education, recreation and the origin of martial arts

In primitive forms of human culture, religion, education, and recreation were usually intertwined. This integrated pattern of primitive culture is closely related to the origin of martial arts. The two main forms of primitive religion, witchcraft and totemism, were usually embodied by martial dances. *Explaining Graphs and Analyzing Characters* describes witchcraft as a way of communication with gods, which is realized when the witches exert their imagination by dancing.[15] Martial dances played a significant role during witchcraft activities. Before or after hunting or warring, people performed martial dances in order to produce a sense of supernatural power and achieve victory by imagining that they were killing beasts and defeating enemies through performance of the movements of striking, stabbing or killing.

Martial dances in totemism were important activities in the sacrificial ceremonies of primitive tribes, who danced in a warlike manner to worship their earliest ancestors and gods. The engagement of primitive religion and martial arts can also be traced from some ethnic customs still in their original forms in modern times. For instance, for Dongbatiao, a martial dance practiced by the Nakhi people in Yunnan Province, thousands of people dance frenziedly with weapons in their hands in order to offer sacrifices to the gods. In some areas inhabited by the Dai people in Yunnan Province, people hold knives while dancing to defeat beasts at the annual Buddha-worshipping ceremony. In primitive sacrificial ceremonies, there is also another martial dance that mimics the images and movements of beasts. According to *Book of Documents*, a chieftain named Kui said: 'Come on! Let's rock the stone drums and dance like the movements of all kinds of beasts.' This may be a primitive form of Xingyiquan (See Chapter 8).[16]

In primitive religious activities, martial skills competitions incorporated with witchcraft also emerged. According to *Book of Origins*:

> People in the Ba County and Nan County [both in south-west China] didn't have a tribal leader. In order to manifest deities, they conducted a sword-throwing contest. The person who was able to throw a sword into a hole in rocks was selected as the tribal leader.[17]

It seems that conducting a sword-throwing contest for the purpose of manifesting deities can be regarded as the infancy of martial arts contests.

During primitive religious activities, education was often engaged with entertainment. Martial dances in the sacrificial ceremony were also an important component of education. *Rites of Zhou* notes that masters taught their warriors martial dances and led them to perform martial dances to worship the deities in the mountains and rivers.[18] Although these activities were conducted in the Western Zhou dynasty (c.1029–771 BC),[19] they mirrored primitive customs. *Records of the Grand Historian* records that 'starting from the era of Huangdi to the Qin dynasty ... contests had been held in the winter sacrificial ceremony'.[20] It is also cited in the work that the purpose of these contests was to make sacrifices to the gods.[21] Although there are no detailed records in the ancient works about the programme of the contests, there is no doubt that martial arts, which were in close relation with sacrificial ceremony, made up a part of these contests. Martial arts originated in and grew within the holistic culture of primitive society, which in turn constituted an important part of this culture.

The invention of primitive weapons

Using tools is the most important sign of the evolution of humankind. As human culture came into being and developed, so did the invention and improvement of tools. In primitive China, there was no boundary between tools and weapons. Wood and stones used to strike objects were regarded as tools, but became weapons in combat. The earliest primitive weapons were made of wood and stone. Archaeologist Jia Lanpo points out that for the Sinanthropus, the most useful hunting weapons were probably wooden cudgels and torches.[22] Primitive people lived in the jungle, so tree branches were most accessible to them. Therefore, wooden cudgels and spears fashioned from these branches were the earliest weapons made by mankind.

However, wood decayed easily, so these weapons were difficult to preserve. As depicted in Figure 1.2, the wooden spears excavated from the Hemudu ruins in Yuyao City in Zhejiang Province are among the few that remain. Additionally, archaeologists have discovered stone spearheads that date back to approximately 30,000 years ago. A spear was made when a wooden cudgel was fixed on the spearhead. The emergence of these compound weapons indicated great progress in the history of weapon production.

The sabre is also one of the earliest weapons. A lot of primitive stone sabres and bone sabres have been excavated from Sinanthropus sites. The primitive stone sabres in the Neolithic Age from about 10,000 years ago took various shapes, for instance rectangular, half-moon-shaped, and strip. At the back of the blades of some of these sabres, up to seven holes were drilled. If equipped with long handles, they became long-handle sabres that could be used to hack (see Figure 1.3). Other stone weapons that proliferated in the Neolithic Age include spears, spearheads, dagger-axes, axes, adzes, spades and mallets (see Figure 1.4).[23]

Figure 1.2 A wooden spearhead from the Neolithic Age, excavated in the Hemudu ruins in Yuyao, Zhejiang Province.

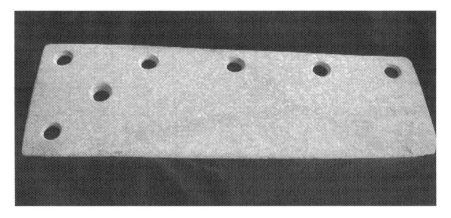

Figure 1.3 An image of a seven-hole broadsword from the Neolithic Age, excavated in Nanjing, Jiangsu Province.

Figure 1.4 An image of a stone axe on a painted pottery vat from the Neolithic Age, excavated in Linru, Henan Province.

A significant number of primitive stone axes in large and small sizes were also in use in primitive China. Most of these axes had a sharp double edge, taking the form of a trapezoid, rectangle or oval. Some had holders, while some had drills. They were devastating weapons capable of causing major injury if equipped with a long wooden handle. *Miscellaneous History of the State of Yue and Wu* also notes that jade weapons were used in the age of Huangdi, which has been verified by archaeologists.[24] As soon as weapons were put into use, people began to generate and accumulate experience using them, which was the germ of tactical fighting arts.

The invention of the bow and arrow greatly advanced the progress of weapons in primitive society. Engels argues that 'the bow and arrow was for savagery what the iron sword was for barbarism and firearms for civilization – the decisive weapon'.[25] The primitive Chinese people invented the bow and arrow about 30,000 years ago, and it is assumed that they were inspired by throwing spears and resilient tree branches.[26] They then combined spear with bow to invent the bow and arrow. The exquisite sharp stone arrowheads made of flint unearthed from Zhiyu Village in Shuo County, Shanxi Province are more than 20,000 years old. A great number of stone arrowheads and bone arrowheads from the Neolithic Age have been excavated, which indicates that the bow and arrow was a very popular weapon among the ancient Chinese. Ancient works also reveal that bows were used to launch ball-like objects. In *Miscellaneous History of the State of Yue and Wu*, an archer named Chen Yin mentions he has heard that the crossbow derives from the bow, while the bow derives from the slingshot.[27] *Spring and Autumn Annals of Wu and Yue* records a ballad said to be from the Huangdi era: 'Cut the bamboo to make the bow, trigger the projectiles, shoot the beasts'.[28]

Many primitive tribes also invented the spear-launcher to shoot spears a longer distance, implying that they were in desperate need of ranged weapons. *Book of Origins* records that officials appointed by the Huangdi were in charge of making arrows and bows.[29] This generally reflects the long history of the invention of the bow and arrow, and also highlights the great wisdom of the ancient Chinese people.

Ancient legends include many tales of archery, especially the tale of a skilful archer named Houyi, leader of the Yi people in the Xia dynasty, who was known for his excellent shooting skills. It was said that ten suns scorched the grass and trees, nine of which were shot by Houyi. He was also a good killer of vipers and beasts, inspiring all the people. These myths demonstrate that primitive people had considerable proficiency in archery, which enhanced their confidence to conquer nature. Meanwhile, myths eulogized heroes with superb martial skills.

Martial arts in the Shang and Zhou dynasties

The application and evolution of bronze weapons

In the Shang and Zhou dynasties, bronze manufacture achieved a high level. In addition to the ongoing wars, the development of military martial arts was significantly promoted, highlighted by the wide use and improvement of bronze weapons.

Chariot battle was the primary campaign mode in the Shang and Zhou dynasties. The use of the chariot in China dates back to the Xia dynasty more than 2,000 years ago. In the Shang dynasty, it made great progress. It is recorded in *Annals of Master Lv* that King Tang of Shang (c.1670–1587 BC) defeated the Xia people by using 70 superior chariots.[30] According to *Records of the Grand Historian*, the Western Zhou dynasty defeated the Shang dynasty by using 300 well-equipped chariots.[31] Ancient chariots consisted of two wheels, four horses and a square carriage which held three warriors. The warrior on the left was the chief. He held the bow and arrow and was mainly in charge of shooting. The warrior on the right held the dagger-axes and spears to attack. The warrior in the middle was in charge of controlling the chariot. Besides bow and arrow, weapons used in chariots mainly included dagger-axe, spear, halberd, and lance. *Classic of Poetry* says, 'The king is about to lead the armies to war, it is time we made dagger-axes and spears'; 'The king is about to lead the armies to war, it is time we made spears and halberds'.[32]

Dagger-axe, spear, and halberd were the most widely used weapons at that time. During chariot battles in the Shang and Zhou dynasties, the distance between opposing chariots was over four metres, so they couldn't kill or hurt each other unless their horses collided. Therefore, warriors couldn't fight their enemies until their chariots had intersected with each other. *Songs of Chu* depicts a lively scene of chariot battle: the warriors hold dagger-axes made in the State of Wu and wear armour, the chariots intersect with each other, and the warriors begin to fight with short weapons; many warring flags are waved in the air, the number of warriors is uncountable, arrows keep falling from the air, but the warriors keep striving to fight.[33]

The spear was an important type of long weapon in the Shang and Zhou dynasties. All the unearthed bronze spears from the Ruins of Yin (Shang dynasty) have double blades with two rings for buckling ribbons on the sleeve, and are exquisite and sharp. The blade of the bronze spear in the Zhou dynasty was longer, but the sleeve was a little shorter. There were two types of spears in the Zhou dynasty, based on length. The shorter spears were probably used in infantry battle, with the longer spears used in chariot battle. This change in spear shape during the Zhou dynasty demonstrates the improvement of stabbing skills.

Archaeological findings have shown that the dagger-axe was the most widely used bronze weapon during the Shang and Zhou dynasties. As depicted in Figure

1.5, the dagger-axe was a unique weapon in ancient times, and its cutting hook and sharp head were usually used to resist the enemy. There were two types of bronze dagger-axes in the Shang and Zhou dynasties, depending on how the wooden handle was fixed to the blades. For one kind of dagger-axe, the handle of the dagger was inside the wooden handle. This was made by chiselling the wooden handle and inserting the handle of the dagger into it. They were then fastened together tightly (see Figure 1.6). Another kind of bronze dagger-axe had the wooden handle inside a hole cast in the dagger. The first kind of dagger-axe was the most commonly used in practical combat, so most unearthed dagger-axes are that type.

A further evolution of the bronze dagger-axe in the Zhou dynasty involved elongating its lower end and increasing the number of the holes. Elongating the lower end enhanced its capacity for cutting and sawing, while increasing the number of holes further fastened the dagger and the wooden handle. This evolution reflects the development and improvement of dagger-axe skills. As the dagger-axe was the most widely used weapon in the Shang and Zhou dynasties, all Western Zhou dynasty warriors were required to practice using the shield to defend and the dagger-axe to attack. As late as the Spring and Autumn and Warring States periods, the dagger-axe was still an important bronze weapon.

Figure 1.5 Bronze dagger-axes with crooked blades from the Shang dynasty, Liaoning Provincial Museum.

Figure 1.6 Bronze dagger-axes from the Western Zhou dynasty, Tianjin Museum.

As a spear could only stab straight, whereas a dagger-axe could only hook and peck, people made an effort to combine the spear and dagger-axe to make a new weapon that could stab, hook and peck, thus inventing the halberd. The earliest halberds found so far were unearthed in an ancient Shang dynasty tomb in Taixi Village in Gaocheng, Hebei Province. Figure 1.7 shows the structure of a halberd with a bronze spearhead mounted on top of a wooden handle, below which is a lateral dagger-axe head. This shows that this kind of compound weapon was invented in the Shang dynasty. In the Western Zhou dynasty, a kind of cruciform bronze halberd cast with a bronze spear and bronze dagger-axe emerged. However, a larger number of halberds were mounted with both spear and dagger-axe. Their wooden handles decayed easily, therefore only the spearheads and dagger-axe heads can be unearthed. As a result, they are often mistakenly regarded as two separate weapons.

The halberd was first used as a main weapon in chariots in the Shang and Zhou dynasties, but it was not until the Spring and Autumn and Warring States periods that they became popular. Although a halberd could be used to stab, peck and cut, hooking with the lower blade was its major function. This can be verified by some of the unearthed bronze halberds, with their upper ends equipped with crooked blades rather than sharp spearheads (see Figure 1.8). *Annals of Master Yan* adds that a halberd can hook one's neck, and a sword can stab one's heart.[34]

The lance, one of the Five Weapons, was also in use in the Western Zhou dynasty. *Explaining the Ancient Characters* describes the lance as being about 2.8 m long without blade. Lances were used to separate two chariots when they

Figure 1.7 A mid-Shang dynasty bronze halberd, excavated in Taixi Village in Gaocheng, Hebei Province.

intersected with each other.[35] *Rites of Zhou* says a lance looks like a cudgel, about 7.4 m long.[36] However, the lance was not equal to a cudgel.

There are a good number of ball-like objects among the unearthed bronze weapons from the Western Zhou dynasty. Nails are cast on the surface of the ball, and a hole in the centre of the ball allows a wooden handle to be inserted, making a weapon that can be used to strike enemies. The balls are about 500–800 g in weight, with three to 18 nails. A lance was produced when a wooden handle was inserted into the bronze ball, and this could then be used as an attacking weapon in a chariot battle.

Lances were found among the weapons unearthed in an ancient tomb from the Warring States period in Sui County in Hubei Province. The heads of these lances are in the shape of a triangular pyramid, with a flower-ball-like band and a spiky-ball-like band at each end of the lance's handle. The handles are 3.4 m in length. The lance was used like a hammer to hit enemies (see Figure 1.9). Besides, those equipped with an acuminate object in the head are a derivative of lance.[37]

The sword, which originated in the Shang dynasty, plays a very important role in the history of Chinese martial arts. A chariot was equipped with three types of weapons, as found in Shang dynasty relics. The bow and arrow were long-range shooting weapons, whereas the dagger-axe and spear were used in melee. The sword, however, was used as a weapon of self-defence. As bronze

Pre-Qin period 13

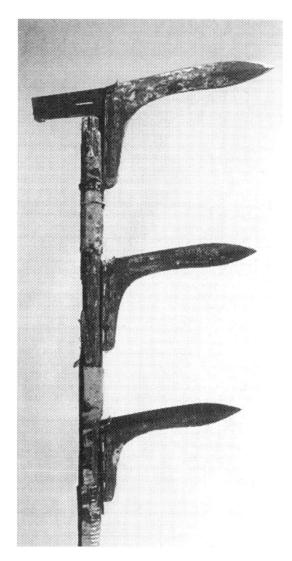

Figure 1.8 A halberd with three bronze spearheads from the Warring States period, excavated in Sui County, Hubei Province.

smelting technology improved during the Shang dynasty, people began to cast daggers. These looked roughly like sabres or spears, with a crooked handle that looked like the head of a horse or sheep. Both sides were sharp, about 30 cm long. In general, they are considered the earliest form of sword. In the Western Zhou dynasty, bronze swords were developed into various shapes, for instance with the appearance of horse heads and salix-leaves, or spiniform. As with those

14 Pre-Qin period

Figure 1.9 A bronze lance from the Warring States period, excavated in Sui County, Hubei Province.

in the Shang dynasty, they were short and used for self-defence in melee. The sword remained at an early stage of its evolution in the Shang and Zhou dynasties; it was not until the Spring and Autumn and Warring States period that swordsmanship took a leap forward.

Armour and shield, also as defensive weapons, took their earliest shape in the Shang and Zhou dynasties. In this period, armour was mainly made of leather, though there was also some smart-looking armour made of bronze. Shields were handheld weapons to ward off blades and stones. In the *Oracle*, there is a lively portrait depicting a warrior holding a spear in one hand and a rectangular shield in the other. By the time of the Zhou dynasty, shields had diversified into different forms. *Rites of Zhou* notes that five main types of shield of different sizes were in use in the Zhou dynasty.[38] They were also made of different materials, for example, wood or leather, and used in different modes of battle – chariot or infantry battle, for instance.

In Chinese history, the Shang and Zhou dynasties opened the first page of Chinese civilization and took it into the splendid bronze age. It is in this era that Chinese martial arts enter the period of culturalization. The diversification and advancement of bronze weapons set the scene for the glorious history of Chinese martial arts.

Unarmed combat and Jiaodi[39]

Although barehanded fighting had been budding since the primitive period, the skills and tactics for unarmed combat didn't take form until the Shang and Zhou dynasties. When ancient people went to fight or hunt, although they mainly relied on weapons in general circumstances, occasionally they had to fight hand to hand when their weapons were not available. As such, waiving weapons to fight barehanded became a form of martial contest to demonstrate power. It is recorded that King Jie of Xia (?–1595 BC) and King Zhou of Shang (c.1105–1046 BC), both of whom were the last king of their dynasty, had extraordinary strength. *Records of the Grand Historian* notes that Jie and Zhou managed to fight wolves with bare hands and chase down four horses; their strength was immense.[40] Zhou's extraordinary strength enabled him to defeat wild animals.[41] All these ancient writings praise the bravery and strength of fighting beasts with their bare hands. In the Western Zhou dynasty, field hunting, a way of fighting beasts, was adopted in military training. Certainly, people did not generally fight wild animals with bare hands, but they still tended to eulogize those heroes who did. For instance, *Classic of Poetry* depicts the younger brother of Duke Zhuang of Zheng (757–701 BC), a renowned politician in the Spring and Autumn period, beating a tiger to death without any weapons or armour, and then presenting it to the king.[42]

Nevertheless, the development of unarmed combat was mostly advanced by inter-personal combat. In the Shang and Zhou dynasties, Jiaodi and unarmed combat were among the most important military training modules. *Book of Rites* records that in the first month of winter, the king ordered his generals to train soldiers in martial arts, including archery, riding, and Jiaodi. They were also invited to compete in archery and riding with their arms and legs bare.[43] It shows that martial skills and strength were included in the examinations for recruiting soldiers in the Zhou dynasty, and that soldiers were required to attend military training that included Jiaodi.

Classic of Poetry indicates that in the people's eyes, a true man has strength and courage.[44] *Guanzi* notes that martial spirit prevailed at that time, and that the king called for recommendations of those who had a strong body and outstanding fighting skills and strength.[45] Unarmed combat was very popular in the Zhou dynasty. *Commentary of Zuo* records that Duke Wen of Jin (c.671/697–628 BC) dreamed that he defeated King Cheng of Chu (?–626 BC).[46]

16 Pre-Qin period

In the Zhou dynasty, adequate unarmed combat skills were indispensable in arresting criminals to subdue their resistance. *Rites of Zhou* says the principal mission of the official guard was to patrol and grapple with criminals.[47] *Book of Rites* says that in the first month of autumn, orders should be given to prepare prisons and instruments of torture to cope with criminals.[48] Criminals resisted when arrested, so unarmed combat and grappling skills were needed. This also reflects that unarmed combat developed to a higher level in the Zhou dynasty.

The development of archery and archery rites

The widespread use of bronze in the Shang and Zhou dynasties offered superior conditions for making arrows, which further promoted the development of archery. The unearthed bronze arrows in the Ruins of Yin are ridged in the middle and in inverted-beard style, which greatly improves killing ability. The *Oracle* indicates that certain officials were specifically in charge of archery, and that archery teams were an important part of armies in the Shang dynasty. During the Zhou dynasty, archery not only became an essential skill for a warrior, but also played an important role in the daily lives of ordinary people (see Figure 1.10). *Book of Rites* records that people would hang a bow on the left

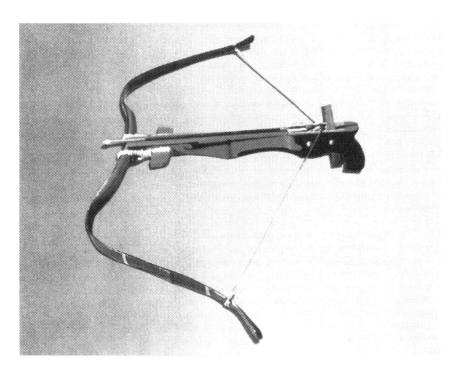

Figure 1.10 A restored image of a crossbow from the Warring States period, excavated in Changsha, Hunan Province.

side of the door if they had given birth to a boy. They would also shoot six arrows – one each to the heaven, the earth, the east, the south, the west, and the north – to proclaim that the boy would become a strong warrior dedicated to protecting their homeland.[49] In people's minds, all heroes were adept at archery. *Classic of Poetry* eulogizes Duke Zhuang of Lu (c.706–662 BC), saying that he was an excellent dancer and archer, all his four arrows could hit the centre point, and he was a hero that could defeat the enemies.[50]

The kings of the Zhou dynasty often practiced archery in order to inspire people to follow, and they gave orders to build archery ranges, known as archery cottages or archery palaces. The king usually gifted people of merit with exquisite bows and arrows. Archery was the primary examination in recruiting warriors throughout the country; *Book of Rites* writes that the dukes recommended potential archers to the king and the king then examined them in the archery palace, and that the king and dukes were all dedicated to practicing archery.[51]

Another notable feature of the development of archery in the Western Zhou dynasty was the formation of archery rites. Rites were extremely serious in the Zhou dynasty. Rites refer to the rules and norms that people in their daily lives abide by in order to regulate behaviour and maintain social order. As early as during late primitive society, people started to share the prey they had hunted with those in their social circle, rather than keep it for themselves. This is normally regarded as the birth of rites; *Book of Rites* shows rites emerging in the behavioural norms of eating and drinking.[52]

In the Zhou dynasty, many forms of rites developed, suggesting ideas of social hierarchies used to cultivate morality and maintain the sovereignty of kings. Various rites were conducted in sacrifices, funerals, and weddings in the Zhou dynasty. Since archery played an important role in social life, it was thereby integrated into the rites. Archery rites refer to the archery activities integrated with the sense of morality and rules. It is recorded in *Book of Rites* that archery is designated for men and combined with rites and might be the most appropriate routine to be integrated with rites in order to establish morality, which is why the king pays so much attention to it – indicating that archery rites were closely associated with moral education.[53] This may have been the infancy of martial virtue. Therefore, the requirements for archery rites, as noted in *Book of Rites*, were: in ritual archery, whether participants go forwards or backwards, whether they turn left or right, their actions must be well disciplined. They need to keep quiet in mind so as to hold the bow and arrows tightly and hit the target. That is why people say that one's inner virtue can be reflected in one's exterior archery actions.[54]

There were four types of archery rites in the Zhou dynasty. Dashe was held by the king and his dukes to select archers to perform in royal sacrificial ceremonies. Binshe was held by dukes before being received by the king or visiting each other. Yanshe was held by the king or dukes as entertainment during banquets. Xiangshe was held by the *dafu*[55] in rural drinking ceremonies. Archery contests during these drinking ceremonies were very popular.

These four kinds of archery rites were in reality archery contests. During archery rites in the Zhou dynasty, the king, the dukes, and the dafu or common people used different targets. The king used the Tiger Target, the dukes used the Bear Target, and the dafu used the Panther Target. Each archer was given four arrows. A number of staff were appointed to administrate the contests, from regulating contest rules to playing music during the event. In general, contests involved two teams. Each team selected one participant to compete against one participant from the other team, called paired. The losers were punished by being made to drink wine.

In fact, archery rites in the Western Zhou dynasty were a kind of institutionalized Chinese sporting competition dating back more than 2,000 years. They were not only significant for embedding body-building and morality in martial arts, but also had a rich entertainment function. Therefore, they became important cultural and recreational sporting activities in ancient times.

Martial dances in the Shang and Zhou dynasties

Culturally, in primitive society martial dances and martial arts were in essence the same thing. In the Shang and Zhou dynasties, despite martial dances and martial arts having demonstrated their own cultural characteristics and begun to demarcate from each other, it was sometimes still hard to completely distinguish between them, for the reason that the utility of the martial dancing was still of great importance, while the artistry had yet to be fully developed. Although martial dances were partly an expression of emotion and a form of recreation, they had a pragmatic function in the Shang and Zhou dynasties. Many combinations of movements in martial dances were very close to those in martial arts. *Xunzi* emphasizes that practicing martial dances with Ganqi in hand not only improved body-building and martial skills, but that these skills could also be applied in the battlefield. It greatly affirmed that martial dances were seen as having as much utility as martial arts.[56]

Dancing prevailed in the Shang dynasty, mostly applied to sacrificial ceremony and celebration. According to the *Oracle*, people in the Shang dynasty often danced to pray for rain and to make sacrifices to the Earth God and the Harvest God. They also danced to demonstrate a warlike spirit and martial skills.[57]

Historical documents recorded a series of dances named Six Dynasties Dance before the Zhou dynasty. These were named Yunmen for the Huangdi, Dazhang for the Yaodi, Dashao for the Shundi, Daxia for the Yudi, Dahu for the Shang dynasty, and Dawu for the Zhou dynasty. The first four dances were civil dances, while the last two were martial dances. Dahu showed the achievements of the Shang dynasty in conquering the Xia dynasty, while Dawu was a history-telling performance eulogizing King Wu of Zhou's (?–1043 BC) great victory over the King Zhou of Shang. *Classic of Poetry* notes that Dawu was created in the era of King Wu of Zhou.[58] In *Records of the Grand Historian*, Confucius (551–479 BC) elaborates that the dancers of Dawu held weapons such as the Ganqi in their hand, with indignation in their faces, which expressed the military prowess of King Wu in defeating King Zhou. He further explains that Dawu was divided into six sections, covering the entire course that the King Wu's armies set out to the battlefield where they achieved victory, and King Wu establishing a new regime. In addition, Dawu included one movement and four steps.[59] The movement refers to beating a big bell for rhythm, while each step is composed of one striking and one stabbing, according to *Book of Rites*. It indicates that there were many striking and stabbing movements with dagger-axe and spear performed in martial dances.[60] It is seen from Confucius' interpretation that Dawu was a kind of large-scale martial dance including a large number of martial arts movements.[61]

In the Zhou dynasty, martial dances had a certain practicality in the battlefield, which can be illustrated by the case of Bayu Dance being applied on the battlefield in King Wu's conquest of the Shang dynasty. Legend goes that on the night before King Wu defeated the King Zhou, the Zhou armies camped outside the palace of Shang, where they sang and danced until dawn with their fighting spirit soaring aloft. Singing and dancing was on the one hand an expression of the warriors' soaring fighting spirit, and on the other hand a means of practicing their martial skills. *Chronicles of Huayang* argues that the warriors of Zhou defeating the enemies through singing and dancing in the battlefield may refer to their rushing towards them, shouting loudly and brandishing their weapons.[62] In fact, this was actual combat to make enemies surrender.

The Xiang Dance was another martial dance in the theme of the Zhou dynasty overthrowing the Shang dynasty. *Classic of Poetry* indicates that the Xiang Dance derived from the movements of hitting and stabbing in martial arts and was invented by King Wu of Zhou. An inscription titled 'Kuang You' found on bronze ware reads that King Yi of Zhou (937–892 BC) performed the Xiang Dance in the archery palace.[63] That the king personally took part in the performance of the Xiang Dance was recorded as a significant event, showing that it may have been an important assembly where the Xiang Dance was used to train soldiers.

In the Zhou dynasty, people were keen to practice martial dances and began to learn them in childhood. *Book of Rites* shows that people began to learn dancing at 13 years old, then learned the Xiang Dance at 15–16 and Daxia when they reached the age of 20.[64] *Book of Rites* says that Ji Chang (later King Wen of Zhou) practiced martial arts with weapons in spring and summer, and studied military strategy and tactics in autumn and winter.[65] Holding weapons to dance was a way of practicing martial skills; instruments employed in martial dances included bow and arrow, spear, and broadax.

Warrior-like education in the Shang and Zhou dynasties

In the Shang and Zhou dynasties, sacrifices and the military were the two most important affairs for the state, as noted in *Commentary of Zuo*.[66] Nobles tended to educate their children to be warriors with versatile martial arts. Schooling emerged as early as in the Xia dynasty. In the Shang dynasty, schools were the sites provided for the aged, as well as for the aged to educate young people, in which martial skills were fundamental courses. The *Oracle* records a Shang dynasty king ordering one of his generals to teach 300 people to shoot in the school,[67] indicating that archery was crucial to the warrior-like education in the Shang dynasty.

According to *Yinqi Cuibian* by Guo Moruo (1892–1978, a writer and historian), neighbouring states also sent people to the state of Shang to learn martial arts.[68] This shows that the level of martial arts in the Shang dynasty was higher.

Most Zhou dynasty chariot warriors were selected from the nobles. Warrior-like education was as important in the Zhou dynasty as in the Shang dynasty. Jin Wen[69] records a large quantity of historical evidence that the kings of the Zhou dynasty emphasized the importance of archery education. For instance, *Jingyin Mingwen* shows King Xuan (?–783 BC) studying archery in school as a prince.[70]

The Six Arts taught in schools during the Zhou dynasty were rites, dancing, archery, riding, calligraphy, and math, with the first four containing rich amounts of martial skill. Archery and riding were the most important military skills in chariot battle. The Five Archeries refers to five shooting methods and requirements, showing that there was rich content in the education of archery.[71] Riding referred to the skills taught to drive the chariots, which was an important course in martial skills education. There were also the Five Ridings, referring to the skills and requirements of riding horse and chariot.[72] Rites in the Six Arts were carried out in a large number of martial arts, including archery rites and field hunting. Martial dance, a fundamental part of dancing, was a combination of martial arts and dance. Many martial dances carried out with weapons in hand, such as bow and arrow, Ganqi, and broadax, were virtually armed martial arts practice. In summary, while Six Arts education in the Zhou dynasty valued literature as well as martial arts and the cultivation of morality. Its main objective was to develop well-rounded warriors. This is why martial arts were the main component of education in the Zhou dynasty.

The initial systematization of Chinese martial arts in the Spring and Autumn and Warring States periods

The Spring and Autumn and Warring States periods (770–221 BC) was a distinct epoch in Chinese history, featuring first, greatly improved productivity with the unprecedented development of the economy; second, flourishing cultural and academic development underpinning the development of traditional Chinese culture; third, ongoing war dramatically giving rise to the ethos of the warlike spirit. It was in this historical situation that the system of martial arts, as part of the macro system of Chinese culture, began to develop.

If we consider Chinese martial arts a kind of cultural form, they were in their embryo form in the Spring and Autumn and Warring States periods.[73] Their development exhibited the following features: first, multidimensional development of the social functions of martial arts; second, diversification of martial skills (both armed and unarmed); third, development of the self-awareness and theorization of martial arts. These features paved the way for Chinese martial arts to become a unique cultural system.

Diversification of the functions of martial arts

That martial arts bear multiple social functions is one of the most essential characteristics of the culturalization of martial arts. In the Spring and Autumn and Warring States periods, military martial arts employed in array-oriented battle undoubtedly made great progress with the transformation of campaign modes. More important, however, was the emergence of other social functions of martial arts – performance, athletics, recreation and fitness, for example. This advancement broke through the constraint of being simply a military pursuit. From skills to organizations, from forms to ideas, great changes and development created a rich martial arts culture.

War invigorated the ethos of the warlike spirit and propelled the development of military martial skills in this period, as the scale of war grew. In the Spring and Autumn period, the number of soldiers in battle ranged from tens of thousands to hundreds of thousands. Approaching the Warring States period, this increased to as many as a million. Recruitment, selection, and training of soldiers immensely facilitated the martial arts ethos and enhanced military skills. The nature of military campaigns also changed. Chariot battle was mainly adopted in the Shang and Zhou dynasties. Both chariot battle and infantry battle were used in the Spring and Autumn period, while infantry and cavalry battle dominated in the Warring States period.

The king of each warring state highly emphasized military power in order to conquer other states and avoid being conquered. In particular, the outcome of war was largely determined by the quality of the selection and training of soldiers, once infantry battle became the principal campaign mode. Therefore, kings enacted various decrees to encourage the development of military martial arts, so as to build a powerful state. *Guanzi* records that the king in the State of Qi ordered local officials to recommend people who were mighty or had a strong body; officials who discovered such people but did not recommend them were declared guilty of wasting talent.[74] High appreciation and recommendation of elite martial artists drove the development of martial arts. In the State of Qi, Guan Zhong (also named Guanzi, c.723–645 BC) devoted himself to systematizing the state's military system by enrolling military forces and martial talents from the public society. *Discourses of the States* notes that competent martial artists with superb martial skills in archery, riding, running, and Jiaodi were honoured as one of the Five Wisdoms and well-respected in the State of Jin.[75]

Mozi advocated promoting martial arts by awarded property and honour in all states.[76] As recorded in *Hanfeizi*, Li Kui (55–395 BC) of the State of Wei gave an order for the purpose of inspiring people to learn archery: to settle a dispute at law, the parties would compete in shooting; the one who hit the target was the winner.[77] Under this order, everyone practiced archery day and night, and consequently the State of Wei defeated the State of Qin. These historical records show that military martial arts were further disseminated to meet the needs of war.

In the Spring and Autumn and Warring States periods, the multidimensional development of the functions of martial arts was prominently highlighted by their new roles in performance, competition, and entertainment. The purpose of practicing martial arts was not only its battlefield application, but also as a kind of martial arts competition. Killing and fighting in martial arts contests were no longer only for the battlefield, but to perform and compete in the arena.

Sword-fighting is a good example. The sword is short and handy, suitable for stabbing and hacking. In chariot battle, the sword tended to be limited in terms of defence, compared to long weapons such as the dagger-axe and spear. In the Spring and Autumn and Warring States periods, however, small, exquisitely sharp swords resulted from improvements in metal smelting techniques and manufacturing, becoming the most favoured weapon. Moreover, swordsmanship developed rapidly.

Nobles and dukes liked the sword. As recorded in *Records of the Grand Historian*, the chancellor of the State of Wei was fond of martial arts, so he ordered all officials to carry a sword.[78] Mencius says that Duke Wen of Teng liked playing with his sword and riding horses when he was prince.[79] *The School Sayings of Confucius* notes that Zilu, a student of Confucius who was a skilled swordsman, once took out his sword to dance in front of Confucius, proudly claiming that a noble should wear a sword to protect himself.[80] Even the famous patriotic poet Qu Yuan (c.340–278 BC) enjoyed wearing a long sword. It is worth noting that they loved the sword not for its battlefield application, but rather as an instrument to portray a brave and heroic spirit – they wore a sword for recreation purposes.

An article in *Zhuangzi*, 'On the Sword', concerns sword-fighting.[81] Although it aims to explain the principles of state governance through the metaphor of sword-fighting, in fact it reflects the ethos and institutions of sword-fighting in the Warring States period, and provides important historical data for research into the competitive and recreational aspects of martial arts. It says that King Wen of Zhao (c.308–266 BC) was a sword-fighting enthusiast who housed over 3,000 swordsmen in his palace and loved to watch them fight each other. Despite hundreds of deaths each year, he continued with the contests. As a result, after three years the state began to decline, and the dukes hatched plans to topple him. Zhuangzi (c.369–286 BC), renowned for his wisdom, was asked to persuade the king to halt the contests and focus on affairs of state. Dressed as a sword-fighter, he came to the palace and claimed to the king that he was such a superb practitioner that he could kill a man from ten steps away – nobody within 1,000 miles can stop him. Furthermore, he presented part of a very insightful theory of swordsmanship. At this, King Wen launched a statewide selection process to pick the best swordsmen to fight Zhuangzi. This contest lasted for seven days, with five to six men to be selected, and resulted in more than 60 deaths. When the formal contest was due to begin, Zhuangzi did not appear for the fight. Instead, he explained that the sword was a metaphor for politics, expounding this through the analogy of 'The Sword of the King', 'The Sword of the Duke', and The Sword of the People'. King Wen now understood the proper attitude and behaviour needed to govern the state, and gave up his hobby of sword-fighting. The selected swordsmen felt dishonoured and killed themselves in anger.[82]

In general, academics believe that 'On the Sword' was invented by Zhuangzi's followers and used to allegorically illustrate the principles of state governance. Nevertheless, it mirrors people's social lives and helps us to have a concrete understanding of the development of martial arts in the Warring States period.

First, the purpose of sword-fighting was not for military training, but for entertainment, and even to meet rulers' need to watch sword-fighting contests. It vividly reveals that martial arts entailed competition, performance, and recreation.

Second, it shows that sword-fighting contests were institutionalized to a great extent in the Warring States period, with sword-fighting uniforms, recruitment systems, rules, and awards.

Third, the idea of swordsman as a profession appeared in the Warring States period. Although there is no explicit description in *Zhuangzi*, it still can be seen from the book that swordsmen wore short clothes and had dishevelled hair on the head, protuberant hair on the temples, glowering eyes, and loud, harsh voices. They cut the head and penetrated the liver and lung of opponents, and were so fiery and forthright that they would commit suicide to demonstrate a brave and dauntless spirit when dishonoured. This portrays professional swordsmen in a way that is very close to the reality of the period.

Fourth, 'On the Sword' states that the essentials of swordsmanship are to generate advantage by showing disadvantage to the opponent on purpose, and to take action after the opponent only to stab the opponent before being stabbed. This reveals that sword-fighting tactics had achieved a high competitive level.

In the Spring and Autumn and Warring States periods, people often entertained themselves by watching martial arts contests, and this practice gradually grew into a general trend. *Liezi* records that Fan Zihua, a nobleman in the State of Jin, hosted a large number of martial fighters who often conducted martial art contests. Injury caused in the fights did not matter, but doing this day and night led to the decline of the state.[83] This kind of martial arts contest as a form of entertainment gradually developed into Jiaodi and vaudeville in the Qin dynasty and the Han dynasty. This tells us that the engagement of martial arts with entertainment derived from the ethos of emphasizing a warlike spirit in the Spring and Autumn and Warring States periods. This engagement not only increased the frequency of practice of martial arts, but also enhanced the attractiveness of martial arts contests and advanced the development of martial arts towards a multifunctional social effect.

The diversification of martial skills

In order to accommodate the multidimensional social functions of martial arts, martial arts skills inevitably followed. By the Warring States period, the skills included in Chinese martial arts had diversified and developed.

Diversification first entailed the development of non-military martial skills. The emergence of array-oriented military martial skills and non-military skills is a major benchmark in the development of martial arts. As discussed, infantry and cavalry battle gradually took the place of chariot battle as the major campaign mode between the Shang and Zhou dynasties and the Warring States period. However, the basic features of chariot battle did not change fundamentally. That is, chariot battle tended to be collectively organized and pragmatic, with a single function. In contrast, individuality was a fundamental feature of non-military martial skills, which consequently became increasingly complicated and varied.

In ancient times, the formation of troops and the line-up for battle were the most stressed aspects of war; *The Methods of Sima* explains that to prepare for battle, it is necessary to arrange the soldiers into certain ranks and arrays.[84] According to *Book of Documents*, before King Wu of Zhou led 300 chariots and 300 veteran soldiers to do battle with the army of King Zhou of Shang, he earnestly warned them to strictly maintain the order of the ranks. To stabilize the ranks, soldiers should stop after taking six to seven steps and making four to seven strikes or stabs.[85]

To maintain stability, collectivism and uniformity were strongly stressed. *The Art of War* says that the drum and the flag were put to use to avoid soldiers not hearing or seeing each other. Beating drums and waving flags to direct the battle mainly highlighted the strong uniformity of the operation. In this way, the individual was subsumed by the collective. Braver soldiers were not allowed to go forward, while more fearful soldiers were not allowed to retreat.[86] Every soldier was required to take action in his own fixed position. Therefore, although various short and long weapons were used together in this collectively organized military operation, such as bow and arrow, dagger-axe, halberd, and spear, only those martial skills that were simple and useful were applicable, since they could highly unify the soldiers in the ranks so as to increase combat effectiveness. In consequence, even though various movements and patterns of martial skills had developed in martial arts of the public society, they were useless on the battlefield.

In contrast to martial arts in array-oriented battle, the martial arts that originated from the needs of daily life were composed of individual (one on one) skills of attack and defence. Such individuality diversified and enriched Chinese martial arts. In the Spring and Autumn and Warring States periods, different features emerged in the prevailing martial arts of various regions. *Book of Han* points out that martial skills in the State of Qi, the State of Wei, and the State of Qin each had their own character, with the Qi people in particular developing their own arts of individual attack and defence.[87] However, these martial skills emphasized individuality more than the collectivity required in battle, so were only applicable in fighting a single opponent. If used against a troop of enemies, the soldiers would scatter, and teamwork and cohesion would break down.

In the Spring and Autumn and Warring States periods, individual martial arts gained momentum, contributing to an increasing demand for martial arts in people's social and daily life. In the Shang and Zhou dynasties, warrior-like education was widely conducted for the children of the nobility. Their aim in learning martial arts was to become warriors. In the Spring and Autumn and Warring States periods, however, intellectuals emerged, and intellectuals and martial artists entered different careers – the former developed a political career through knowledge and wisdom, while professional warriors made a living from their martial skills. It became rare for warriors to come from the nobility; they mostly came from ordinary families and came to be known as *wuxia*.[88]

In the Spring and Autumn and Warring States periods, vassal states fought each other, and noble families in every state fostered their own armed forces to protect clan interests. The most notable figures involved in this political campaign were Tian Wen of the State of Qi, Zhao Sheng of the State of Zhao, Wei Wuji of the State of Wei, and Huang Xie of the State of Chu, known as the Four Noblemen of the Warring States. They each had up to 1,000 followers, a great number of warriors who made a living from their martial strength and loyalty.

At that time, warriors were helpful in various circumstances: as back-up in negotiations, as assassins, as avengers, as bodyguards. They put loyalty before their own lives, and they solved problems and difficulties for their masters. They treated others as they treated themselves, and they faced death unflinchingly. In this period, celebrated warriors included Cao Mo of the State of Lu, who forced Duke Huan of Qi (?–643 BC) to return the land he had occupied; Zhuanzhu of the State of Wu, who hid a dagger in a fish belly in order to assassinate King Liao of Wu (?–515 BC); Nie Zheng, who assassinated a chancellor of the State of Han named Xialei (?–397 BC) with a sword; and Jignke, who sacrificed himself after failing to assassinate King Yingzheng of Qin (259–210 BC, later Emperor Yingzheng) (see Figure 1.11).

Warriors in the pre-Qin period were proficient in martial skills, which drove the further development and diversification of martial arts in public society. Taking the armed martial arts as an example, in contrast to the weapons used in

Figure 1.11 Jing Ke's assassination attempt on Emperor Yingzheng of Qin, a stone inscription in Wushi Temple in Jiaxiang, Shandong Province.

military battle – dagger-axe, halberd, and spear, for example – lighter and shorter weapons were preferred in martial arts of public society. Moreover, the features of these weapons varied from region to region, as indicated in *Rites of Zhou*. People in the State of Zheng tended to use sabres, whereas axes were often used in the State of Song, and swords were the weapon of choice in the State of Wu and Yue. These weapons would not be improved if they were disseminated to other regions, for the sake of cultural diversity.[89] In addition to sabre and sword, short weapons prevailing in martial arts of public society in the Spring and Autumn and Warring States periods also included those weapons that were easy to carry and hide – dagger, iron hammer, axe, hook, and slingshot, for example.

The sword drew extra emphasis and development. *Mozi* states that the advantages of swords are that they can stab through something, cut something into pieces, and can't be broken by other weapons.[90] To increase the effectiveness of martial skills, people paid equal attention to the excellence of weapons and the skills of using them. *Annals of Master Lv* points out that a sharp sword is of little use without appropriate swordsmanship, but a sharp sword is indispensable regardless of how superb the swordsmanship.[91] At that time, the State of Wu and Yue was famous for manufacturing swords (see Figure 1.12). *Miscellaneous History of the State of Yue and Wu* details the distinguishing features and mystery of treasured swords, namely being able to pierce a bronze axe and cut iron weapons.[92] That the Sword of Goujian, unearthed in the early 1990s, was found still to be extraordinarily shiny and sharp after more than 2,000 years, serves as reliable evidence.[93] The period also saw the appearance of specialized sword connoisseurs such as Xue Zhu and Zeng Congzi, who were responsible for confirming the authenticity of treasured swords.

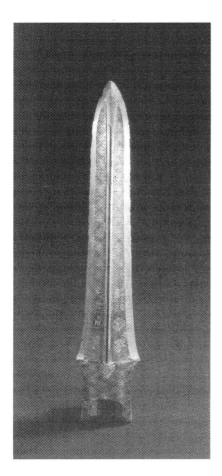

Figure 1.12 A sword of a king named Fuchai of the State of Wu in Warring States, Hubei Provincial Museum.

The development of martial arts in public society in the Spring and Autumn and Warring States periods also dramatically advanced the diversification of skills. In this period, swordsmanship was extremely well developed. For instance, *Records of the Historian* concerns swordsmanship in fighting against long weapons with short swords. Some families with superb skills earned fame by teaching martial arts, demonstrating that rich, essential swordsmanship skills had developed, and that swordsmanship had become a specialized field.[94] These historical records indicate that swordsmanship was widely diffused and developed.

Likewise, unarmed combat skills witnessed great development. *Zhuangzi* records that people fought righteously with recognized skills, but tended to use surprising skills afterwards, which reveals the multidimensional development of unarmed combat at the time.⁹⁵ *Spring and Autumn Annals* offers an illustration. Nangong Changwan, a military official of Duke Min of Song (?–682 BC) who was in charge of the South Palace, was hot tempered. On being humiliated by Duke Min of Song, he wrung the duke's neck in anger. Another official named Qiu Mu came quickly, indignantly denouncing Nangong with a sword in his hand. Nangong killed Qiu Mu with a side-arm strike, and Qiu Mu's head was broken into pieces.⁹⁶

Development of awareness of martial arts

In the pre-Qin period, Chinese martial arts became a kind of cultural form symbolized by the emergence of an awareness of martial arts and the initial formation of martial arts theories. This was principally expressed in terms of athletic, ethical, and theoretical awareness and was prominent in the Spring and Autumn and Warring States periods.

At this time, people obtained a sense of satisfaction by participating in martial arts activities and pursuing victory over an opponent. As such, the athletic awareness was conveyed by people's desire for self-fulfillment through involvement in martial arts. The sense of achieving victory through martial arts competition was often associated with social mentality, such as people's sense of heroism, pleasure, honour, and aesthetics. This association not only provided an opportunity for martial arts to have multiple social functions in the perspective of social psychology, but also paved the way for athletic martial arts to fill multidimensional social demand. There is a representative example in *Spring and Autumn Annals*. Jiyou, a prince of the State of Lu, defeated an army led by Ju'na. After capturing Ju'na alive, however, Jiyou insisted on a barehanded fight with Ju'na to determine the winner. Battlefield victory was unable to satisfy Jiyou; he still sought victory in one-on-one martial arts competition.⁹⁷ This suggests that athletic awareness of martial arts had become an important social awareness.

In the Spring and Autumn and Warring States periods, another kind of athletic awareness formed from martial skills competitions. They fought fairly, respected the strong, and determined social status through martial skills. Shaoshi Zhou was such a warrior, as recorded in the *Hanfeizi*. Zhou was a warrior of King Xiang of Zhao who was defeated by Xu Zi from Zhongmou County in a Jiaodi contest. Zhou was so genuinely convinced by Xu Zi's martial skills that he recommended him to his master as his own replacement.⁹⁸ This historical document not only implies an awareness of fair play, but also an athletic awareness related to faith and righteousness. This clearly demonstrates a highly valued feature of Chinese martial arts.

This athletic awareness also demonstrates a sense of ethics, indicating that ethical awareness was an important component of the concept of martial arts. Upholding ethics and morality is traditionally considered a characteristic of the Chinese people. Within martial arts, this is reflected in the emphasis on the ethics of martial arts, clearly seen in the Spring and Autumn and Warring

States periods. Sima Qian (145–?BC) stated that favourable moral characteristics were the precondition for a person to learn martial arts, and that learning martial arts was both a way of achieving internal physical enhancement and an acquisition of flexibility in external behaviors.[99] This statement demonstrates the ethical characteristics of the culture of Chinese martial arts, characteristics which are still very important.

With the multi-functional development of martial arts and the increasing complexity of martial skills, the practice began to be theorized. In the history of Chinese martial arts, theories of swordsmanship were probably the earliest to emerge. *Records of the Grand Historian* describes Jingke paying a visit to Ge'nie to exchange views on swordsmanship. However, the debate between the two celebrated swordsmen ended in an intense wrangle.[100] Presumably, each had a profound but incompatible theory of swordsmanship, which reveals that people had their own views and intensive interest in the theories of martial skills.

According to *Spring and Autumn Annals of Wu and Yue*, an outstanding civil swordswoman in the State of Yue was called in by the king to train his soldiers in swordsmanship, and was honoured by being named the Maiden of the Southern Forest. She was also asked to share her theories of swordsmanship.[101] She replied that she had been born in a remote mountainous area where there were no schools or government oversight, but people there were still keen on the arts of fighting. It can also be reckoned from her words that theories of martial arts were widely diffused in public society.

She further elaborated to the king that the movements of sword-fighting are easy, but the principle is profound. The movements in sword-fighting operate as a door opens and closes, and can be strong or weak. In a fight, one should express calmness externally and make adequate preparation internally. One should appear as a gentle woman but attack as a fierce tiger. One's movement in brandishing the sword should be coherent with the breath and mind. One should stab the opponent as straight as the sun stabs; one's movements to the right or the left should be as agile as those of a jumping rabbit. The process of stabbing should be quick and decisive; all movements should be completed at once, without breath. No changes in the movements are allowed. Once in command of this theory, one person can resist 100 enemies, and 100 people can resist tens of thousands of enemies.

The theories of swordsmanship stated by the Maiden of the Southern Forest generally illuminate the rationale of swordsmanship, which stresses staying calm before taking action and taking action while staying calm, so as to integrate staying calm and taking action – though her statement is somewhat attached to mysterious features and exaggerated description. She describes well the experience of sword-fighting through the example of the operating principles of Yin and Yang – meaning that the movements of advancing, retreating, attacking, and defending ought to be conducted with flexible behaviour and a calm mentality. *Zhuangzi* also contains a very famous theory of swordsmanship: the essentials of swordsmanship are to generate advantage by showing disadvantage to the opponent on purpose, and to take action after the opponent only to stab the opponent before being stabbed.[102]

This theory in swordsmanship is regarded as the guiding principle of attack and defence in martial arts. Its significance goes far beyond swordsmanship; it can be viewed as an all-round theory of the strategies and tactics of martial arts. Therefore, it is seen that the theories of martial arts emerged and gradually developed with the impetus of martial arts practices in the Spring and Autumn and Warring States periods. This progress is an important benchmark in the initial systematization of Chinese martial arts.

Philosophers and martial arts in the pre-Qin period

The Spring and Autumn and Warring States periods saw various schools of philosophical thought contend, leading to a golden age in the cultural history of ancient China. These thoughts also endowed Chinese martial arts with rich cultural connotations. They served not only as a crucial historical condition for the development of Chinese martial arts, but also as underlying ideologies and philosophies for more than 2,000 years.

Confucianism and martial arts

Chinese martial arts have been deeply and profoundly influenced by Confucianism. The great philosopher and educator Confucius was born into a martial arts family. *Records of the Grand Historian* notes that he was about 2.2 metres tall. It is also recorded in many ancient books of the pre-Qin period that Confucius was accomplished with both pen and sword.[103] For instance, in *Mozi* it is stated that Confucius once lifted the bar[104] of the castle gate easily when serving as a judicial official in the State of Lu.[105] Other records indicating Confucius was a warrior of extraordinary power can be found in *Liezi*,[106] *Annals of Master Lv*,[107] and *Huainanzi*.[108] *Book of Rites* adds that Confucius was particularly proficient in riding and archery.[109]

Confucius stressed benevolence and morality in governance, as he was an educator. However, he was well aware of the importance of both literacy and martial education in the Spring and Autumn and Warring States periods.[110] With this in mind, Confucius regarded the Six Arts as an important component of education. As mentioned, martial dances and martial arts were closely related to rites and dancing, while archery and riding were essential martial skills. The ultimate goal of Confucius' mentorship of his students was to cultivate well-rounded men. He considered that a noble man should be knowledgeable, benevolent and brave, but a perfect man should also be adept in various skills, including martial arts. In *Records of the Grand Historian*, Confucius names four representative examples of well-rounded men.[111] A prominent warrior named Bian Zhuangzi in the state of Lu represents the brave man, while Confucius's student Ranqiu represents the skilful man well versed in both literacy and martial arts. Two other students, Zilu and Youruo, are also brave warriors, with Zilu once serving as Confucius' guard.

The far-reaching influence of Confucianism on Chinese martial arts is also demonstrated in the concept of benevolence, which is regarded as the core value of the ethics of martial arts. Advocating ethics, pursuing benevolence, righteousness, loyalty, and trustworthiness are the distinguishing features of Chinese martial art. These values make Chinese martial arts not only a form of combat skills and body-building, but also a method of spiritual development.

Benevolence means loving people and forgiving. In *Analects of Confucius*, Confucius indicates that benevolence means kindness, tolerance, self-discipline, and humility. He also links boldness with benevolence in saying that people with benevolence are sure to be brave, while people who are bold but without benevolence will be sinners.[112] Martial arts are employed in fighting and killing, so must be restricted by ethical codes. Chinese martial arts contain rich ethical reflection which still has tremendous practical meaning in modern times.

Mohism and martial arts

Among the various schools of pre-Qin philosophical thought, Mohism has a closer relationship with martial arts, and accounts for some of the *wuxia* quality of martial arts. Mozi, the founder of Mohism, was a remarkable ideologist, educator, and militarist in the early Warring States period. He advocated universal love, pursuing peace without conflict, respect for the distinguished, and frugality. But in the age of incessant wars and chaos, he also advocated using force against all forms of invasion and disloyalty. His followers were all adept in martial arts and had a strong sense of loyalty. They cared for others more than for themselves, and valued brotherhood more than their own lives. The spirit of faith, loyalty, and boldness in Mohism is regarded as the origin of *wuxia*, which has been deeply embedded in Chinese martial arts for more than 2,000 years.

In the book *Mozi*, bravery is highly valued. The opening sentence of the 'Self-cultivating' chapter points out that bravery is the most essential winning factor in fighting.[113] In the 'Respecting the Distinguished' chapter, he ranks those of outstanding archery and riding skills as top talents.[114] In the 'Pursuing Peace without Conflict' chapter, he also elaborates the features of the sword and the self-defence function of swordsmanship.[115] Other chapters also expound on military theories and methods of defending the castle gate and repelling enemies, and were of great importance to the development of military martial arts.

Taoism and martial arts

Yang Chengfu (1883–1936), a prominent Taijiquan master in modern China, once said that the basic spirit in Chinese quan is embedded with philosophies despite the rich variety of quan schools.[116] Taoism is a major philosophical source for Chinese martial arts.

Laozi (c.571–471 BC), the founder of Taoism, was a great ideologist in the Spring and Autumn period who was born in Ku County in the State of Chu (now Luyi City, Henan). He was the author of *Tao Te Ching*,[117] also known as *Laozi*. Zhuang Zhou (c.369–286 BC) of the Warring States period later succeeded Laozi's theories, authoring *Zhuangzi*. Laozi and Zhuangzi are the two main representatives of Taoism.

Taoism has had a great influence on Chinese martial arts in terms of epistemology and methodology. In respect to epistemology, Chinese martial arts have aligned themselves with theories on the ultimate source of space from Taoism, namely the theories of Tao, Qi,[118] and Oneness of Heaven and Men. *Taijiquan Treatise* argues that infinity coexists and interconnects with the ultimate in Taijiquan.[119] This argument stems from the theories of Taoism. Regarding methodology, Chinese martial arts have adopted some theories of Taoism as guiding principles, namely 'things will develop in the opposite direction when they become extreme'; 'coping with all motions by remaining motionless'; 'conquering the unyielding with the yielding'; and 'gaining mastery by striking only after the enemy has struck'. The previously mentioned theories of swordsmanship of Zhuangzi and the Maiden of the Southern Forest are also embodiments of Taoism. As for the internal quan[120] that later emerged, such as Xingyiquan and Bagua Quan,[121] they originated from the methodologies of Taoism.[122]

Military strategists and martial arts

Martial arts share the same origin as ancient Chinese military strategies, explaining their common fundamental feature of applying tactical fighting arts. The classic pre-Qin works on military strategy include *The Art of War*,[123] *Wuzi*,[124] *Sun Bin's Art of War*,[125] *The Methods of Sima*,[126] *WeiLiaozi*,[127] and *Six Secret Teachings*.[128] According to these works, pre-Qin military strategists tended to emphasize the selection and training of soldiers.

In *Sun Bin's Art of War*,[129] it is recorded that Sun Bin (?–316 BC) highlighted the significance of soldiers with martial talent who were able to cut into the enemy and capture the general. Therefore, he also believed that mastery of martial skills rather than social status was the chief criterion for recruiting soldiers. *Six Secret Teachings* was one of the most important military works in the pre-Qin period, written in the form of conversations between King Wen and King Wu and Jiang Ziya of the Western Zhou dynasty. The 'Farming Weapons' chapter notes that martial arts in the army and the people had close interaction, because many weapons derived from farm tools.[130] The 'Chariot Riders' chapter notes that different selection criteria were made according to the requirements for different kinds of riders – chariot riding and horse riding.[131] The 'Training the Soldiers' chapter also notes that soldiers were classified into different categories according to fitness, martial skills, and personality, so that they could be trained to adapt to different kinds of missions.[132]

Pre-Qin military strategists had a deep understanding of the relationship between military tactics and martial skills in wars. *The Methods of Sima*, written during the early Warring States period, argues that a battle is first a contest of wisdom, followed by a contest of strength and skill.[133] Therefore, applying strategies and tactics comes first, whether in war or non-military fights. Martial skills are certainly important, but they must be combined with appropriate strategies and tactics to achieve victory. Of the works on military strategy, *The Art of War* is the one that has gone on to have the greatest influence on later ages.

Sunzi (c.545–470 BC), born in the State of Qi in the late Spring and Autumn period, was an approximate contemporary of Confucius. His masterpiece *The Art of War* is a book of profound wisdom which has been widely accepted as a code of conduct, and certain strategies and tactics of Chinese martial arts derive directly from it.[134] In general, the integration of Sunzi's thoughts with Chinese martial arts manifests in the following eight ways: first, being acquainted with both oneself and the enemy; second, becoming undefeatable before taking action; third, unveiling the enemy's weakness by deceptive movements; fourth, making good use of both regular and irregular tactics and strategies; fifth, seizing the initiative within the bilateral actions; sixth, making changes according to the changes of the enemy; seventh, taking action by surprise towards the unprepared enemy; eighth, forming a holistic view of all kinds of tactics and strategies.

Qi Jiguang, a famous Ming Dynasty general, applied this idea to martial skills and proposed that learning martial arts should not be confined to one school. People should study extensively, learn the advantages of all the schools, and use them in practice. The sparkling thought of Sunzi is unquestionably an inexhaustible source for Chinese martial arts. It has not only greatly enriched the cultural aspect, but has also strongly empowered the development of Chinese martial arts.[135]

Yin and Yang and martial arts

During the Spring and Autumn and Warring States periods, the philosophy of Yin and Yang emerged. Yin and Yang first referred to the status of being seen and unseen of sunshine. Later, this was further conceptualized to describe the status of all objects. In *Laozi*, it is recorded that all objects on earth consist of both Yin and Yang.[136] *Esoteric Scripture of Huangdi* adds that Yin and Yang is the basic operating principle of all objects in nature, and that it runs through the process of origin, evolution, decline and death.[137]

The philosophy of the Five Elements – metal, wood, water, fire, and earth – was also put forward in the pre-Qin period. It posits that these five elements make up all objects of the world and determine their changes or transformation. At the end of the Warring States period, Zou Yan (c.305–240 BC) of the State of Qi combined Yin and Yang with the Five Elements. He explained political changes and the rise and fall of a dynasty by illustrating how the five elements mutually generate and neutralize each other. Hence, he was venerated as the representative of the School of Yin and Yang for his remarkable contribution.

Book of Changes from ancient times is the comprehensive embodiment of Yin and Yang, the Five Elements, and the Eight Trigrams.[138] It is said that the Eight Trigrams were painted by Fuxi (one of the Three Sovereigns and Five Emperors in Chinese mythology) and was later developed into 64 hexagrams by King Wen of Zhou (c.1152–1056 BC). The integration of Yin and Yang with the Five Elements and the Eight Trigrams was deeply infused into and has advanced all fields of Chinese traditional culture, including martial arts.

The philosophy of Yin and Yang is fully presented in *Book of Changes*. A series of dialectical thoughts such as static and dynamic, hardness and softness, open and closed, advance and retreat, in and out, up and down, show and hide, attack and defend have been widely used in many theories and skills of all schools of Chinese martial arts. The Eight Trigrams theory in *Book of Changes* has been widely adopted as well and is regarded as an important guiding principle in combat. The emergence of Baguazhang serves as a good case.

The kernel of the Five Elements is interaction, which contains two functions. One plays a positive role as 'mutual promoting', where the five elements present a cyclic effect – water promotes wood, wood promotes fire, fire promotes earth, earth promotes metal, metal promotes water. The other plays a negative role as 'mutual restraining' – water restrains fire, fire restrains metal, metal restrains wood, wood restrains earth, earth restrains water. Chinese martial arts are also deeply influenced by the Five Elements, as seen in the Xingyiquan, with systematic and rigorous tactics and martial skills employed.

Flow of martial arts between peoples in pre-Qin period

Chinese martial arts were originally initiated by the Han people and expanded with the influx of various types of martial arts during the long-term cultural communication between the Han and other peoples. In ancient times, the Han lived in the fertile and flat central plains, where agricultural civilization developed. To all sides, there were many other people. They lived in the deserts and mountains, or near the water. These harsh environments and the consequent production and living modes had made them braver than the Han and given them more martial skills, such as stabbing, throwing and shooting. As a result, these martial skills were often adopted by the Han into their own martial arts. The Han named Chiyou, a non-Han, God of War – rather than Huangdi, chieftain of Han.

Martial arts of the Hu

Scholars tend to regard horseback archery in China as beginning with the 'Horseback Archery in Hu Dress' revolution launched by King Wuling of Zhao (c. 340–295 BC). The replacement of chariot battle by cavalry and infantry as the primary battle mode in the ancient central plains didn't take place until the late Warring States period. However, cavalry and horseback archery can be found much earlier. Many northern nomadic peoples who lived by hunting in the desert or grassland, such as the Xiongnu, Xianbei, Kok Turks, and Khitan, were good at horseback archery. The Han were often defeated by northerners, and gradually learned from their warlike spirit and horseback archery skills. According to *Book of Changes*, cavalry battle can trace its history back to the early Zhou dynasty.[139]

Nevertheless, it was not until King Wuling of Zhao's advocacy of 'Horseback Archery in Hu Dress' that the Han began the large-scale practice of horseback archery and cavalry training. In particular, Wuling regarded horseback archery as a way of demonstrating and promoting a warlike spirit. *Records of the Grand Historian* records that Wuling made up his mind to reinforce the state's military force in the face of the threat of the Hu people.[140] In so doing, he launched a stern military revolution in 302 BC. At his orders, Han people began to wear the Hu-style short dress with narrow sleeves, rather than the former long and wide Han gown, in order to better practice horseback archery. This eventually led to military power and prosperity. 'Horseback Archery in Hu Dress' was not only a way of learning shooting skills from the north but, more importantly, an innovation of ideology that diffused the intense warlike spirit of the northern peoples among the Han. Moreover, it showcases the communication of martial arts between different peoples in the pre-Qin period.

Martial arts of the Ba and Shu

The Ba and Shu people have a long history. They lived between Sichuan and Hubei provinces, between the Yangtze and Han rivers, with the Ba to the east and the Shu to the west. Both were good at martial arts. Fu Hao, a famous female militarist and a queen in the Shang dynasty, succeeded in conquering the Ba area. The *Oracle* shows that the Shu once made a tribute of 300 well-trained archers to the Shang dynasty. They joined the Shang army,[141] which contributed to the communication of martial skills among various peoples. A large amount of bronze ware, such as dagger-axes, spears, and broadaxes, has been unearthed in Sichuan Province, which indicates that the martial arts of the Ba and Shu made great achievements in an early time (see Figure 1.13).

The Ba and Shu were given priority to be sent to the battlefield on account of their being brave and skilful fighters, as shown in the case of King Wu of Zhou's conquest of the Shang dynasty. Adding to the depiction of the legend in the previous section, it's worth a reminder that the Zhou army was mostly made

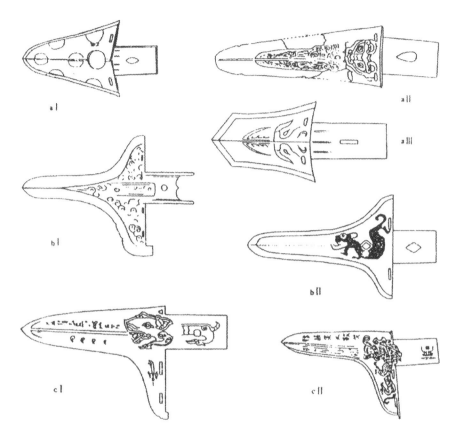

Figure 1.13 Various bronze dagger-axes of the Ba and Shu peoples in the Warring States period.

up of Ba and Shu soldiers. Later in the Han dynasty, Emperor Gaozu ordered the officials in charge of dance to combine martial arts and martial dances, which brought the Bayu Dance into being. Involving wielding swords and spears to display a warlike spirit, the Bayu Dance enjoyed a widespread reputation. It won great affection from kings from ancient times and was popular for thousands of years.

Martial arts of the Yue

The Yue inhabited the southern coastal areas of the Yangtze River; records of them can be found in the *Oracle*, dating back to the Shang dynasty. The broadax was their primary weapon. They used stone axes in the Neolithic Age, which became bronze in the Shang and Zhou dynasties. Their name is said to have originated from the axe, for it has the same pronunciation as 'yue' in

Figure 1.14 A bronze broadax from the Warring States period, excavated in Qinhuangdao, Hebei Province.

Chinese pinyin (see Figure 1.14). Most Yue lived near the water, so they were skilled in naval battle.

In the regions that are now Guangxi and Guangdong provinces, there were two Yue peoples, the Xiou and the Luoyue. In most circumstances, they are called the Ouluo. During the Spring and Autumn and Warring States periods, the Ouluo frequently communicated with the central plains. The Ouluo were brave, tenacious, and skilful in battle; *Huainanzi* records that the Yue hid in the jungle to avoid capture by the Qin army, and eventually defeated them through their storm troops.[142]

The rock paintings in Flower painted between the Warring States period and the Qin and Han dynasties. Mountain near Zuo River in Guangxi were These paintings show Ouluo martial activities, with weapons including sabre, sword, spear, dart, and bow and arrow. Postures in the paintings are similar to those in martial arts, such as a horse stance, a short sword worn at the waist, raising hands, and stretching the body as if unfolding wings (see Figure 1.15).

In 1976, a lacquer bronze plate was unearthed in Gui County in Guangxi, where the Ouluo had lived. On the outside surface of the plate, there is an image of 18 people in four groups practicing both armed and unarmed forms of martial arts. This depicts martial activities in the late Warring States period and the early Han dynasty. The plate may have been brought to the Ouluo during the early Han dynasty, which reflects the cultural communication, including martial arts, between the Yue areas and the central plains.

Figure 1.15 Rock paintings of martial dance from Guangxi Province painted between the Warring States period and the Qin and Han dynasties.

Martial arts of the Dian

The Dian, one of the Man[143] peoples in the south-west, lived along Dian Lake in what is now Yunnan Province. At the end of the Warring States period, Zhuang Jiao of the State of Chu led thousands of soldiers to Dian Lake and declared himself King of Dian. The subsequent cultural exchanges enriched Chinese martial arts with a Dian character.

The Shield Dance was a popular martial dance among the ancient Dian, similar to the martial skills with shield and sword of later ages. In the 1950s, a number of ancient Dian relics were unearthed outside Kunming in Yunnan Province, among them a bronze drum. On the waist of the drum are a large number of martial dances, such as the Shield Dance and the Spear Dance. The Shield Dance is considered a type of Ganqi Dance. The dancer wears a short skirt, with the upper body naked and feathers on the head. This kind of martial dance was widely practiced by various peoples in the south. Many Shield Dance rock paintings can be found around Awa Mountain in Cangyuan County in Yunnan Province.

Swordsmanship was another popular martial art among the Dian. Hundreds of bronze swords have been unearthed by archaeologists. Most are short, but in

Figure 1.16 A bronze plate from the Han dynasty, excavated in Yunnan Province.

different specifications, such as with a flat grid and broad blade or without a grid. They are well-made, with gorgeous decoration. Fan Chuo of the Tang dynasty wrote in *Book of the Southern Man* that the ancient Dian people were fond of wearing a sword, regardless of their social status.[144] As did the Han, the Dian not only employed the sword in war, fighting and hunting, but also wore it to demonstrate heroism and courage. The unearthed relics also include a bronze plate which shows a vivid image of two people dancing with a long sword at the waist (see Figure 1.16). This indicates that the long sword was in use among the ancient Dian people, but whether it was introduced from the central plains has yet to be further researched.[145]

Notes

1. (Warring States) Han Feizi. Hanfeizi•Wudu (韩非子•五蠹). Ancient Chinese classics are generally named using classic name followed by chapter name (if applicable) and article name (if applicable), separated by '•'.
2. (Western Han) Liu An *et al.* Huainanzi•Lanmingxun (淮南子•览冥训).
3. (Warring States – Han). Shanhaijing•Haineijing (山海经•海内经).
4. (Warring States) Lv Buwei *et al.* Lvshi Chunqiu•Mengqiu Ji•Dangbing (吕氏春秋•孟秋纪•荡兵).
5. (Western Han) Sima Qian. Shiji•Wudi Benji (史记•五帝本纪).
6. Shiben•Zuopian (世本•作篇).
7. (Han). Longyu Hetu (龙鱼河图).
8. (Southern Liang) Ren Fang. Shuyi Ji (述异记).
9. (Warring States) Yan Ying. Yanzi Chunqiu•Neizapian Xia (晏子春秋•内杂篇下).
10. (Western Han) Liu An *et al.* Huainanzi•Daoyingxun (淮南子•道应训).
11. Ganqi Dance: 干戚舞, a martial dance with a large axe and shield.
12. (Warring States – Han). Shanhaijing•Haiwai Xijing (山海经•海外西经).
13. (Eastern Jin) Tao Yuanming. Du Shanhai Jing Shisan Shou (读山海经十三首).
14. (Western Han) Liu An *et al.* Huainanzi•Miuchengxun (淮南子•缪称训).
15. (Eastern Han) Xu Shen. Shuowen Jiezi•Wubu (说文解字•巫部).
16. (Spring and Autumn). Shangshu•Yushu•Yaodian (尚书•虞书•舜典). Xingyiquan is a major school of traditional Chinese quan. The quan (拳) refers to Chinese-style boxing, which contains more barehanded fighting skills than boxing in the English-speaking world.
17. Shiben•Shixing Pian (世本•氏姓篇).
18. (Warring States) Zhougong Dan. Zhouli•Diguan•Wushi (周礼•地官•舞狮).
19. Western Zhou dynasty: 西周, during the later stage of the Zhou dynasty, the capital city was moved eastwards; before the relocation, the dynasty is named Western Zhou; after the relocation, it is named Eastern Zhou (770–256 BC).
20. (Western Han) Sima Qian. Shiji•Fengshan (史记•封禅).
21. *A Reference for the Records of the Grand Historian* (Tang) Sima Zhen. Shiji Suoyin (史记索隐).
22. Jia Lanpo, *Zhoukoudian: the Cave Home of the Sinanthropus* (Beijing: Beijing Publishing House, 1975), 40.
23. Zhou Wei, *The History of Chinese Weapons* (Tianjin: Baihua Literature and Art Publishing House, 2006). (Note: The translators failed to find the 2006 edition, but found the quotation on p. 12 of the 2015 edition.)
24. (Eastern Han) Yuan Kang and Wu Ping. Yuejueshu•Yuejue Waizhuan Ji Baojian (越绝书•越绝外传记宝剑).

25 Friedrich Von Engels, *The Origin of the Family: Private Property and the State* (Beijing: Foreign Languages Press, 1978), 25.
26 (Eastern Han) Ying Shao. Fengsu Tongyi•Taishan Pian (风俗通義•泰山篇); (Three Kingdoms) Qiao Zhou. Gushi Kao (古史考).
27 (Eastern Han) Yuan Kang and Wu Ping. Yuejueshu•Goujian Yinmou Waizhuan (越绝书•勾践阴谋外传).
28 (Eastern Han) Zhao Ye. Wuyue Chunqiu•Dange (吴越春秋•弹歌).
29 Shiben•Zuopian (世本•作篇).
30 (Warring States) Lv Buwei et al. Lvshi Chunqiu•Zhongqiu Ji (吕氏春秋•仲秋纪).
31 (Western Han) Sima Qian. Shiji•Zhou Benji (史记•周本纪).
32 (Western Zhou). Shijing•Guofeng•Qinfeng (诗经•国风•秦风).
33 (Warring States) Qu Yuan. Chuci•Jiuge•Guoshang (楚辞•九歌•国殇).
34 (Warring States) Yan Ying. Yanzi Chunqiu•Neipian Za Shang (晏子春秋•内篇杂上).
35 (Eastern Han) Liu Xi. Shiming•Shibing (释名•释兵).
36 (Warring States) Zhougong Dan. Zhouli•Xiaguan•Sigedun (周礼•夏官•司戈盾).
37 Luo Xizhang, 'A Brief Study of Weapons from the Zhou dynasty Excavated in Fu Feng', *Archaeology and Cultural Relics*, no. 1 (1985): 1–10.
38 (Warring States) Zhougong Dan. Zhouli•Xiaguan•Sibing (周礼•夏官•司兵).
39 Jiaodi (角抵) refers to the Chinese-style wrestling that emerged in pre-modern times. Similar to the quan, Jiaodi contains more barehanded fighting skills than wrestling in the English-speaking world. A number of Chinese phrases that refer to Jiaodi can be found in different phases of Chinese history as well as in the original text of this work, such as 角力 (Jiaoli), 摔跤 (Shuaijiao), 摔角 (Shuaijiao), 争交 (Zhengjiao), and 相扑 (Xiangpu). The translators have employed the unified term 'Jiaodi' in this book. However, the term 'Xiangpu' or 'Jiaoli' are kept in the names of the classics.
40 (Western Han) Sima Qian. Shiji•Bashu•Lvshu (史记•八书•律书).
41 (Western Han) Sima Qian. Shiji•Yin Benji (史记•殷本纪).
42 (Western Zhou). Shijing•Guofeng•Zhengfeng•Dashu Yutian (诗经•国风•郑风•大叔于田).
43 (Western Han) Dai Sheng. Liji•Yueling (礼记•月令).
44 (Western Zhou). Shijing•Xiaoya•Qiaoyan (诗经•小雅•巧言).
45 (Warring States-Han) Guanzi. Guanzi•Xiaokuang (管子•小匡).
46 (Warring States) Zuo Qiuming. Zuozhuan•Xigong Ershiba Nian•Jinchu Chengpu Zhizhan (左传•僖公二十八年•晋楚城濮之战).
47 (Warring States) Zhougong Dan. Zhouli•Xiaguan•Huanren (周礼•夏官•环人).
48 (Western Han) Dai Sheng. Liji•Yueling (礼记•月令).
49 (Western Han) Dai Sheng. Liji•Neice (礼记•内侧); (Western Han) Dai Sheng. Li ji•Sheyi (礼记•射义).
50 (Western Zhou). Shijing •Guofeng •Qifeng •Yijie (诗经•国风•齐风•猗嗟).
51 (Western Han) Dai Sheng. Liji•Sheyi (礼记•射义).
52 (Western Han) Dai Sheng. Liji•Liyun (礼记•礼运).
53 (Western Han) Dai Sheng. Liji•Sheyi (礼记•射义).
54 Ibid.
55 In the pre-Qin period, the officials in the vassal states were divided into three ranks: minister, dafu, and shi (士).
56 (Warring States) Xunzi. Xunzi•Yuelun (荀子•乐论).
57 Kuang Wennan, 'Sports in the Shang and Western Zhou dynasties', in *Records for the Study of Sport History*, ed. the Institute for Sport History of Chengdu Institution of Physical Education (Sichuan: Chengdu Institution of Physical Education).
58 (Western Zhou). Shijing•Zhousong•Wu (诗经•周颂•武).
59 (Western Han) Sima Qian. Shiji•Yueshu (史记•乐书).

60 (Western Han) Dai Sheng. Liji•Yueji (礼记•乐记).
61 (Western Han) Sima Qian.Shiji•Yueshu (史记•乐书).
62 (Eastern Jin) Chang Qu. Huayang Guozhi•Bazhi (华阳国志•巴志).
63 (Western Zhou). Shijing•Zhousong•Weiqing (诗经•周颂•维清).
64 (Western Han) Dai Sheng. Liji•Neze (礼记•内则).
65 (Western Han) Dai Sheng. Liji•Wenwang Shizi (礼记•文王世子).
66 (Warring States) Zuo Qiuming. Zuozhuan•Chenggong Shisan Nian (左传•成公十三年).
67 Chen Mengjia, *Reviewing the Oracle Inscriptions of the Yin Ruins* (Shanghai: Zhonghua Book Company,1988).
68 Guo Moruo, *Yinqi Huibian* (Japan: Wenqiutang Book Company,1937).
69 Jin Wen: 金文, transcriptions of the inscriptions on ancient bronze.
70 Jingyin Mingwen (静殷铭文).
71 There are various interpretations of the Five Archeries. The book *Shejing* by Li Chengfen is preferred; Li has given a reasonable interpretation of the characteristics of archery.
72 For a concrete introduction to the Five Ridings, please refer to the annotations of *Zhouli* by both Zheng Xuan and Jia Gongyan.
73 Kuang Wennan, *Introduction to the Culture of Chinese Martial Arts* (Chengdu: Sichuan Education Press, 1990), 22–23.
74 (Warring States-Han) Guanzi. Guanzi•Xiaokuang (管子•小匡).
75 (Warring States) Zuo Qiuming. Guoyu•Jinyu (国语•晋语).
76 (Spring and Autumn – Warring States) Mozi et al. Mozi•Shangxian (墨子•尚贤).
77 (Warring States) Han Fei. Hanfeizi•Neichu Shuo Shang (韩非子•内储说上).
78 (Western Han) Sima Qian. Shiji•Zhang Chengxiang Liezhuan (史记•张丞相列传).
79 (Warring States) Meng Zi et al. Mengzi•Tengwengong Shang (孟子•滕文公上).
80 Kongzi Jiayu•Haosheng (孔子家语•好生).
81 (Warring States) Zhuangzi et al. Zhuangzi•Shuojian (庄子•说剑).
82 (Warring States) Zhuangzi et al. Zhuangzi•Shuojian (庄子•说剑).
83 (Warring States) Lie Zi et al. Liezi•Huangdi (列子•黄帝).
84 (Spring and Autumn – Warring States) Jiang Ziyang. Simafa•Yanwei (司马法•严位).
85 (Spring and Autumn). Shangshu•Zhoushu•Mushi (尚书•周书•牧誓).
86 (Spring and Autumn) Sun Wu. Sunzi Bingfa•Junshi (孙子兵法•军事).
87 (Eastern Han) Ban Gu. Hanshu•Xingfa Zhi (汉书•刑法志).
88 Wuxia (武侠) is a unique popular culture in China. The Wuxia culture is characterized by various types of martial heroes and martial arts skills that advocate a chivalrous spirit.
89 (Warring States) Zhougong Dan. Zhouli•Kaogong Ji (周礼•考工记).
90 (Spring and Autumn – Warring States) Mozi et al. Mozi•Jieyong (墨子•节用).
91 (Warring States) Lv Buwei et al. Lvshi Chunqiu•Zhongqiu Ji•Lunwei (吕氏春秋•仲秋纪•论威).
92 (Eastern Han) Yuan Kang and Wu Ping. Yuejue Shu•Yuejue Waizhuan Ji Baojian (越绝书•越绝外传记宝剑).
93 The Editorial Committee of Chinese Bronze Ware, *The Chinese Bronzes* (volume 4) (Beijing: Cultural Relics Press,1973).
94 (Western Han) Sima Qian. Shiji•Zhang Chengxiang Liezhuan (史记•刺客列传).
95 (Warring States) Zhuangzi et al. Zhuangzi•Renjianshi (庄子•人间世).
96 (Western Han) Gongyang Gao. Chunqiu•Gongyang Zhuan•Zhuanggong Shier Nian (春秋•公羊传•庄公十二年).
97 (Western Han) Guliang Zi. Chunqiu•Guliang Zhuan•Xigong Yuannian (春秋•谷梁传•僖公元年).

98 (Warring States) Han Fei. Hanfeizi•Waichu Shuo (韩非子•外储说).
99 (Spring and Autumn) Sun Wu. Sunzi•Wuqi Liezhuan (孙子兵法•吴起列传); (Western Han) Sima Qian. Shiji•Taishigong Zixu (史记•太史公自序).
100 (Western Han) Sima Qian. Shiji•Cike Liezhuan (史记•刺客列传).
101 (Eastern Han) Zhao Ye. Wuyue Chunqiu•Goujian Yimou Waizhuan (吴越春秋•勾践阴谋外传).
102 (Warring States) Zhuangzi et al. Zhuangzi•Shuojian (庄子•说剑).
103 (Western Han) Sima Qian. Shiji•Zhongni Dizi Liezhuan (史记•仲尼弟子列传).
104 Bar: The long and sturdy bar used for bolting a castle gate in ancient China.
105 (Spring and Autumn – Warring States) Mozi et al. Mozi•Feiru (墨子•非儒).
106 (Warring States) Lie Zi et al. Liezi•Shuofu (列子•说符).
107 (Warring States) Lv Buwei et al. Lvshi Chunqiu•Shenda (吕氏春秋•慎大).
108 (Western Han) Liu An et al. Huainanzi•Zhushuxun (淮南子•主术训).
109 (Western Han) Dai Sheng. Liji•Sheyi (礼记•射义).
110 *The Analects of Confucius*. (Western Han) Sima Qian. Shiji•Kongzi Shijia (史记•孔子世家); (Warring States) Confucius et al. Lunyu•Yanyuan (论语•颜渊); (Warring States) Confucius et al. Lunyu•Zilu (论语•子路).
111 (Western Han) Sima Qian. Shiji•Zhongni Dizi Liezhuan (史记•仲尼弟子列传).
112 (Warring States) Confucius et al. Lunyu• Taibo (论语•泰伯).
113 (Spring and Autumn – Warring States) Mozi et al. Mozi•Xiushen (墨子•修身).
114 (Spring and Autumn – Warring States) Mozi et al. Mozi•Shangxian (墨子•尚贤).
115 (Spring and Autumn – Warring States) Mozi et al. Mozi•Jieyong (墨子•节用).
116 *The Practice of Taijiquan*. (Qing) Yang Chengfu. Taijiquan Zhi Lianxi Tan (太极拳之练习谈).
117 (Spring and Autumn) Laozi. Daode Jing (道德经).
118 Qi (气) is believed to be a vital force forming part of any living entity. It is the central underlying principle in traditional Chinese medicine and in Chinese martial arts.
119 (Ming) Wang Zongyue. Taijiquan Lun (太极拳论).
120 Internal quan is a major school of traditional Chinese quan which integrates the operation of inner qi (breath) exercises and external body movements, drawing on the Yin-Yang thesis.
121 Baguazhang is a major school of traditional Chinese quan which is mainly based on changing palms and circle walking.
122 Kuang Wennan. *Introduction to the Culture of Chinese Martial Arts* (Sichuan: Sichuan Education Press, 1990), 43.
123 (Spring and Autumn) Sun Wu. Sunzi Bingfa (孙子兵法).
124 (Warring States) Wu Qi. Wuzi Bingfa (吴子兵法).
125 (Warring States) Sun Bin. Sun Bin Bingfa (孙膑兵法).
126 (Spring and Autumn – Warring States) Jiang Ziya. Simafa (司马法).
127 (Warring States) Wei Liaozi. Weiliaozi (尉缭子).
128 (Warring States) Jiang Ziya. Liutao (六韬).
129 (Warring States) Sun Bin. Sun Bin Bingfa•Cuanzu (孙膑兵法•篡卒).
130 (Warring States) Jiang Ziya. Liutao•Longtao•Nongqi (六韬•龙韬•农器).
131 (Warring States) Jiang Ziya. Liutao•Quantao•Wucheshi (六韬•犬韬•武车士).
132 (Warring States) Jiang Ziya. Liutao•Quantao•Lianshi (六韬•犬韬•练士).
133 (Spring and Autumn – Warring States) Jiang Ziya. Simafa•Dingjue (司马法•定爵).
134 (Spring and Autumn) Sun Wu. Sunzi Bingfa (孙子兵法).
135 Kuang Wennan, 'The Art of War and the Fighting Art of Chinese Martial Arts: Militarists and Martial arts Culture II', *The Journal of Sport History and Culture*, no. 5 (1990): 47–51.
136 (Spring and Autumn) Laozi. Laozi • Di Sishier Zhang (老子•第四十二章).

137 (Warring States – Han). Huangdi Neijing•Suwen (黄帝内经•素问).
138 (Western Zhou) Wangbi. Zhou Yi (周易).
139 (Western Zhou) Wang Bi. Zhou Yi•Jin (周易•晋).
140 (Western Han) Sima Qian. Shiji•Zhaoshijia (史记•赵世家).
141 (Qing) Liu E. Tieyun Canggui (铁云藏龟).
142 (Western Han) Liu An *et al.* Huainanzi•Renjianxun (淮南子•人间训).
143 Man (蛮) refers to the people living to the south of the central plains in the pre-Qin period.
144 (Tang) Fan Chuo. Manshu•Yunnan Guanwu Neichan (蛮书•云南管内物产).
145 The Museum of Yunnan Province, An Excavation Report of Ancient Tombs at Shizhai Mountain in Jinning of Yunnan Province (Beijing: Cultural Relics Publishing House, 1959).

Chapter 2

Martial arts in the Qin and Han dynasties and Three Kingdoms periods (221 BC–280)

During the reign of Emperor Yingzheng (259–210 BC), martial arts were prohibited among normal people, with all weapons confiscated. However, the trajectory of Chinese martial arts continued, and the Qin dynasty collapsed after only two emperors. The Han dynasty (202 BC–220) is considered a splendid era of Chinese feudal society, with political, economic, and cultural prosperity. Martial arts achieved great progress in this phase. Both military and non-military martial arts were further promoted by the Han emperors as a result of their dependence on military force during the wars with the Xiongnu.

With the development of Chinese martial arts in the Qin and Han dynasties and Three Kingdoms periods (220–280), a great number of classics on martial arts emerged; various schools of martial arts took their initial shape; the role of the sword in military application was gradually replaced by the sabre, but remained active in non-military use; the sabre, the skills of practicing sword and sabre, and Jiaodi were introduced into Japan.

Martial arts in the Qin and Han dynasties

In 221 BC, the State of Qin defeated the last warring state, Qi, and established the first unified 'Chin'. Emperor Yingzheng issued a series of decrees to consolidate the unification of the state and his autocratic power. Notably, he gave the order to confiscate weapons from his people. *Records of the Grand Historian* notes that Emperor Yingzheng destroyed famous cities and killed the able-bodied. He also confiscated all weapons in the capital city Xianyang, melted them into 12 metal statues, and used them to decorate the palace. Clearly, his purpose was to inhibit people from martial practice in order to weaken their power.[1]

This movement achieved great success. The public were deprived of any sort of weapons, as shown in records of the peasant uprising led by Chen Sheng and Wu Guang at the end of the Qin dynasty, when the insurgent troops had no military weapons and had to cut wood to make weapons.[2] But Emperor Yingzheng eventually failed, and the Qin dynasty collapsed.

Nevertheless, there was martial practice among the armies of Qin. In defeating all the warring states, Qin had built a very compelling army comprising millions of armoured soldiers, thousands of chariots, and tens of thousands of horses.[3] Its scale can be seen in the Terracotta Warriors excavated in Xi'an in Shaanxi Province in 1974. Tens of thousands of ceramic soldiers and horses were found. The soldiers are classified into four branches of armed forces: infantry, crossbow troop, chariot troop, and cavalry, holding different kinds of weapons such as bows, crossbows, bronze swords, dagger-axes, spears, and halberds, each in a heroic posture facing the east. It is vivid evidence of military training in the Qin dynasty.

In general, the development of Chinese martial arts in the Qin and Han dynasties was largely perpetuated by the wars with the northern peoples, in particular the Xiongnu. Before the establishment of the Qin dynasty, the Xiongnu often invaded the states in and around the central plains, such as Qin, Zhao, and Yan, which consumed great military effort from these states. After the establishment of the Qin dynasty, Emperor Yingzheng expelled the Xiongnu invaders in the north and built the Great Wall so as to further hold back invasion. During the transition between the Qin and Han dynasties, the Xiongnu, led by Batur Tengriqut (234–174 BC), conquered many other peoples in the north, such as the Loufan and Donghu. These defeated peoples were forced to invade the south together with the Xiongnu. They later conquered the southern area of Hetao (the upper reaches of the Yellow River in north-western China), previously occupied by the Qin dynasty. With a strong military force – they claimed to have 300,000 soldiers – the northerners kept invading the south.[4] In the early Han dynasty, the Han rulers had to ingratiate themselves with the Xiongnu with a policy of 'intermarriage for pacification' after several defeats, but this compromise didn't stop the invasions. During the reign of Emperor Wen (203–157 BC), the Xiongnu people even occupied the central part of Han, which posed a huge threat to the capital Chang'an. The Han rulers had to make advances in the development of weapons and military training to cope with the strong invaders.

Chao Cuo (200–154 BC), a Minister of Ceremonies of Han, pointed out the main reason the Xiongnu forces had the advantage over the Han: they were nomadic. When they found borders not fully guarded, they attacked. If the emperor didn't send troops to rescue the people living there, they might surrender to the Xiongnu. Sending small numbers of troops did not guarantee victory, while sending large numbers was time-consuming. By the time the troops arrived, the invaders might have already left. If they stayed on the borders, it was costly; if they didn't, the Xiongnu invaded again.

Chao Cuo suggested sending more people to settle near the borders. In doing so, these people were trained to be regular military forces.[5] Emperor Wen adopted this suggestion. In a tomb discovered in Chengdu in 1975, there is a stone sculpture of people of the Han dynasty weaving, riding, and making liquor, along with others keeping domestic animals, showing a picture of 'combining farming with military' and 'farmers trained to be fighters'. On the sculpture, there are also weapon stands with trident, halberd, sword, shield, and bow and arrow.

The strategy of militarizing the border people was effective in holding back the invaders from the north. However, the Han had to take the initiative to fight against the Xiongnu and eliminate their main military force to solve the long-term invasion problem, meaning a mighty army was urgently required. In fact, the rulers had already realized that training and evaluation of the army was very important in the early Han dynasty. During the reign of Emperor Gaozu (256–195 BC), the government had begun to recruit martial talents and warriors as various kinds of soldiers.[6]

The Han dynasty highly stressed building up the cavalry. Emperor Gaozu set up and improved institutions in charge of horse raising and riding. In the reign of Emperor Wen, Chao Cuo encouraged horse raising among the public, with immediate benefits in building the cavalry.[7] Later, Emperor Wu (156–87 BC) set up two specialized troops in Chang'an, one to guard the emperors and the other to guard the capital. The majority were cavalry. In fighting the Xiongnu, cavalry replaced infantry as the major force; the *Book of Han* records the Han sending 30,000 to 180,000 cavalry soldiers to war.[8]

With the emphasis on military force, coupled with other political and economic advantages, the Han eventually defeated the Xiongnu. In some ways, the attention given to military affairs promoted the development of martial arts. The advancement of crossbow techniques in the Han dynasty was closely related to the battles with the Xiongnu, while the replacement of the sword by the sabre is attributed to its being more suited to cavalry. This strong military ethos persisted throughout the Han dynasty.

Schools, classics, and theories of martial arts in the Han dynasty

Ban Gu (32–92), a distinguished historian and intellectual of Han, classified the military classics into the following categories in his *Book of Han*: 259 articles of 13 schools on military strategy; 93 articles of 11 schools on battlefield tactics; 249 articles of 16 schools on military Yin and Yang; 199 articles of 13 schools on military skills. The works in the category of military skills can be regarded as martial arts classics, among which archery skills play a dominant role. There are also six articles on unarmed combat, 38 articles on swordsmanship, and 25 articles on Cuju.[9,10] These are the earliest writings on Chinese martial arts that we know of. They indicate that as early as during the Han dynasty, Chinese martial arts were theorized in written form, in addition to methods of oral inheritance.

Besides, the fact that many articles were written about a single martial art also demonstrates the emergence of various schools of martial arts in this period. Emperor Wen of Wei (Cao Pi, 187–226) claims in *Classic Thesis* that he learned sword skills from childhood from different masters, and that sword skills varied in different regions but those in the capital were the best.[11] This clearly reveals that different schools of swordsmanship had formed at that time. Moreover, *Book of Han* also says that the schools of quan and other weapon techniques were initially formed during the Han dynasty.[12] Both *Complete Classics Collection of Ancient China* and *Records of the Three Kingdoms* use the term 'wuyi'

(武艺), which generally refers to all kinds of martial skills.[13] This seems to be evidence that Chinese martial arts had been conceptualized and systematized.

Unfortunately, some of the military classics have been lost to the ages, and their original content is unknown to us. But we can still have a brief look at martial arts theories in the Qin and Han dynasties from the limited records in other ancient writings. For instance, Chao Cuo had penetrating and incisive comments on military affairs. He stated that three factors should be considered in war: first, occupying a favourable geographical position; second, having a well-drilled troop; third, acquiring favourable weapons. He also analysed which geological environment was suitable for what kind of soldiers and weapons, and he emphasized the significance of weapons and martial arts.[14] His comments are not only military theories but also martial arts theories. Besides, *Classic Thesis*, *Inquiring Balance*, *Swordsmanship* also reveal the systematization and theorization of sword skills in the Han dynasty.[15]

Han dynasty martial arts forms, paired fights, and contests of strength

Forms

Chinese martial arts often appeared in the form of martial dances in ancient times. The Han dynasty, in particular the Eastern Han period (25–220), witnessed great progress in many kinds of martial dances, such as the sword dance, the axe dance, and the broadax dance. Despite these martial dances being generally performed freely, they expressed the meaning of attack and defence through the combination of basic movements such as chasing and jumping, advancing, and striking. In this sense, some early martial arts forms emerged.

The sword dance performed by Xiang Zhuang (who intended to assassinate Liu Bang) at Hongmen Banquet was a typical martial dance[16] demonstrating a casual martial arts form of swordsmanship. On some brick portraits from the Han dynasty, we can also see the performance of this kind of sword dance. For example, a portrait found in a tomb in Yi'nan County, Shandong Province shows the emperor watching a sword dance. The swordsman is performing a skilful gesture, making an attack with sword in hand, lifting his knee, and turning his body.

There is a vivid image of a broadax dance with the performer's knee and body raised in an Eastern Han stone coffin unearthed in Pi County, Sichuan Province in 1972. In 1954, a stone portrait titled 'Da-nuo-tu' was found in Linyi in Shandong Province, with famous Chinese dramatist Ouyang Yuqian (1889–1962) commenting:

> We can see from this portrait the demons and deities in people's imagination. Some of the deities are holding axes while some have short swords. They are chasing and jumping, while the demons are fleeing. This reveals

the supreme power of the deities. The theme of this ritual is to expel demons, so most of the movements involved in the dance are chasing, jumping, shooting, etc.[17]

As a dance performance, these movements must be combined. Therefore, broadax, axe, and sword dance can be regarded as simple forms of Chinese martial arts.

Paired fights

Martial arts combat and performances, which originated from the warlike ethos in particular swordplay since the Spring and Autumn and Warring States periods, were very popular in the Han dynasty. Besides unarmed combat and Jiaodi, paired fights also included the following activities:

Swordplay

Swordplay was very popular among the nobility as well as the common people in the Han dynasty. There were specialized masters of swordsmanship. *Book of Han* records that Prince Liu An (179–122 BC) was addicted to swordsmanship and seemed to be good at swordplay.[18] There is no doubt that Emperor Wen of Wei was a master of swordsmanship, according to the aforementioned description in *Classic Thesis* in section two of this chapter.

A good number of stone portraits have shown scenes of swordplay in the Han dynasty, as in the case of a picture in Shaoshi Tower in Dengfeng in Henan Province, where two swordsmen in narrow clothes and pants are fighting against each other. Two swordsmen are also fighting each other with long swords in a stone portrait unearthed in Nanyang in Henan Province (see Figure 2.1).

Animal fights

The Han nobility was keen on watching animal fights. For instance, Emperor Wu once gave the order to trap bears, boars, and wolves in order to show the Hu people how to fight them with bare hands. He would watch the fights in person.[19] Cao Zhang (?–223), son of Cao Cao (posthumously honoured as Emperor Wu of Wei, c.155–220), was capable of fighting wild animals,[20] as was Liu Xu (?–54 BC), the fourth son of Emperor Wu of Han.[21]

Sword versus halberd

Sword versus halberd play was very popular in the Han Dynasty, as can be seen from the excavations. For instance, a brick portrait unearthed in the Yangzi Mountain District of Chengdu shows a man stabbing his opponent's abdomen with a long halberd. The opponent is dodging and warding off the halberd, and trying to stab back with his sword.

Figure 2.1 An image of Han dynasty swordplay.

Sword versus broadax

A portrait of sword versus broadax play was found in a stone tomb in Tanghe County in Henan Province in 1971. It depicts a man striking his opponent's helmet with the broadax. The handle breaks off from the strength exerted (see Figure 2.2).

Figure 2.2 An image of two men fighting from the Han dynasty, excavated in Tanghe, Henan Province.

Halberd versus sword and halberd versus hook-shield

A picture of halberd versus sword and halberd versus hook-shield was found in Zhengzhou in Henan Province, in which a sword and hook-shield holder is forced back against a tree by a halberd holder. He uses the hook-shield in his left hand to ward off the halberd, and attacks with the sword in his right hand. A similar portrait was also found in Miao Mountain in Tongshan County, Jiangsu Province (see Figure 2.3).

Figure 2.3 Halberd vs. sword fights from the Han dynasty, excavated in Tongshan County, Jiangsu Province.

Unarmed versus armed

In the preface of *Classic Thesis*, Cao Pi says General Deng Zhan was good at fighting unarmed against armed opponents.[22] A stone portrait discovered in Xuzhou, Jiangsu Province in 1964 depicts a fight between an unarmed man and a halberd-holding man. Also, a stone portrait of an unarmed man fighting a spear-holding man was found in Nanyang, Henan Province. From portraits, we can also see other Han dynasty paired fights, such as cudgel versus cudgel, halberd versus halberd, sword and shield versus double halberd, and so on.

Strength contests

It can be inferred from the excavations and the literature that bar-lifting and ding-lifting[23] were the major forms of strength contest in the Han dynasty. Zuo Si (250–305), a Western Jin writer (265–316, coinciding with the late Eastern Han), notes the rules of bar-lifting contests in his *Overview of the State of Wu*.[24] The participants competed to use one hand to lift the long and heavy bar of the castle gate by holding one end. It seems to have been very difficult.

In *Overview of the Capital of Western Han*, Zhang Heng (78–139) describes the grand scene of the Han Hundred Skills Show,[25] with ding-lifting one of the most eye-catching contests.[26] There are also many written records of Han ding-lifting, such as in *Records of the Grand Historian* and *Book of Han*,[27] indicating that it was a very popular strength training and contest. From Han portraits, we can see the scene and rules. There were two methods of lifting. One was to hold one leg of the ding with a single hand, stretching the arm to lift it up. The ding used in this contest was usually small. This method is shown on a stone portrait unearthed in Nanyang, Henan Province. The other was to hold the two handles of the ding, turn it upside down and lift it up with three legs in the air. This method is shown in a stone portrait unearthed in Xuzhou, Jiangsu Province.

There were also other kinds of strength contest in the Han dynasty. For instance, a stone portrait unearthed in Xuzhou shows three strong men: the man on the left with a thick beard is uprooting a willow whose trunk is as big as a bowl; the man standing in the middle is holding the tail of a large deer in his hand and the body on his shoulder; the man on the right is lifting a ding with both hands over his head (see Figure 2.4). There was a huge bell during the period of Emperor Wen of Wei, and a man named Wang Zhang was so strong that he could run while holding it.

Jiaodi and unarmed combat

Jiaodi was mainly for entertainment, not only for the common people but also for the palace in the Qin dynasty (see Figure 2.5). Jiaodi tended to be a form of unarmed contest on strength and tumbling techniques. Therefore, Jiaodi not only survived the weapon confiscation campaign launched by Emperor

Figure 2.4 An image of strength training from the Han dynasty, excavated in Xuzhou, Jiangsu Province.

Figure 2.5 A Jiaodi mural excavated in Mi County, Henan Province.

Yingzheng, but also developed further. Jiaodi was so popular in the Qin palace and attracted so much enthusiasm from the rulers, *Records of the Grand Historian* describes Emperor Huhai (230–207 BC) deserting his government affairs to watch Jiaodi.[28]

At the beginning of the Han dynasty, Taoism was upheld by Emperor Gaozu. He suggested that people should live in a harmonious and peaceful society and live a simple life, so Jiaodi was prohibited. During the reign of Emperor Wu, Jiaodi became popular again. *Book of Han* records that a Jiaodi contest held in 108 BC drew a large crowd of spectators, and that another large-scale Jiaodi contest took place in the summer three years later.[29]

The reign of Emperor Wu was a strong and prosperous era for the Han dynasty. The rulers were so proud of this that they often welcomed foreign guests in an extravagant way. Jiaodi was an important element at grand banquets,[30] particularly during the reign of Emperor Shun (115–144). *Book of the Later Han* notes that emperors liked to invite people of merit to watch Jiaodi during commemorations.[31] *Book of Han* adds that some officials of Emperor Wu were good at Jiaodi.[32]

Jiaodi was prohibited as part of money-saving measures after an outbreak of natural disasters in 44 BC.[33] However, this was temporary. Up to the Eastern Han period, the development of the Hundred Skills, including Jiaodi, again made great progress.

A Jiaodi scene can be found on a silk painting unearthed in a Han dynasty tomb in Linyi, Shandong Province. There are three men in the picture, two of them strong wrestlers with broad shoulders and impressive muscles. They are arm in arm and staring at each other as they wait for the start of the contest. The other man stands in the middle and seems to be the referee (see Figure 2.6). This silk painting was buried with the dead, and the Jiaodi scene takes up one fifth of the whole painting. Some thus argue that it reveals the dead person's love for Jiaodi, in that the descendant arranged a Jiaodi performance for him. Other archaeological excavations also show that Jiaodi was popular in the Qin and Han dynasties. Furthermore, we learn from Yu Pu's *Records of Jiangbiao*[34] that female practitioners of Jiaodi emerged during the Three Kingdoms period.

Unarmed combat is recorded in the historical writings of the Han dynasty, such as the drunken fight between Grand Administrator of Huaiyang Guan Fu and Commander of Guards Dou Fu during the reign of Emperor Wu, in *Book of Han*.[35] Zuo Si says in *Overview of the State of Wu* that the people liked unarmed combat.[36] Notably, unarmed combat had detached from Jiaodi by the time of the Han dynasty.[37] The annotations of *Book of Han* by Meng Kang, a Three Kingdoms scholar, show that unarmed combat was an element of soldier selection.[38]

Capable unarmed combat fighters of the Han dynasty and the Three Kingdoms period are also recorded in historical documents. For example, *Records of the Three Kingdoms* says that General Dong Zhuo (?–192) took out his halberd to attack General Lv Bu (?–199), but Lv's hands were so flexible that he could

Qin and Han dynasties and Three Kingdoms 55

Figure 2.6 An image of a silk painting of Jiaodi from the Western Han dynasty, excavated in Lingyi, Shandong Province.

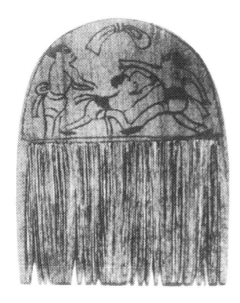

Figure 2.7 A wooden comb with lacquer painting of Jiaodi from the Qin dynasty, excavated in Phoenix Mountain in Jiangling County, Hubei Province.

avoid being attacked.³⁹ This was because he was well trained in unarmed combat.

Qin dynasty excavations and Han dynasty murals and brick portraits also show scenes of unarmed combat. For example, on a Qin dynasty wooden comb unearthed in Phoenix Mountain in Jiangling County, Hubei Province in 1975, there is a colour lacquer painting of unarmed combat. All three men in the painting are topless and wearing short pants, a belt on the waist and a pair of warped head shoes. The two men on the right are fighting each other, while the man on the left is stretching his hands flat as the referee (see Figure 2.7).

The transformation of the sword and the rise of the sabre

Bronze sword manufacturing techniques had their heyday during the Warring States period. A number of bronze swords, of 81–94.4 cm in length and 3.14–3.6 cm in width, have been unearthed with the Terracotta Warriors. The ridges and blades of these swords are primarily made of bronze with different percentages of tin, so as to make the sword body pliable but strong while the blade is sharp. It is rather remarkable that some of these swords were dark gray or pitch dark and completely stainless, with a surface of a very high degree of gloss finish and strong wear resistance. Studies have revealed that these bronze swords were treated by chromate salt oxidation and coated with a compact oxide film ten microns thick. Such an important scientific discovery shocked the world's researchers, because this technology was classified as a patent by Germany in 1937 and the US in 1950. The excavation of substantial numbers of bronze swords in the Terracotta Warriors vaults suggests that Qin armies were well equipped with these bronze swords (see Figure 2.8).

Iron swords were widely used during the Warring States period. By the Han dynasty, the specification and application of iron swords had basically been established. Two iron swords owned by Liu Sheng (165–113 BC), son of Emperor Jing of Han (188–141 BC), were unearthed in a Han dynasty tomb in Mancheng County, Hebei Province. Each measures more than 1 m, with a well-preserved scabbard. The blade remained sharp through quenching and the ridge kept good toughness through the addition of carbon.

The sword remained a very important weapon in the early stages of the Han dynasty. According to *Records of the Grand Historian*, when Emperor Gaozu was in danger during the Hongmen Banquet, his general Fan Kuai (242–189 BC) broke into the banquet area, dressed in full armour with sword and shield in hand.⁴⁰ At the time, Han soldiers were widely equipped with sword and shield. A *Biographical History of Eastern Han* also notes that the nomad Xiongnu people also used swords.⁴¹

Originating in the Spring and Autumn and Warring States periods, the custom of wearing a sword prevailed in the Qin and Han dynasties. Taking the Hongmen Banquet as an example again, Xiang Zhuang pretended to perform a

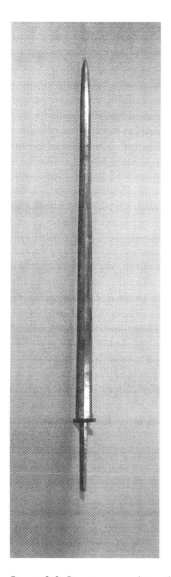

Figure 2.8 Bronze swords in the Terracotta Warriors vaults.

sword dance in order to find an opportunity to assassinate Liu Bang (later Emperor Gaozu), then Xiang Bo offered to join the performance with a sword in order to block Xiang Zhuang with his body. At the same time, Xiang Yu (232–202 BC) grasped his sword. All the people present in the banquet, including Xiang Yu, Liu Bang, Xiang Zhuang, Xiang Bo, Fan Zeng, Fan Kuai, and Xiahou Ying, carried swords. *Book of Jin* writes that carrying a sword was the etiquette of the Han dynasty, and all officials, civil or military, were required to do so. Later, they only carried them at court.[42] Dong Zhongshu, a scholar of the Han dynasty, in his *Luxuriant Dew of the Spring and Autumn Annals* says that the sword was on the left while the sabre was on the right.[43] A sword on the left was regarded as a sign of dignity. This suggests that there were rules about how to wear a sword.

The swords worn by emperors were considered precious treasures. For instance, the sword of Emperor Yingzheng of Qin was honored for its role in the 'united Qin dynasty', and Emperor Gaozu of Han wore a sword named Scarlet which had been used to hack up a white boa constrictor. There was a treasured sword named Turtle owned by Emperor Wen of Han, and Wang Mang (45 BC–23), a Han official who later seized the throne from the Liu family and founded the Xin Dynasty (9–23), even had a sword named Holy Sword. Sun Quan (182–252), founder of the state of Eastern Wu, collected six exquisite and valuable swords that he was passionate about.[44] Liu Bei (161–223), who founded the state of Shu Han in the Three Kingdoms period and became its first ruler, was a sword enthusiast too, and had eight different swords cast.[45] During the Han dynasty and the Three Kingdoms period, people connected the emperor's sword to divination, as in the anecdotes of Liu Xiu (5 BC–57), Emperor Guangwu of Han. Liu Xiu was merely a common person when he chanced to acquire a sword on Mount E in Nanyang, naming it the Supreme Xiu. Mysteriously, he then became the founding emperor of the Eastern Han dynasty. Furthermore, one of the four peculiar swords named Retrieval cast by Emperor Ling of Han (c.156–189) suddenly disappeared. This was believed to be a heavenly signal that the recovery of the dynasty would never take place during his reign, as turned out to be historical fact.

A warlike ethos prevailed during the Han dynasty, and masters of swordsmanship in the public society emerged. Both *Records of the Grand Historian*[46] and *Records of the Three Kingdoms*[47] note that many people began to learn swordsmanship from childhood, including Xiang Yu and Lu Su.

Refined scholars also had a passion for swordsmanship. For example, Dongfang Shuo (154–93 BC) said he started learning how to wield a sword at age 15,[48] while Sima Xiangru (c.179–118) also kept up with sword training.[49] With the prevailing warlike ethos, teaching sword skills could bring glory and higher social status, as *Book of Han* records that people were ranked by their competence in sword instruction in the State of Zhao.[50]

In the Han dynasty, swordsmanship began to be stylized as martial performance for a single person or a pair. Pair fighting further developed Han swordsmanship. Moreover, theoretical writings on swordsmanship emerged in this period.

The sword seems to have been gradually abandoned in war, but to have gained greater popularity both in the upper classes and among the common people from the Han dynasty on. One reason is that swords had thin, light blades likely to break in military battle. Also, as the use of cavalry increased, the main way to attack the enemy changed from stabbing to hacking. The sword was thus gradually replaced by the heavy and hard ring-headed sabre from the Western Han period on.

A number of ring-headed sabres were excavated in 23 Western Han tombs in western Luoyang in Henan Province between 1957 and 1958.[51] They are iron, and 85–114 cm in length. Vivid scenes of using the sabre in the Han dynasty can be seen in relics. Whether cavalry or infantry, every soldier holds a shield in one hand and a sabre in the other in a picture carved at the lintel of a stone tomb in Yi'nan County, Shandong Province. The sword was replaced by the sabre to complement the shield for military application. The picture also shows that the Han dynasty ring-headed sabre had a straight ridge and blade. There is no hand-protection between the handle and the body, but there is a ring at the head.

The tradition of wearing the sabre formed in the Western Han period. Han literature also shows that many significant figures, such as Emperor Guangwu, wore a sabre instead of a sword. Sabres were also worn by some ordinary people. For example, *Book of the Later Han* documents that 15-year-old Peng Xiu drew his sabre to protect his father who was robbed.[52] Additionally, it is common to see the farmer figurines excavated from the tombs of the late Eastern Han period wearing the ring-headed sabres.

By the Three Kingdoms period, the sabre had become the major short weapon in the army. *A Supplementary Biography of Zhuge Liang* says that Pu Yuan, a renowned craftsman, made 3,000 sharp sabres for Zhuge Liang (181–234), a famous military strategist.[53] Sun Quan gave the order to craft 10,000 high-quality sabres in 226.[54]

The development of crossbows and archery

The war between the Han and the Xiongnu stimulated the development of crossbow and archery technology. Many Western Han army generals were good at archery, with the most famous being Li Guang (?–119 BC). It was written that when hundreds of Xiongnu soldiers were trying to capture him, he managed to snatch a bow from one of them and use it to fight back, and finally got away.[55] Since then, Li has been a symbol of excellent archery in ancient China.

The Xiongnu were also good at archery. Chao Cuo analysed the contrast between the Han army and Xiongnu army, and found that the terrain of Xiongnu was of great strategic importance, since it meant the people living there were especially good at riding and shooting. Because they were such good archers, almost all of them could be regarded as warriors. Thus, Han dynasty records often describe them as an enormous army of 300,000 archers. In view of this situation, Chao Cuo came up with the idea that the Han should ally with other peoples who were good at archery, such as the Yiqu, to resist the Xiongnu.[56]

There were many good archers in the Eastern Han and Three Kingdoms period. Sun Quan once killed a fierce tiger with a single arrow; Taishi Ci

(166–206), an Eastern Wu general, never missed the target. *Records of The Three Kingdoms* adds that Cao Pi adapted archery as a method of daily exercise.[57]

Crossbow techniques were much more advanced than bow techniques during the Qin and Han dynasties and Three Kingdoms periods. Thirty-four crossbows have been unearthed in the pits of the Terracotta Warriors. Beside the second pit stands an army of archers. *Book of Han* claims that crossbows were first among all weapons during the Han dynasty.[58] Chao Cuo also pointed out that crossbows and long halberds were the potential weapons to defeat the Xiongnu.[59]

The crossbow was even regarded as a token of rituals in the Han dynasty. For example, when Emperor Wu appointed Sima Xiangru as General of the Palace Gentlemen in charge of the Shu area in the south-west, officials welcomed him with a crossbow and arrow.[60] Similarly, when General Huo Qubing (140–117 BC) of the Western Han visited Hedong, the County Magistrate carried a crossbow to give directions to Sima Xiangru, to show respect.[61]

There were many different types of crossbows in the Han Dynasty, such as the Dahuang Crossbow, Lian Crossbow, Yao Crossbow, Shilian Crossbow, Wanjun Shen Crossbow, and Yuanrong Crossbow. The Lian was the most famous, because it could continuously fire tens of arrows, according to many texts. However, we lack specifications and information about methods.

Regarding methods of triggering the crossbow, crossbowman used their hands to draw the bow for light crossbows and their feet, using mechanical devices, for heavy crossbows.[62] People could also choose to sit on the ground and use a pedal,[63] or draw from the waist[64] (see Figure 2.9). However, Yuan Tingdong, author of *The Ancient Warfare of China*, argues that such inefficient and inflexible approaches were not commonly applied, judging from the stone portraits in Shandong and Sichuan provinces and some illustrations in *Treatise on Armament Technology*.[65] In the Han dynasty, the crossbow already had a scale plate. Yuan considered its usage to be similar to that of modern rifles, and that it could significantly improve the accuracy of the crossbow.[66] This reveals that archers and craftsmen of the time understood the relationship between the projecting angle and the range of oblique projectile motion, and it can be regarded as a great achievement in the Chinese history of ancient weapons and physics.

In the Han dynasty, there were specialized generals and guards in charge of the crossbow as well as other officials responsible for teaching crossbow skills,[67] and a number of good crossbow archers emerged. For instance, the previously mentioned General Li Guang was not only skilful with bow and arrow, but also with the crossbow.

The arrow is essential for both the bow and the crossbow. In the Han dynasty, arrowheads were made of iron in most areas, but some non-Han people used bluestone.[68] There are records of poisonous arrows in the Han dynasty. *Book of the Later Han* records that General Geng Gong used them successfully against the Xiongnu.[69] The famous General Guan Yu (160–220) of Shu Han in the Three Kingdoms period was once shot by a poisonous arrow; to save him,

Qin and Han dynasties and Three Kingdoms 61

Figure 2.9 An image of sitting on the ground to draw a crossbow from the Han dynasty, excavated in Yinan County, Shandong Province.

the doctor had to scrape the poison from his bones.[70] Moreover, there are also records of fire arrows in the late Han dynasty, such as when Zhuge Liang attacked Chencang County in 228.[71] They were apparently produced by binding combustible objects to the arrowhead, and were shot manually rather than triggered by gunpower.

Other weapons

Long halberd

The long halberd was the most important long weapon in Han dynasty armies.[72] The many iron halberds unearthed in Hebi in Henan Province and Xi'an in Shaanxi Province are also evidence of the wide use of long halberds. Moreover, the long halberd was also used as a kind of ceremonial mace by Han emperors and officials.[73]

Double halberd

People in the Han dynasty used the double halberd. *Records of The Three Kingdoms* documents that General Dian Wei was able to carry a double halberd weighing 17.6 kg[74]; General Gan Ning could dance with double halberd[75]; and Sun Quan once succeeded in subduing a tiger with a double halberd.[76]

Hand-held halberd

The hand-held halberd was a short weapon used during the Han dynasty. Cao Cao was adept with it.[77] Throwing was a significant function of this kind of halberd, as indicated in *Records of The Three Kingdoms*, which describes General Sun Ce (175–200) killing his opponent by throwing hand-held halberd.[78]

Spear

The spear was the most common long weapon in the Qin and Han dynasties. Many spears have been unearthed with the Terracotta Warriors. In the Han dynasty, the spear was widely used in military training, and by the Three Kingdoms period, it had begun to replace the halberd. It's noteworthy that spears for military use in this period were generally long – in the Spring and Autumn and Warring States periods they measured around three metres, rising to over four metres in the Han dynasty. The longest spear unearthed with the Terracotta Warriors is 6.7 m long.

Other weapons widely used in this period include the long sabre, double-head spear, axe, hook-shield, full-length shield, wolf-toothed mace, iron hammer, dagger, and cudgel.

Early spread of Chinese martial arts into Japan

Starting in the Han dynasty, a relationship between the Japanese and Chinese was established. Thereafter, Chinese culture in a variety of forms was introduced to Japan, and the development of Japanese martial skills has been deeply influenced by Chinese martial arts since then. *Book of the Later Han* notes that in

236 Queen Himiko sent an ambassador to the State of Wei to establish a relationship, and the Wei presented two long sabres to the Japanese in return.[79] Between 238 and 248, the Yamatai-koku again sent ambassadors to the State of Wei four times. Sabres were also included in the many gifts given by the Wei emperors.[80] From a comparative study of the Han sabres unearthed in China and in Japan, as well as the ancient sabres handed down in Japan today, we know that Han sabres spread to Japan as far back as the Wei state period.

Japanese Weapon Prevue says that weapons in early Japan, like the Han sabres, came from mainland China via the Korean peninsula, and have been unearthed almost everywhere in Japan.[81] *On Bronze Swords and Bronze Spears* says that the vast majority of bronze swords and bronze spears discovered along Hakata Bay were probably made in China, specifically in East Liao County[82] during the Han dynasty.[83] It is apparent that quite a few sabres spread to Japan from the Han dynasty on, exerting a deep influence on the formation of the Japanese sword known as a Tachi. Since the Japanese characters for this sword are similar to those used for the sabre in Chinese, some Chinese scholars argue that the two weapons have a shared origin.

In terms of swordsmanship, there are also many similarities between Japanese and Chinese martial arts in terms of written characters and practical fighting skills. Some Chinese scholars assert that this is no coincidence.[84]

Foreign guests were entertained with various activities, including Jiaodi, in the Han dynasty. Having watched so many Jiaodi performances, the Japanese messengers are likely to have brought it back to their country. *Japanese Sports Information Chronology* indicates that Japanese sumo existed as early as 23 BC – the end of the Western Han period – which implies that this is when Jiaodi spread to Japan, though why the Japanese named it sumo remains to be discovered.[85]

Notes

1 (Western Han) Sima Qian. Shiji•Qinshihuang Benji (史记•秦始皇本纪).
2 (Western Han) Sima Qian. Shiji•Chenshe Shijia (史记•陈涉世家); Shiji•Qinshihuang Benji (史记•秦始皇本纪).
3 *Strategies of the Warring States*. (Western Han). Zhanguoce•Qince (战国策•秦策).
4 (Eastern Han) Ban Gu. Hanshu•Xiongnu Zhuan (汉书•匈奴传).
5 (Eastern Han) Ban Gu. Hanshu•Chao Cuo Zhuan (汉书•晁错传).
6 *Book of the Later Han*. (The Southern) Fan Ye. Houhanshu•Guangwu Diji (后汉书•光武帝纪).
7 (Eastern Han) Ban Gu. Hanshu•Shihuo Zhi (汉书•食货志), annotated by Yan Shigu (581–645) in the Tang dynasty.
8 (Eastern Han) Ban Gu. Hanshu• Wudi Ji (汉书•武帝纪).
9 Cuju (蹴鞠), an ancient code of football with similarities to soccer which originated in China.
10 (Eastern Han) Ban Gu. Hanshu•Yiwen Zhi (汉书•艺文志).
11 (Three Kingdoms) Cao Pi. Dianlun•Lunwen•Zixu (典论•论文•自序).
12 (Eastern Han) Ban Gu. Hanshu•Yiwen Zhi (汉书•艺文志).
13 (Qing) Chen Menglei. Gujin Tushu Jicheng•Guiqibu Liezhuan (古今图书集成•闰

奇部列传); (Western Jin) Chen Shou. Sanguozhi•Shuzhi•Liu Feng Zhuan (三国志•蜀志•刘封传).
14 (Eastern Han) Ban Gu. Hanshu•Chao Cuo Zhuan (汉书•晁错传).
15 (Three Kingdoms) Cao Pi. Dianlun•Lunwen•Zixu (典论•论文•自序); (Eastern Han) Wang Chong. Lunheng•Bietong (论衡•别通); Jiandao (剑道).
16 (Western Han) Sima Qian. Shiji•Xiangyu Benji (史记•项羽本纪).
17 Ouyang Yuqian, *Dances in the Tang Dynasty* (Shanghai: Shanghai Literature and Art Publishing House, 1980), 165.
18 (Eastern Han) Ban Gu. Hanshu•Huainanwang Liu An Zhuan (汉书•淮南王刘安传).
19 (Eastern Han) Ban Gu. Hanshu•Yang Xiong Zhuan (汉书•杨雄传).
20 (Western Jin) Chen Shou. Sanguozhi•Weizhi•Cao Zhang Zhuan (三国志•魏志•曹彰传).
21 (Eastern Han) Ban Gu. Hanshu•Wuwangzi Zhuan (汉书•武王子传).
22 (Three Kingdoms) Cao Pi. Dianlun•Lunwen•Zixu (典论•论文•自序).
23 Ding (鼎), a large three-leg kettle used for cooking and later for ceremonial purposes in ancient China, often made of bronze.
24 (Western Han) Zuo Si. Wudufu (吴都赋).
25 Hundred Skills (百戏), a general name for various folk performances and pastimes of the Han people since the Han dynasty, during which Jiaodi was a significant form of entertainment.
26 (Eastern Han) Zhang Heng. Xijingfu (西京赋).
27 (Western Han) Sima Qian. Shiji•Xiang Yu Benji (史记•项羽本纪); (Eastern Han) Ban Gu. Hanshu•Wuwangzi Zhuan (汉书•武王子传).
28 (Western Han) Sima Qian. Shiji• Li Si Liezhuan (史记•李斯列传).
29 (Eastern Han) Ban Gu. Hanshu•Wudi Benji (汉书•武帝本纪).
30 (Eastern Han) Ban Gu. Hanshu•Xiyu Zhuan (汉书•西域传); (Eastern Han) Ban Gu. Hanshu•Zhang Qian Zhuan (汉书•张骞传).
31 (The Southern) Fan Ye. Houhanshu•Liyi Zhi (后汉书•礼仪志).
32 (Eastern Han) Ban Gu. Hanshu•Jin Midi Zhuan (汉书•金日磾传).
33 *Book of Han*. (Eastern Han) Ban Gu. Hanshu•Yuandi Ji (汉书•元帝纪).
34 (Western Jin) Chen Shou. Sanguozhi•Jiangbiao Zhuan (三国志•江表传).
35 (Eastern Han) Ban Gu. Hanshu•Guanfu Zhuan (汉书•灌夫传).
36 (Western Han) Zuo Si. Wudufu (吴都赋).
37 Annotation of '(Eastern Han) Ban Gu. Hanshu•Shuaidi Ji (汉书•哀帝纪)' by Su Lin. Since Su was a famous intellectual official in the late Han, this argument tends to be reliable.
38 (Eastern Han) Ban Gu. Hanshu•Gan Yanshou Zhuan (汉书•甘延寿传).
39 (Western Jin) Chen Shou. Sanguozhi•Weishu•Lv Bu Zhuan (三国志•魏书•吕布传).
40 (Western Han) Sima Qian. Shi Ji•Xiangyu Benji (史记•项羽本纪).
41 (Eastern Han) Ban Gu, Chen Zong *et al*. Dongguan Hanji•Zhuan Si•Deng Zun (东观汉记•传四•邓遵).
42 (Tang) Fang Xuanling, Chu Suiliang *et al*. Jinshu•Yufu Zhi (晋书•舆服志).
43 (Western Han) Dong Zhongshu. Chunqiu Fanlu•Fuzhi (春秋繁露•服制).
44 (Qing) Chen Menglei. Gujin Tushu Jicheng•Daojian Bu (古今图书集成•刀剑部).
45 *Records of the Ancient and Contemporary Sabres and Swords*. (The Southern) Tao Hongjing. Gujin Daojian Lu•Xu (古今刀剑录•序).
46 (Western Han) Sima Qian. Shiji•Xiangyu Benji (史记•项羽本纪).
47 (Western Jin) Chen Shou. Sanguozhi•Wuzhi•Lu Su Zhuan (三国志•魏志•鲁肃传).
48 (Eastern Han) Ban Gu. Hanshu•Dongfang Shuo Zhuan (汉书•东方朔传).
49 (Eastern Han) Ban Gu. Hanshu•Sima Xiangru Zhuan (汉书•司马相如传).
50 (Eastern Han) Ban Gu. Hanshu•Sima Qian Zhuan (汉书•司马迁传).

51 Chen Jiuheng and Ye Xiaoyan, 'Excavations of Han Tombs in the Western Suburbs of Luoyang', *The Journal of Archeology* no. 2 (1963): 1–58, 111–124, 138–153.
52 (The Southern) Fan Ye. Houhanshu•Peng Xiu Zhuan (后汉书•彭修传).
53 Zhuge Liang Biezhuan (诸葛亮别传).
54 (The Southern) Tao Hongjing. Gujin Daojian Lu•Xu (古今刀剑录•序).
55 (Eastern Han) Ban Gu. Hanshu•Li Guang Zhuan (汉书•李广传).
56 (Eastern Han) Ban Gu. Hanshu•Chao Cuo Zhuan (汉书•晁错传).
57 (Western Jin) Chen Shou. Sanguozhi•Weizhi•Wendi Ji (三国志•魏志•文帝纪).
58 (Eastern Han) Ban Gu. Hanshu•Dili Zhi (汉书•地理志).
59 (Eastern Han) Ban Gu. Hanshu•Chao Cuo Zhuan (汉书•晁错传).
60 (Western Han) Sima Qian. Shiji•Sima Xiangru Zhuan (史记•司马相如传).
61 *Readings of the Taiping Era.* (Song) Li Fan, Li Mu *et al.* Taiping Yulan•Juan 348 (太平御览•卷348).
62 (Eastern Han) Ban Gu. Hanshu•Shen Tujia Zhuan (汉书•申屠嘉传).
63 (Western Han) Sima Qian. Shiji•Su Qin Liezhuan (史记•苏秦列传).
64 (Tang) Fang Xuanling, Chu Suiliang *et al.* Jinshu•Ma Long Zhuan (晋书•马隆传).
65 Yuan Tingdong, *Decryption of the Warfare in Ancient China* (Ji'nan: Shandong Pictorial Publishing House, 2008), 185.
66 Ibid.
67 (Eastern Han) Ban Gu. Hanshu•Dili Zhi (汉书•地理志).
68 (Western Jin) Chen Shou. Sanguozhi•Weish•Yilou Zhuan (三国志•魏书•挹娄传).
69 (The Southern) Fan Ye. Houhanshu•Geng Gong Zhuan (后汉书•耿恭传).
70 (Western Jin) Chen Shou. Sanguo Zhi•Guan Yu Zhuan (三国志•蜀志•关羽传).
71 (Western Jin) Chen Shou. Sanguozhi•Weizhi•Mingdi Ji (三国志•魏志•明帝纪).
72 (Western Han) Sima Qian. Shiji•Xiang Yu Benji (史记•项羽本纪); (Eastern Han) Ban Gu. Han Shu•Chao Cuo Zhuan (汉书•晁错传); *Ode to Zixu*. (Western Han) Sima Xiangru. Zixufu (子虚赋); (Western Jin) Chen Shou. Sanguozhi•Weizhi•Zhang Liao Zhuan (三国志•魏志•张辽传).
73 (Eastern Han) Ban Gu. Hanshu•Dongfang Shuo Zhuan (汉书•东方朔传); (The Southern) Fan Ye. Houhanshu•Yufu Zhi (后汉书•舆服志).
74 (Western Jin) Chen Shou. Sanguozhi•Weizhi•Dian Wei Zhuan (三国志•魏志•典韦传).
75 (Western Jin) Chen Shou. Sanguozhi•Wuzhi•Gan Ning Zhuan (三国志•吴志•甘宁传).
76 (Western Jin) Chen Shou. Sanguozhi•Weizhi•Wuzhu Zhuan (三国志•魏志•吴主传).
77 (Western Jin) Chen Shou. Sanguozhi•Weizhi•Wudi Ji (三国志•魏志•武帝纪).
78 (Western Jin) Chen Shou. Sanguozhi•Wuzhi•Sun Polu Taoni Zhuan (三国志•吴志•孙破房讨逆传).
79 (The Southern) Fan Ye. Houhanshu•Dongyi Zhuan (后汉书•东夷传).
80 Ibid.
81 *Japanese Weapon Prevue* (日本武器概说), is a book by Moyongyaxiong, a Japanese scholar.
82 East Liao County (辽东郡), located in present-day Liaoning Province. Mugong Taiyan (木宫泰彦, きみややすひこ), *Cultural Communications Between Japan and China* (Beijing: Commercial Press, 1980), 13.
83 *On Bronze Swords and Bronze Spears* (关于铜剑、铜铧), is a book by Umehara Sueji, a Japanese archaeologist.
84 Tang Hao. 'Some Observations on the Exchange of Swordplay between China, Korea and Japan', in *References of the History of Chinese Sports* (Volume 6), ed. by the Sport Committee of China (Beijing: People's Sports Press, 1958), 54.
85 *Japanese Sports Information Chronology* (日本体育资料年表), is a book by Jincun Jiaxiong, a Japanese scholar.

Chapter 3

Martial arts in the Jin and the Southern and Northern dynasties (265–589)

The Jin (265–420) and the Southern and Northern dynasties (386–589), lasting over 300 years, were a turbulent epoch and a great period for the fusion of Chinese nations. The so-called Upheaval of the Eight Princes broke out only 30 years after the establishment of the Western Jin (265–316) dynasty. Peoples from the west and the north began to invade the central plains, including the Xiongnu, Xianbei, Jie, Di, and Qiang. They established the regimes which came to be known as the Sixteen States. After the Han people moved south, five dynasties – the Eastern Jin (317–420), Liu Song (420–479), Southern Qi (479–502), Southern Liang (502–557), and Southern Chen (557–589) – were established, while in the north, dynasties including the Northern Wei (386–534), Eastern Wei (534–550), Western Wei (535–556), Northern Qi (550–577), and Northern Zhou (557–581) were established by different ethnic groups.

Conflict between the south and the north lasted for about 300 years, officially known as the Southern and Northern dynasties. War was frequent, which promoted the development of military martial arts. Another feature of Chinese martial arts in this period was that the Han, who lived mostly around the Yangtze River in the south, were obsessed with entertainment like music and dance, which also promoted the development of recreational martial arts. Also, with the rapid development of Buddhism and Taoism, martial arts were increasingly embedded with religious activities. Most significantly, the fusion into Chinese culture of different peoples greatly enhanced the development of Chinese martial arts in this period.

The evolution of military martial arts

The incessant conflicts and wars of this era required stronger military forces, which advanced the development of Chinese martial arts. The military of the Jin dynasty followed the hereditary system of the state of Wei during the Three Kingdoms period. In this system, all family members of soldiers were registered with the army and their career as a soldier could be passed down to later generations. This system was beneficial to the development and inheritance of military skills, including martial skills. Furthermore, large aristocratic families tended to build their own forces in order to consolidate power. The farmers, as followers of these families, often practiced martial skills. It was largely in this way that Xiao Yan (464–549) overthrew the Southern Qi dynasty and established the Southern Liang dynasty. In the Western Wei of the late Northern dynasties, this kind of private force was replaced by a centralized government military system.

Cavalry played the most important role on the battlefield in this period, as the preference of the northern peoples (see Figure 3.1). In the south, however,

Figure 3.1 A Dunhuang mural of fighting between heavy cavalry and infantry during the Western Wei dynasty, number 285 mural in Dunhuang, Gansu Province.

people tended to jointly use cavalry and infantry. Cavalry required proficient long weapon skills, such as with spear, while the infantry mainly used short weapons such as the sabre, shield, and double halberd.

From the late Han dynasty on, military use of the halberd gradually diminished, and the spear became more widely used. There was a distinct long spear over 5.7 m long during the Han–Wei period,[1] which was mostly used by the cavalry to stab their enemies.[2] Since a longer spear made it easier to strike enemies on horseback, it was gradually lengthened. Moreover, it was sharp enough to be better suited to stabbing armoured cavalry and horses, compared to the halberd. These long spears were primarily used in war by the Xianbei in the north. During the Wei–Jin period,[3] the longer spear became a most lethal weapon, and Emperor Wu of Wei Cao Cao and his first son Cao Pi (later Emperor Wen) enjoyed using them. In *Horseback Spearing Guide*, Emperor Jianwen of Southern Liang (503–551) writes that in the Southern Liang, long spear skills developed quickly despite the weapon's short history. In the preface, he also says that the horseback spearing skills included in the book were collected and compiled in his spare time.[4]

From the Three Kingdoms period, the sabre became an important weapon of war. The ring-headed sabre was largely used in the Han dynasty (see Figure 3.2). Up until the Jin and the Southern and Northern dynasties, the sabre and shield were mainly employed by the infantry. Furthermore, the sabre became a day-to-day weapon, since it was short and handy, and sabre craftsmanship greatly improved. *Book of Jin* describes people regarding the sabre as a treasured sword. It was not only a kind of weapon, but also a demonstration of the spirit of bravery and heroism.[5] Therefore, a sabre was often awarded by emperors to officials, or given as a gift between friends. For instance, Emperor Yuan of Eastern Jin (276–323) granted a sabre to Liu Kun, a newly-promoted military official.[6]

At that time, sabres were made of refined steel; some had inscriptions and some were even decorated with gold carving. The popularity of the sabre led to myth. For instance, Lv Qian of the Jin dynasty owned a treasured sabre, and an

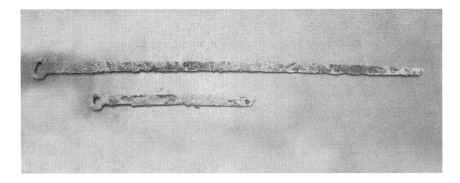

Figure 3.2 Two iron ring-headed sabres in Nanyang, Henan Province.

expert said whoever wore it would be successful. Lv presented it to his friend Wang Xiang, and later Wang Xiang gave it to his younger brother Wang Lan. It is said that the Wang family became rich and powerful for generations.[7] Wearing a sabre also became a form of rite in the Jin and the Southern and Northern dynasties.[8] *Book of Song* points out that some wooden sabres were worn as a kind of adornment in Jin,[9] which demonstrates a decrease in martial arts spirit in this era, with priority given to literary rather than martial arts.

Since ancient times, archery had been an important martial art (see Figure 3.3). The northern peoples were fine archers, and emperors attached great importance to it. The archery rites of the Han people were adapted into military archery by the northerners, who used archery in selecting and training soldiers and in determining military proficiency. At that time, accuracy and distance were the two most important elements, and consequently the hard-bow was widely used.[10]

Hand-fighting skills are fundamental to military martial arts, and a great number of generals were good at hand-fighting skills talented in the Jin and the Southern and Northern dynasties. *Book of Northern Wei* documents that Emperor Xiaowen (467–499) was able to smash a femur into pieces as a teenager.[11] Yang Kan, a renowned general of Emperor Wu (464–549) in the Southern Liang dynasty, was also a brilliant figure with extraordinary hand-fighting skills and strength.[12] *Spring and Autumn Annals of the Sixteen States*

Figure 3.3 A mural of horseback archery from the Sui dynasty, excavated in Ji'an, Jilin Province.

describes a master named Guo Mo who was able to break leather armour with his bare hands.[13]

During the Jin and the Southern and Northern dynasties, literary pursuits outweighed the development of martial arts. However, in this turbulent era, there still emerged a great number of enlightened intellectuals who diligently practiced martial arts in order to serve the country. For instance, the story of Zu Ti (266–321) of the Eastern Jin period rising at the sound of the roosters to practice martial arts gave rise to a commonly used expression.

The development of recreational martial arts

Recreation had been an important function of Chinese martial arts since the pre-Qin period, gaining greater momentum in the Jin and the Southern and Northern dynasties. It was realized both through the performers of martial activities and through the spectators who watched such activities. Recreational martial arts were not only about fitness, but also more closely related to athleticism in this historical phase.

Unarmed combat and Jiaodi were popular in this period. According to *Book of Jin*, Yu Jian, father of renowned literary official Yu Chan, was known for his strength and barehanded fighting skills. During the reign of Emperor Wu of Jin (236–290), a master from the west was so strong that nobody dared fight him, so the emperor recruited brave men to challenge him. Only Yu Jian responded to the call, and eventually he killed that master.[14] During this contest, lethal barehanded fighting skills rather than tumbling skills were used. *Book of Northern Wei* records that in March 512, Empress Ling sat in the garden with the officials on both sides. Drinking happily, the officials took turns dancing for amusement. When it was General Kangsheng's turn, he performed a Lishi Dance. Whenever he turned to look at the queen, his movements and expression made it seem as if he was killing someone.[15] This was a performance of barehanded fighting.

During this period, Jiaodi performances took place formally in the palace, as *Book of Northern Wei* notes that in 404 Emperor Daowu (371–409) ordered that Jiaodi be made a recreational programme.[16] Jiaodi was also popular among the common people. *Accounts of Marvels* states that Jiaodi traces its roots from the legend of Chiyou. The author also introduces a Chiyou game widely played in Jizhou (now in Hebei Province), during which people wore a bull horn to charge at each other.[17]

Notes on the Jingchu Areas by Zong Lin records that people in this district (now in Hubei Province) were also keen on Jiaodi, showing it was also popular in the south.[18] In certain areas, Jiaodi also became a competitive sport. According to *Book of Jin*, the counties of Yingchuan and Xiangcheng often conducted Jiaodi contests. Xiangcheng was often defeated by Yingchuan, and the Official of Merit Liu Zidu was blamed by Grand Administrator of Xiangcheng. He defended himself by saying that Jiaodi could not be used to determine the value of the two counties.[19] This shows that people at the time paid attention to the results of regional Jiaodi contests.

Jin and the Southern and Northern dynasties 71

The archaeological findings of that period offer further insight into Jiaodi and unarmed combat. A Northern Zhou dynasty mural in the Mogao Grottoes in Dunhuang, Gansu Province depicts a vivid Jiaodi scene (see Figure 3.4). Two men, shirtless and wearing shorts, are bent at the waist, having exhausted their strength trying to knock each other down. Another person nearby who looks like a referee is raising his hands and observing. In the third Anyue Grave in the Datong River area of North Korea, which was the territory of General Dong Shou of the Western Jin as verified by archaeologists, there is a mural of unarmed combat. The two fighters are also shirtless and wearing shorts, raising their hands to fight. This shows that Jiaodi and unarmed combat were similar but different martial skills, and that they were introduced into ancient Koguryo (now on the Korean Peninsula) at that time.[20]

There was also a kind of unarmed martial art performance called Paizhang. *Book of Southern Qi* says that Wang Jingze of the Southern dynasty was such a good Paizhang performer that he was appointed as a military official.[21] *The Origin of Words and Phrases* calls Paizhang a sword-catching game,[22] while

Figure 3.4 A Jiaodi mural from the Northern Zhou, number 290 mural in Dunhuang, Gansu Province.

History of Jiaodi considers it a form of Jiaodi.[23] However, these descriptions are inappropriate. This author sees Paizhang as a kind of individual unarmed combat performance.

In the Southern and Northern dynasties period, there were also plenty of entertaining performances with weapons, with both sabre and shield, long spear, sabre, and sword. There were also acrobatics-like weapon-throwing performances – sabre-jumping, sword-jumping, and halberd-throwing – generally included in the Hundred Skills Show. Performers threw these weapons into the air and caught them with dancing movements. *Comprehensive Mirror in Aid of Governance* records that when Zhang Chang gathered a crowd to rebel against the local government, the soldiers he commanded were all able to hold a sabre in each hand, moving back and forth to stab, then throw the sabres high in the air and catch them again. They were also expert in using the double halberd with two hands, and could sprint in every direction while rotating it swiftly around the body; they were able to jump onto and make performance on the handle of the stick of a head-in-earth halberd.[24] These descriptions show martial arts in the public society as a combination of martial arts and acrobatics.

In this period, martial dances also developed further. The artistic nature of martial dances was stronger than the martial arts nature. The palace martial dance of the pre-Qin period was inherited by the Jin dynasty. For example, the pre-Qin martial dance about King Wu of Zhou's victory over King Zhou of Shang was adapted as Bayu Dance in the Han dynasty and Xuanwu Dance in Jin. Fu Xuan, a Jin dynasty writer, depicts in *On Short Weapons* that the sword dance combined thrilling and quick movements, and that the colliding swords burst into flame.[25]

The development of entertaining martial arts was also reflected in the integration of martial arts and Chinese opera. Chinese opera originated in the Han dynasty with martial arts as a significant element; for example, *Old Man Huang of the Eastern Sea* contained a lot of Jiaodi. In the Three Kingdoms period, martial arts were also included in court opera. In the Southern and Northern dynasties, court opera developed further. *Prince of Lanling* of Northern Qi, for instance, had a lot of scenes of acrobatic fighting. *Good Words of Sui and Tang* records that the opera refers to Prince of Lanling, who failed to frighten his enemies due to being handsome rather than intimidating, so wore a ferocious mask in battle.[26] *Records of the Music Bureaus* adds that there were many scenes of combat in this opera, in particular sabre play.[27]

Archery was a major competitive martial art. The state tended to promote archery, due to its important military role. Rich rewards were offered to participants to inspire a sense of competition rather than mere entertainment, and archery contests were plentiful. For instance, Xiao Ye, the fifth son of Emperor Wu of Southern Qi (440–493), was a skilful archer. Emperor Wu convened an archery contest and offered 50,000 Qian (monetary unit of Northern Qi) for one successful shot. Xiao made five out of six shots and won the large prize.[28]

Notably, probably the first documented archery contest in the history of Chinese martial arts, the Archery Silver Cup, was held in this period. Tuoba Shun of the Northern Wei, duke of Puyang, was an archery master. Early in the reign of Xiaowu (510–534), the emperor organized an archery contest in a garden in Luoyang, now Henan Province. He hung a silver cup of wine at a distance of more than 100 steps and ordered the 10-plus participants to shoot at it. The first to hit it would be given the cup. An archer named Shun won, and the cheerful Emperor Xiaowu also awarded him with gold, as well as having his name engraved on the cup.[29]

Archery is a representative martial art in China. In this period, archery competition was also a major martial competition between the Southern and Northern peoples. For instance, the masters of the Northern Qi once competed with the visiting masters of the Southern Liang. The Liang lost both the strength contest (drawing the hard-bow) and the horseback archery contest.

Origin of Shaolin martial arts, the early Taoism and martial arts

Chinese martial arts have a close relationship with ancient religions, particularly Buddhism and Taoism. Buddhism was introduced into China from ancient India in the Eastern Han period. During the Jin and the Southern and Northern dynasties, Buddhism developed significantly due to emperors paying great attention to it. Emperor Wu of Southern Liang (464–549), for example, devoted himself to serving in the temple four times, and many temples were constructed and renovated under him. There were eventually thousands of temples and hundreds of thousands of monks and nuns throughout the north and south. In 493, Emperor Xiaowen of Northern Wei relocated the capital from Pingcheng to Luoyang. He carried out large-scale temple construction, with hundreds built in Luoyang alone.

The frequent wars and prevailing warlike ethos gave rise to the practice of martial arts in the temples. Many temples had their own military force. Perhaps one of the pivotal reasons for the monks' practice of martial arts was to protect the temple's possessions. Due to the emperors' advocacy of Buddhism, many temples were endowed with land and property. *Sequel of Biographies of Eminent Monks* recounts the story of a monk named Minggong, a master of martial arts. Minggong lived in Huishang Temple in Zhengzhou, and the monks in this temple had a dispute with the monks of Chaohua Temple. When Chaohua Temple gathered over 100 thugs to rob grain from Huishang. Minggong easily lifted a huge stone which could otherwise only be moved by 30 strong men. The thugs ran away the moment they saw this.[30] This demonstrates that not only did temples need to be defended from mutinous soldiers and thieves, but also that monks would safeguard their property with the use of force.

Among the great number of monks who practiced martial arts, some took part in rebellious activities.[31] Once defeated, these monks were forced into exile or to resume a secular life. For instance, Emperor Taiwu of Northern Wei (408–452) found a large cache of weapons in a temple in Chang'an in 438, and suspected the monks of conspiring with traitors.[32] He compelled all monks under 50 years old in the city to serve the army or resume their secular lives. However, once the rebellion was over, the emperors would often return to Buddhism and the monks could return, as in the case of Emperor Wencheng of Northern Wei (440–465), an advocate of Buddhism. Because these monks had been soldiers, their return may have advanced the development of martial arts in the temples.

The monks' martial arts practice was also to some degree related to fitness and entertainment. *The Record of the Buddhist Monasteries of Luoyang* by Yang Xuanzhi of Northern Wei describes the grand scene at the temple fair, including many performances of martial arts, such as unarmed combat and Jiaodi.[33]

It can be said that the emergence of Shaolin martial arts coincided with the construction of Shaolin Temple. In 493, Emperor Xiaowen of Northern Wei relocated to Luoyang as the capital city, and in 495 he launched the construction of Shaolin Temple on Song Mountain for Buddhabhadra, a celebrated monk from ancient India. Buddhabhadra had a preference for a quiet place and was determined to settle down on Song Mountain.[34]

Buddhabhadra was erudite in Buddhist doctrine and introduced several Buddhist scriptures into China. In the biographies of Buddhabhadra, there is little mention that he practiced martial arts. But judging from the records of his two disciples, Huiguang and Sengchou, he valued them. According to *Biographies of Eminent Monks*, Buddhabhadra met 12-year-old Huiguang in Luoyang, playing a game on the street kicking a shuttlecock-like object while balancing on the edge of a well. Huiguang made about 500 successive kicks. This game required bravery and skill. In the view of Buddhabhadra, since Huiguang was so proficient at this dangerous game, it would be easy for him to comprehend Buddhist doctrine. Buddhabhadra linked Buddhism acquisition and bravery. He enrolled Huiguang as his disciple because of his excellent skill rather than his knowledge or talent.[35]

Another disciple of Buddhabhadra, Sengchou, was probably one of the earliest monks to be highly skilled in martial arts. In *Anecdotes of the Sui and Tang* by Tang dynasty novelist Zhang Zhuo, it is noted that the young Sengchou was weak when he became a monk, and was often insulted by companions during Jiaodi and fights. Therefore, he prayed to a statue of the bodhisattva Vajrapani in the hall of the temple by wrapping himself around its legs. After six days Vajrapani appeared at dawn, forcing him to swallow a bowl of tendon. Magically, Sengchou gained extraordinary power, with the ability to run on the walls and leap onto the beams of the temple hall. His fists were so agile and powerful that the monks all felt stunned.[36] This is certainly a legendary tale or myth. However, it mirrors the facts in some ways. That is to say, the origin of Shaolin martial arts dates back to the preliminary stage of the Temple, since the two disciples of the first master were skilled in martial arts.

According to some documents such as *Book of Northern Wei*, Bodhidharma, an Indian monk and the founder of Chinese Zen Buddhism, came to China to transmit Buddhism in the Southern Liang dynasty.[37] When he crossed the Yangtze river to the Northern Wei in 520, he went to Shaolin Temple and settled down there. After facing the wall and meditating for nine years, he passed away in 528 and was buried on Xiong'er Mountain. Later generations attributed the invention of Shaolin martial arts to him. They claimed that Bodhidharma imparted the *Yijinjing* and the *Xisuijing* to Shaolin Buddhist monks, making him the founder of Shaolin martial arts. However, this author disagrees, for there are no records in Chinese historical literature and documents to prove Bodhidharma ever practiced or taught martial arts.[38]

Shaolin Temple is the birthplace of Chinese Zen. That the Shaolin monks began to practice martial arts has a relationship to Zen, apart from the martial spirit in time of war. Zen was an integration of Indian Buddhism and Chinese culture. The most significant feature of Zen is that it is transmitted without written words, so that it overcame the abstruse theories of classical Indian Buddhism. This discipline was supposed to lead practitioners to comprehend the eternal mystery and the Buddhist nature of the world. However, how to stimulate such comprehension? Buddhabhadra suggested that one sentence, one movement, even berating or hitting, could be the source of such comprehension, and this was sometimes achieved by the blows of a cudgel. In other words, the acquisition of Zen is largely dependent on self-experience, which is in line with the practice of martial arts. Moreover, both studying Zen and practicing martial arts are methods of self-cultivation. Thus, the relationship between Zen and martial arts grew closer, as seen by their integration, such as comprehending Zen through practicing martial arts and taking martial movements with Zen principles. Many important old Zen scriptures, such as *Record of Linji* and *Record of Biyan*, contain vivid examples of this relationship.

Shaolin martial arts specialized in cudgel techniques, for three reasons. First, Zen advocates the principles of insight and the methods of 'blows with cudgel'. Second, Buddhism advocates leniency. Buddhists carried cudgels for self-defence and cudgels are not as threatening as iron weapons with blades. Third, cudgels seemed more convenient on some special occasions, though they were not major weapons of war during the Jin and the Southern and Northern dynasties.

Taoism, an indigenous religion in China, has a solid cultural background. It came into being by the late Han dynasty and boomed in the late Three Kingdoms period. Taking Lao-Zhuang[39] philosophy as its original thought and inheriting the immortal myths of pre-Qin and the Daoyin,[40] Taoism had a great impact on the common people. Ideologically, the dialectical view of Yin and Yang, the interaction of the Five Elements, and ideas such as 'responding to the enemy's changes', 'coping with motion with inaction', and 'overcoming hardness with softness' in Chinese martial arts all derive from Taoism. Martial arts theories were in line with those of Taiji, the Eight Trigrams, and the Five Elements of Taoism. What's more, having obtained the philosophy and methodology of Taoist health maintenance, Chinese martial arts formed an exercise system based on qi. Nevertheless, both Taoism and martial arts were at early stages of development, so they did not bind to each other closely and deeply in terms of cultural and ideological integration. Generally speaking, the integration of Taoism and martial arts was expressed in two ways in this period. One was that the Taoists began to practice martial arts; the other was the combination of martial arts with Taoist immortal techniques.

Ge Hong (284–364), a great scholar and Taoism theorist of the Jin dynasty from Danyang County (now in Jiangsu Province), was also a superb master of martial arts. *Baopuzi* says he started learning Taoism when young. Ge, who was adept in archery, enlisted in the army and was given the title of General Fubo for his outstanding performances on the battlefield during the reign of Emperor Xiaohui of Western Jin (259–306).[41]

Tao Hongjing (456–536), a famous Southern dynasties Taoist also born in Danyang County, excelled in both literary and military affairs, and made a significant contribution to the development of Taoism. His lifetime covered three dynasties: Liu Song, Southern Qi and Southern Liang. Tao's early career was in politics, but he went to the mountain for monasticism to keep away from the turbulent times. Due to his talent and knowledge, he was appreciated by emperors and addressed as 'Chancellor on the mountain'. Tao's grandfather and father were both martial arts masters, in particular of horseback archery.[42] Tao carried on his family's talent and was learned in military strategy as well as the manufacture of sabres and swords. In *Records of the Ancient and Contemporary Sabers and Swords*, he records the names, inscriptions, sizes, and other features of the swords used by past emperors, from the Xia dynasty to the Han-Wei period. He also records the swords he made himself, 13 swords with a mixture of gold, silver, copper, iron, and tin, each with its own name and usage.[43]

Tao's *Records of the Ancient and Contemporary Sabers and Swords* to some extent features religious mystery and reflects the integration of the miraculous conception of Taoism with martial arts. However, it also reveals Tao's appreciation of the function of the sword; he put effort into studying the sword manufacture and produced some characteristic swords. Tao was also good at casting sabres. According to *Book of Southern Qi*, he cast two fine sabres, Victory and Prowess. These treasured sabres were later presented to Emperor Wu of Southern Liang and in return Tao was rewarded by the emperor.[44]

The incorporation of Taoist immortal thought is one significant feature of Chinese martial arts culture. This incorporation began in the early Taoism of the Wei-Jin period, shown in myths of the sword and Taoist magic arts. From the pre-Qin era, swordsmanship drew much enthusiasm among the Chinese. Practicing swordsmanship or wearing a sword was a representation of heroism and nobility rather than an application of martial arts. Thereafter, the sword gradually took on greater significance. People believed in swords that were supernatural and embodied auspiciousness, and that could vanquish demons and monsters. In this way, many supernatural myths and tales were acted out, paving the way for the creation of the famed legends of swordsmen in the Tang dynasty. Furthermore, the fusion of swordsmanship and Taoism, swordsmen and immortals, became an inexhaustible source for the creation of literary works on swordsmen, from ancient times to now. It should be pointed out that the combination of martial arts and Taoism during the period of the Southern and Northern dynasties made the culture of Chinese martial arts more prosperous.

Martial arts communication between the southern and northern peoples

This long period of war accelerated the development of martial arts among all peoples in the Jin and Southern and Northern dynasties. The northern and western peoples, including the Xiongnu, Xianbei, Jie, Di, and Qiang, invaded the central plains one after another. They were tough and skilful in martial arts. Besides men, not a few women were also masters of martial arts. According to *Book of Northern Wei*, the sister of General Li Bo had brilliant horseback archery skills.[45] Another heroine in the north was named Qin Nvxiu. *Collection of Poems in the Music Bureau* describes her holding a sabre in one hand and a spear in the other to avenge her family at the age of only 14 or 15.[46] Apart from horseback archery, the northerners were also good at both unarmed and armed martial skills.

There were over ten Xiongnu tribes. As they had lived in the central plains (historically inhabited mostly by the Han) for a long time, most of their names followed a Han surname, such as the remarkable general Liu Yuanhai of Western Jin. *Book of Jin* describes Liu Yuanhai as fond of learning, with a particular interest in *Commentary of Zuo*, *Wuzi*, and *The Art of War*, which he had learned by heart. Liu was tough and strong, and tall with a thick beard. He mastered outstanding martial skills and was a good archer. The grandson of Liu Yuanhai, Liu Yuan overthrew the Jin dynasty and claimed the throne to establish the Han Zhao dynasty (304–329). Liu Yao, nephew of Liu Yuan, was also an outstanding master with extraordinary archery skills,[47] as was Liu Yuan's son, Liu Chong.[48]

The Xianbei lived in north-east China, with the Tuoba, Yuwen, and Murong as the major tribes. The Tuoba first built the state of Dai (338–376), predecessor of the Northern Wei. The Xianbei were also known for their brilliant archery skills. *Book of Northern Wei* documents that Emperor Xuanwu (483–515) was able to shoot a distance of 350 feet.[49] There are a lot of historical records about the Murong tribe. Notably, famous archer Murong Han once succeeded in hitting the ring of a sabre that belonged to a rival general. It's recorded in *Readings of the Taiping Era* that Yu Lidi once fought a bear with his bare hands.[50] Lai Dagan, a brave and fierce general, used a long spear to kill a tiger while hunting.[51]

The Jie people, with long noses, deep eyes, and long beards, mostly lived in the Shangdang region (now south-east of Shanxi Province) after they arrived in the central plains. They were excellent in martial arts and fighting skills, especially the Shi family, who built the Later Zhao. *Book of Jin* documents that Shi Le (274–333), first ruler of the Later Zhao, was courageous and burly. His nephew Shi Jilong was not only good at archery, but also proficient with the slingshot. At the age of 17, he enjoyed hitting people with his slingshot. This infuriated some soldiers, who even wished to kill him. But because of his skilled martial arts and young age, Shi Le put up with his behaviour. Shi Min, adopted son of Shi Jilong, was a valiant general. Once, in battle with troops led by Murong Ke of Xianbei, he killed hundreds of opponents with a double-edged spear in his left hand, and a halberd in his right.[52]

The Di and Qiang both accepted Han culture from a relatively early time. There were many martial arts talents among them as well. For example, the Fu family, a big Di clan, established the state of Former Qin in 350, mostly through their superior martial skills. It is recorded in *Book of Jin* that Fu Jian (founder of the Former Qin) was born after his mother dreamed of a big black bear. When he grew up, he became very brave and a good rider and archer.[53] Fu Jian had a son named Fu Sheng, born with only one eye. In his childhood, Fu Sheng's grandfather once made fun of his disability. Fu Sheng was so angry that he stabbed himself until he drew blood. When he grew up, he became an extremely brave and strong general and an outstanding martial arts master.[54]

The Qiang lived mainly in the Ba and Shu areas and Longxi regions of the south-west part of China. The legend of selecting the chief with a sword-throwing contest (as mentioned in Chapter 1) demonstrates their martial spirit. This spirit can also be seen in a man named Li Te, who rebelled in the Ba and Shu areas and established the state of Cheng Han (304–347). Li Te, as recorded in *Book of Jin*, was around 2.4 m in height and good at riding and archery. There were also many other martial artists in the Li family.[55]

The northern peoples began to build their regimes when they invaded the central plains. They strengthened their governing power by learning the culture of the Han people, and also emphasized military training so as to retain their martial traditions. Since the Western Zhou period, the Han people had built a long tradition of archery rites, but the role of these rites gradually diminished. By the time of the Southern dynasties, archery rites were even often cancelled by emperors. However, the Northern dynasties carried this tradition forward and winners of archery competitions were granted gold, silver, silk fabrics, and cotton. *Book of Northern Wei* says that Emperor Xiaowen repeatedly highlighted the importance of archery, even when a well-organized archery contest had to be postponed due to rain in 492.[56] *Book of Sui* records a grand archery contest scene in the Northern Qi of the Xianbei. The contest was held twice a year, in spring and autumn, and all officials were required to attend.[57] Historical materials indicate that the northern peoples attached more importance to the traditional archery contest.

There were also some other entertaining martial contests among the northern peoples. The aforementioned Archery Silver Cup was one. In this period, there were many other martial contests with a gold or silver cup as the prize. For example, *History of the Northern Dynasties* records Emperor Wen of Western Wei (507–551) awarding a gold cup to the winner of an archery contest.[58]

Among the old traditional martial games of the northern peoples, there was one named willow-shooting, first practiced by the Xianbei during the autumn worship ceremony.[59] Participants carried out horseback archery around a tree. A willow branch would be used if there was no tree available. A tree or willow branch was used as the target.[60] This game was very popular in the Northern dynasties, and remained popular in later dynasties in ancient China. Willow-shooting was a representative martial game introduced to the central plains by the northerners in the Southern and Northern dynasties.

Archaeological relics have also exhibited the martial arts of the northern peoples, for instance on a Han-Jin period mural[61] excavated in Hexi (now Jiuquan, Gansu Province). There are two long-nosed, deep-eyed Jie men on the mural; one is drawing a bow to shoot, the other is in a half squat, holding a halberd to stab. This reveals that the halberd and the spear were also widely used weapons, along with the bow, by northerners.

In sum, the Jin and Southern and Northern dynasties witnessed influential cultural communication between different Chinese peoples. In terms of the development of Chinese martial arts, some martial spirits as well as techniques of the northern peoples flowed in. This infusion paved the way for the prosperity of Chinese martial arts in the Tang and Song dynasties.

Notes

1 (Song) Li Fan, Li Mu *et al.* Taiping Yulan•Bingbu (太平御览•兵部). Han-Wei period, a transitional period from the Han dynasty to the Cao Wei period when Cao Cao was dominant.
2 (Eastern Han) Liu Xi. Shiming•Shibing (释名•释兵).
3 Wei-Jin period, a transitional period from the Three Kingdoms to the Western Jin and Eastern Jin dynasties.
4 (Southern Liang) Xiao Gang. Mashuo Pu•Xu (马矟谱•序).
5 (Tang) Fang Yuanling, Chu Suiliang *et al.* Jinshu•Helian Bobo Zaiji (晋书•赫连勃勃载记).
6 (Tang) Fang Yuanling, Chu Suiliang *et al.* Jinshu•Liu Kun Zhuan (晋书•刘琨传).
7 (Tang) Fang Yuanling, Chu Suiliang *et al.* Jinshu•Wang Xiang Wang Lan Zhuan (晋书•王祥王览传).
8 (Tang) Fang Yuanling, Chu Suiliang *et al.* Jinshu •Yufu Zhi (晋书•舆服志).
9 (Southern Liang) Shen Yue. Songshu• Lizhi (宋书•礼志).
10 *Book of Zhou.* (Tang) Linghu Defen. Zhoushu•Dou Luning Zhuan (周书•豆卢宁传); (Northern Qi) Wei Shou. Weishu•Gao Cong Zhuan (魏书•高聪传); (Tang) Fang Yuanling, Chu Suiliang *et al.* Jinshu•Liu Yao Zaiji (晋书•刘曜载记).
11 (Northern Qi) Wei Shou. Weishu•Diji Diqi (魏书•帝纪第七).
12 *Book of Liang.* (Tang) Yao Silian. Southern Liangshu•Yang Kan Zhuan (梁书•羊侃传).
13 (Northern Wei) Cui Hong. Shiliuguo Chunqiu•Qianzhao Lu (十六国春秋•前赵录).
14 (Tang) Fang Yuanling, Chu Suiliang *et al.* Jinshu•Yu Chan Zhuan (晋书•庾阐传).

15 (Northern Qi) Wei Shou. Weishu•Xi Kangsheng Zhuan (魏书•奚康生传).
16 (Northern Qi) Wei Shou. Weishu•Yuezhi (魏书•乐志).
17 (Southern Liang) Ren Fang. Shuyi Ji•Juan Shang (述异记•卷上).
18 (Southern Liang) Zong Lin. Jingchu Suishi Ji (荆楚岁时记).
19 (Tang) Fang Yuanling, Chu Suiliang et al. Jinshu•Liu Zidu Zhuan (晋书•刘子笃传).
20 Liang Mintao, 'Taekwondo originated in China,' *Yangcheng Evening News*. 7 February 1993.
21 (Southern Liang) Xiao Zixian. Nanqi Shu•Wang Jingze Zhuan (南齐书•王敬则传).
22 Lu Erkui *et al.*, *Ciyuan* (Shanghai: Commercial Press, 1915).
23 (Song) Diao Luzi. Jiaoliji (角力记).
24 (Northern Song) Sima Guang. Zizhi Tongjian•Jinji (资治通鉴•晋纪).
25 Duanbing Pian•Jianyu Dier (短兵篇•剑俞第二).
26 (Tang) Liu Su. Suitang Jiahua•Juan Xia (隋唐嘉话•卷下).
27 (Tang) Duan Anjie. Yuefu Zalu•Gujia (乐府杂录•鼓架).
28 (Southern Liang) Xiao Zixian. Nanqishu•Gaodi Shier Wang (南齐书•高帝十二王).
29 *History of the Northern Dynasty*. (Tang) Li Yanshou and Li Dashi. Beishi•Wei Zongshi Changshan Wang Zun Zhuan (北史•魏宗室常山王遵传).
30 (Tang) Shi Daoxuan. Xu Gaoseng Zhuan•Xichan Pian•Sui Jingshi Qingchan Si Shi Tanchong Zhuan (续高僧传•习禅篇•隋京师清禅寺释昙崇传).
31 (Southern Liang) Shen Yue. Songshu•Wang Sengda Zhuan (宋书•王僧达传). (Northern Qi) Wei Shou. Weishu•Suzong Benji (魏书•肃宗本纪).
32 (Northern Qi) Wei Shou. Weishu•Shilao Zhi (魏书•释老志).
33 (Northern Wei) Xian Xuanzhi. Luoyang Jialan Ji•Chengbei•Chanxu Si (洛阳伽蓝记•城北•禅虚寺).
34 *Biographies of Eminent Monks*. (Southern Liang) Hui Jiao. Gaoseng Zhuan•Fotuo Zhuan (高僧传•佛陀传).
35 (Southern Liang) Hui Jiao. Gaoseng Zhuan•Fotuo Zhuan (高僧传•佛陀传).
36 (Tang) Zhang Zhuo. Chaoye Qianzai•Juan Er (朝野佥载•卷二).
37 (Northern Qi) Wei Shou. Weishu•Shilao Zhi (魏书•释老志).
38 *Comprehensive Studies in Administration*. (Song) Ma Ruilin. Wenxian Tongkao (文献通考).
39 Lao Zhuang, combining the names Laozi and Zhuangzi, represents Taoism.
40 Daoyin (导引) was a kind of health preservation practice combined with respiratory movements (dao) and body movements (yin) in ancient China. The practice of Daoyin was a precursor of qigong.
41 (Eastern Jin) Ge Hong. Baopuzi•Waipian Zixu (抱朴子•外篇自序).
42 Liang Mintao, 'Taekwondo originated in China,' *Yangcheng Evening News*. 7 February 1993.
43 (Southern Liang) Tao Hongjing. Gujin Daojian Lu•Daliang Shisan Shenjian (古今刀剑录•大梁十三神剑).
44 (Southern Liang) Xiao Zixian. NanQishu•Wang Jingze Zhuan (南齐书•王敬则传).
45 (Northern Qi) Wei Shou. Weishu•Li Anshi Zhuan (魏书•李安世传).
46 (Three Kingdoms) Zuo Yannian. Yuefu Shiji•Zaqu Geci•Qin Nvxiu Xing (乐府诗集•杂曲歌辞•秦女休行).
47 (Tang) Fang Yuanling, Chu Suiliang et al. Jin Shu•Liu Yao Zaiji (晋书•刘曜载记).
48 (Tang) Fang Yuanling, Chu Suiliang et al. Jinshu•Liu Cong Zaiji (晋书•刘聪载记).
49 (Northern Qi) Wei Shou. Weishu•Gao Cong Zhuan (魏书•高聪传).
50 (Song) Li Fan, Li Mu *et al*. Taiping Yulan•Bingbu (太平御览•兵部).
51 (Tang) Fang Yuanling, Chu Suiliang et al. Jinshu•Li Te Zaiji (晋书•李特载记).
52 (Tang) Fang Yuanling, Chu Suiliang et al. Jinshu•Shi Jilong Xia. (晋书•石季龙下).
53 At that time, a pregnant woman dreaming of a bear was considered an omen that her son would be an outstanding man.

54 (Tang) Fang Yuanling, Chu Suiliang *et al.* Jinshu•Fu Jian Zaiji (晋书•苻健载记).
55 (Tang) Fang Yuanling, Chu Suiliang *et al.* Jinshu•Li Te Zaiji (晋书•李特载记).
56 (Northern Qi) Wei Shou. Weishu•Xiaowendi Benji (魏书•孝文帝本纪).
57 (Tang) Wei Zheng. Suishu•Liyi Zhi (隋书•礼仪志).
58 (Tang) Li Yanshou and Li Dashi. Beishi•Yuwen Gui Zhuan (北史•宇文贵传).
59 (Eastern Han) Ban Gu. Hanshu•Xiongnu Zhuan (汉书•匈奴传).
60 (Eastern Han) Ban Gu. Hanshu•Xiongnu Zhuan (汉书•匈奴传) annotated by Yan Shigu (581–645) in the Tang dynasty.
61 Han-Jin period, a transitional period from the Han dynasty to the Western Jin and Eastern Jin dynasties.

Chapter 4

Martial arts in the Sui, Tang, and Five Dynasties and Ten Kingdoms periods (581–979)

First, the establishment of the Fubing System and the Imperial Martial Examination promoted Chinese martial arts in military training and soldier recruitment. Second, from the governors in the palace to the peasants on the farm, practicing martial arts became popular among the Sui and Tang people, which cultivated the wuxia ethos. Third, Chinese culture developed rapidly, with further overseas exchange, and Chinese martial arts were no exception. Martial dances, archery and Jiaodi, as well as their traditions and rites, began to be influenced by foreign countries such as Japan.

The Sui dynasty (581–618) was short. However, it witnessed the end of the warring age of hundreds of years, as well as the beginning of a state bureaucracy. Therefore, the Sui dynasty is an important historical phase that inherited the past and ushered in the future. Building on this, the Tang dynasty achieved stability of the state and prosperity of the economy during its 289 years' reign. In general, the Sui, Tang (618–907), and Five Dynasties and Ten Kingdoms (907–979) periods play a significant role in the history of feudal Chinese society.

The development of culture in Tang was open with widespread international communication. Therefore, foreign culture enriched the traditional Chinese culture, including its martial arts. Martial dances, archery, and Jiaodi, as well as the ethos of practicing martial arts in Tang were also influenced. Most remarkably, the establishment of the Imperial Martial Examination system is the most important event for Chinese martial arts in this period.

The Fubing System

The Fubing System was first employed during the Western Wei and Northern Zhou dynasties, and was developed during the Sui dynasty. According to the imperial edict issued by Emperor Wen of Sui (541–604) in 590, the households of all soldiers were eligible to register with their local government so that they enjoyed the distribution of farmland as ordinary people, while their military service affairs were still governed by the military commands.[1] As in the Western Wei and Northern Zhou dynasties, the Fubing System of the Sui dynasty followed a framework with 12 military commands as the basic units, each of which was commanded by a senior general in charge of certain military affairs.

During the Tang dynasty, Emperor Taizong (598–649) restructured the Fubing System. There were 634 military commands in total across the country, which were subordinated to 16 central military commands. Each of the central commands was in charge of 40, 50 or 60 military commands. In each of the central commands, there was one senior general and two subordinate generals.

The military command remained the basic unit of the Fubing System in Tang. Those commands of 1,200 soldiers were ranked as premier commands, those of 1,000 soldiers as medium commands, and those of 800 soldiers as junior commands. These military commands were named after the prefecture in which they were located. Within the military commands, 300 soldiers made up a regiment led by a general, 50 soldiers made up a team led by a captain, 30 soldiers made up a group by a leader.[2] The soldiers were required to support themselves with weapons and other instruments and provisions. The soldiers were recruited from the farmers, just as the poet Bai Juyi said in his poem, the government recruited one man if a family had three or more men.[3] Among the households, the commands picked the stronger men when they came from families when they were equally wealthy, picked the men from wealthier families when they were equally strong, and picked the men from the families with more men if they were equally strong and wealthy.[4]

Military training was stressed in the military commands in Tang. The main task in these commands was to train the soldiers, while the soldiers were asked to practice archery in their training.[5] The training in the commands was carried out and led by the senior general in the winter. Some soldiers would also receive military training when they were on duty in the capital.[6] Emperor Taizong even taught some of the on-duty soldiers archery in the palace. The winning soldier was awarded with bows, sabres, silk and so on. In addition, his supervisors would be credited with first class achievement in the grade evaluation.[7] Examinations on military skills were also held on their duty dates. For those soldiers of poor performance, their supervising senior generals, sometimes even the relevant local governors, would be punished.[8]

The Fubing System implemented in the Sui and Tang dynasties was an integration of the military and agriculture, the soldiers and the farmers. The soldiers were usually selected from farming households rather than from the hereditary military households as previously. Effectively, this system extended the development of the reserve pool of soldiers, military instruments, and martial activities to a grassroots level. Besides, the training and examination system for the soldiers evoked the societal ethos on martial arts and martial activities. The Fubing System in the Sui and Tang dynasties definitely spurred the development of Chinese martial arts.

The establishment of the Imperial Martial Examination

In the pre-Qin period, the Chinese character '士' (*Shi*, official) actually referred to a hereditary warrior who was in the lowest rank of the noble class. At the beginning of the Warring States period, *Shi* began to change to simply mean official. People from the civil class could become officials once their capability was recognized by the rulers. In the Han dynasties, there were various ways of selecting officials, including by recommendation and employment. The Nine-rank Official System[9] was adopted during the Wei, Jin, and Southern and Northern dynasties.

The Imperial Martial Examination was established by Empress Wu Zetian (624–705) of Tang in 702. Before then, the martial talents were recruited into the government randomly and without a fixed rule when needed. For instance, in April of 608, Emperor Yang of Sui dynasty issued an imperial edict to regulate the selection of imperial officials through a uniform examination with ten subjects. It can be presumed that there were one or more subjects on martial skills in the imperial exam. But there were no fixed subjects for recruiting officials in Sui. Sometimes the number was two, sometimes four, sometimes ten. Although some form of martial examinations to select the martial talents could always be found. For example, *New Book of Tang* documents that in 638, Emperor Taizong formed his archery team of 100 strong men through various martial contests, such as Jiaodi and archery.[10]

From 702, the Imperial Martial Examination was held annually and the candidates were required to attend different levels of exams with a top-down hierarchy. Ceremonies would be held before the recruited candidates were promoted to the imperial exam or appointed military officials, such as a grand banquet or worship in the Taigong Temple, an important temple dedicated to martial heroes.[11]

The ten examining subjects involved in the Tang dynasty were: (1) ranged archery: the candidates drew their bow to shoot at a target with five rings from a distance of 105 footsteps; (2) horseback archery: the candidates shot at set targets while riding a horse; (3) horseback spearing: the candidates had to knock down wooden boards off the heads of four puppets on their left and right with a 5.5 m and 5.3 kg spear while riding a horse, but were not allowed to knock down the puppets; (4) tube-shaped bow: the bow was about 30 cm long in the shape of a tube.; two-thirds of the tube was cut open so that the arrow could sit in it, and at the end of the tube, there was a small hole for a string which was fastened to the wrist as a trigger for the arrow; once the string was pulled, the arrowed was triggered at the target; (5) foot archery: the candidates shot at scarecrows while walking; (6) armour shooting: to examine the candidates' bow-drawing strength by shooting at armoured targets; (7) bar-lifting: the candidates snatched up a large bar of about 5.2 m in length and 10.7 cm diameter five times, and it increased to ten times later on; the distance between the end of the bar and the candidates' hands was limited to 31.4 cm; (8) weight bearing: the candidates carried a bag of rice weighing about 140 kg while walking 20 steps; (9) physical fitness status; and (10) an interview.[12]

The establishment of the Imperial Martial Examination was an epochal event in the history of Chinese martial arts. On the one hand, the designation of exam subjects reflects the refinement and normalization of the study and development of Chinese martial arts. On the other hand, the establishment of the Imperial Martial Examination popularized martial arts, since the attraction of being a government official drove more people to practice martial arts. The influence and significance of the Imperial Martial Examination is considerable. This method of selecting martial talents from the public was passed down through the succeeding dynasties.

The warlike and wuxia spirits

The prosperity of the Tang dynasty was manifested by its open political strategies and the weak fortification of neighbouring states. The central government had a close relationship with ethnic minorities and foreigners, which provided a free environment for the communication of the wuxias. Consequently, the warlike spirit of the northern peoples which had been diffused into the central plains in the previous dynasties, further stimulated the prevalence of wuxia spirit in the late Sui dynasty and the Tang dynasty.

The *Old Book of Tang* records that the young Chai Shao was strong and brave and earned his fame as a wuxia in Chang'an, the capital of Tang[13]; Qiu He was also a wuxia, whose son, General Qiu Xinggong, was an outstanding horseback archer.[14] *Book of Sui* says Duan Lun, son-in-law of Emperor Gaozu of Tang, was well known as a wuxia when he was young.[15] *New Book of Tang* adds General Li Shentong was chivalrous when he was young.[16] All of them were young wuxia and founding members of the Tang dynasty. It is revealed that the wuxia spirit prevailed at that time. There are many other wuxia legends which can be found in the historical records, such as, Liu Hongji,[17] Liu Quan[18] and Wang Kui.[19]

Members of the royal family of Tang highly valued the warlike and wuxia spirit. Emperor Taizong Li Shimin was a valiant general himself. It is said that he had killed more than 1,000 enemies on the battlefield. And his brothers, Li Jiancheng, Li Yuanji and so on, were all outstanding in martial arts and showed a courageous and skilful performance in war. *Records of Armaments and Military Provisions* say that Emperor Taizong had 1,000 skilful swordsmen who had made great contributions at the crucial moments of his political struggle. In the Incident of Xuanwu Gate, he defeated his opponents and succeeded in becoming the emperor with the help of his swordsmen.[20] Retaining a warlike spirit is a long tradition in the Li family.

In the Sui and Tang dynasties, warlike spirit also prevailed in the people. That the Shaolin monks assisted Li Shimin to defeat General Wang Shichong and establish the Tang dynasty serves as a good example. When Li Shimin led his armed forces to Luoyang to suppress Wang, Wang stationed his army in Huanzhou which was about 25 km from the Shaolin Temple. Wang asked his nephew Wang Renze to defend it, but the Shaolin monks helped the army of Li Shimin defeat the Wang army. Thirteen monks, including Tanzong, Zhicao and Huiyang, captured Wang Renze and presented him to Li Shimin. Consequently, Tanzong was made a senior general. The other 12 monks were not willing to be appointed as government officials, and instead were awarded a purple kasaya.[21] Additionally, the Shaolin Temple was rewarded with riches, including 329.38 acres (about 1.33 km^2) of land and other properties. Since then, the Shaolin Temple has been well known for its martial arts. This history of the Shaolin monks' contribution to the Tang dynasty with their martial arts was recorded in Shaolin Temple Stone Tablet[22] by military commander Pei Zhuo in 728.

Being constantly threatened by the northern Kok Turks people, the Tang dynasty encouraged the people to practice martial arts and advocated a warlike spirit. For instance, Empress Wu Zetian wished to remind the people of the threat of war, thus she advocated martial arts such as horseback archery.[23]

A great number of poems from Tang dynasty were themed on the wuxia. The famous Ode to Gallantry by Li Bai (701–762) depicts the superb martial arts of a wuxia: able to kill one man in every ten steps and nobody can stop him within in a very long distance; and the faith and brotherhood of him: 'making binding promises after drinking three cups of wine' and 'dying for brotherhood'.[24] Li's poems were not just his romantic imagination but a reflection of his real life. It was said that Li learned swordsmanship from famous masters and was good at it. Some historical records, for example in the preface of A Collection of Li Bai's Works, also confirm Li Bai's wuxia spirit and excellent swordsmanship. In addition, the success of novels on wuxia in the Tang dynasty was to a great extent propelled by the prevailing chivalric ethos of that time.

The main weapons of the wuxia were the sabre and the sword, and martial skills were also essential to a wuxia. The wuxia ethos and the respect people showed for the wuxia advanced the development of martial arts.

The flowering of Jiaodi

In the early Sui dynasty, the Hundred Skills Show (Jiaodi being the most significant game involved) was prohibited by Emperor Wen because it was regarded as a form of extravagance and waste, which went against his advocacy of being economical.[25] Besides, the prohibition of Jiaodi probably also stemmed from his orders prohibiting martial arts. However, the prohibition movement was revoked before long. During the reign of Emperor Yang, the Hundred Skills Show revived again, as he himself was a lover of the Hundred Skills. Book of Sui writes that in January (of the Chinese lunar calendar) of 611, there were various Hundred Skills performed on the square at Duanmen Gate, which lasted for about a month. Emperor Yang went to watch the performances in plain clothes several times. The revival of the Hundred Skills was realized by the enthusiasm of both the rulers and the citizens.[26]

Most of the emperors in Tang were keen on the Hundred Skills Show. Emperor Xuanzong (685–762) often arranged various games and acrobatics during the banquets, such as the on-land boating,[27] Xuntong,[28] high-wire walking, sword-jumping, and Jiaodi.[29] There are also many cases to be found of Tang emperors keen on watching the Hundred Skills, for example, Emperor Xian in Jiju[30] and Jiaodi,[31] Emperor Jingzong in Jiaodi and other acrobatics,[32] Emperor Wen in Cuju and Jiaodi[33] and Emperor Wu in field hunting and many other kinds of martial arts performance.[34]

Many emperors of the Five Dynasties and Ten Kingdoms period loved Jiaodi as well.[35] Qian Liu (Emperor of Wu-Yue, 852–932) not only practiced Jiaodi himself, but also cherished the Jiaodi experts, namely, Meng Wanyin and Li Qingzhou.[36] *History of Jiaodi* records that all of the emperors of Southern Tang, Emperor Liezu (889–943), Emperor Yuanzong (916–961), and Emperor Houzhu (937–978) were fond of Jiaodi.[37] Li Cunxu (885–926), an emperor of the Later Tang was the most notable emperor who was addicted to Jiaodi. Both *History of Jiaodi* and *Old History of the Five Dynasties* state that he loved watching Jiaodi as well as participating in it. In 924, he competed with General Li Cunxian in Jiaodi. Although Li Cunxian did not employ all his skills in the fight, he staked a prefectural governor position on the competition. Li Cunxian eventually won and was awarded the post. Although taking a governmental post as a wager is ridiculous, it reveals the extent to which the emperors were fond of Jiaodi.[38]

During the Sui, Tang, and Five Dynasties and Ten Kingdoms periods, Jiaodi was also popular among the people. Before Emperor Wen of Sui gave the order to prohibit Jiaodi previously mentioned, his official Liu Yu had advised that the people had gathered for a carnival for the Lantern Festival. A lot of celebratory activities, including Jiaodi were held, and they should be prohibited.[39] In *History of Jiaodi*, there can be found many records of the grand scenes of popular Jiaodi.[40]

Jiaodi in this period was mostly a celebratory or spectator activity during festivals. *History of Jiaodi* records that Emperor Wen of Tang (809–840) watched Jiaodi during the Cold Food Festival. Ancient writings including the *History of Jiaodi*,[41] *Records of Wuxing*[42] and *Book of Sui*[43] also record many Jiaodi activities during different festivals, including the Lantern Festival and the Dragon Boat Festival.[44]

Two features of the scenes of Jiaodi in this period can be found in the documents *Sequel of Comprehensive Studies in Administration*.[45] One was that the Jiaodi competitions began with the beating of drums; the other was that the participants were partly naked. A Buddhist silk painting of Tang dynasty unearthed in Mogao Grottoes shows that this kind of clothing in Jiaodi at this time was similar to that of Japanese sumo in the present day (see Figure 4.1). *History of Jiaodi* records that a master of Jiaodi named Shi Yanneng suddenly held his opponent's waist to tumble him.[46] Tumbling was still a principal skill in Jiaodi at that time.

88 Sui, Tang, Five Dynasties and Ten Kingdoms

Figure 4.1 A Buddhist silk painting from the Tang dynasty excavated in Mogao Grottoes.

According to *History of Jiaodi*, however, Li Cunxu threw a punch in a Jiaodi competition with Wang Menguan. So it can be seen that tumbling was not the only skill in Jiaodi.[47] Mixing tumbling with punching and kicking skills makes Jiaodi a furious and exciting martial art. In *Comprehensive Mirror in Aid of Governance*, it is written that Emperor Jingzong of Tang (809–826) liked watching Jiaodi, sometimes until late into the night.[48] These combats often resulted in blood, and some participants had their bones snapped or their arms broken.[49]

In the Tang dynasty, there were specialized organizations for Jiaodi. For example, *History of Jiaodi* documents that Emperor Xizong (862–888) convened some martial talents to practice different kinds of Jiaodi. A committee named Xiao-er-yuan worked to train young children for one or more of the Hundred Skills, while the Xiang-pu-peng was also responsible for recruiting talented Jiaodi performers. The famous Jiaodi fighter Meng Wanying was one notable man recruited in the Xiao-er-yuan. Also in *History of Jiaodi*, *She* (社) is mentioned in the popular Jiaodi activities during the Lantern Festival. Here *She* probably means a Jiaodi society.

New Book of Tang and *The Jottings of Tang* note that due to the abolition of the Fubing system under Emperor Xuanzong, some former soldiers had to change their jobs and live off their expertise, namely by performing martial skills including

Jiaodi.[50] It can also be inferred that Jiaodi was probably one of the routine martial skills to be taught in the army of the Tang dynasty.

Apart from military training, recreation and performance, people in this period were also aware of Jiaodi's function in promoting fitness. Weakness of one's body is not good for one's health. Zhang Anguo of the Ming dynasty states in *Records of Wuxing* that people practiced Jiaodi on Ghost Festival in July (of the lunar calendar) so as to get rid of weakness.[51]

During the Sui, Tang, and Five Dynasties and Ten Kingdoms periods, there emerged many superior Jiaodi fighters: Meng Wanying, who earned the name Wanying from his predictable winning performance in Jiaodi[52]; Wang Yuzi, who had been trained in Jiaodi by his father from when he was very young; Shi Yanneng, who was both a literary and martial talent; Li Qingzhou, who claimed to be undefeatable; and Yao Ji'er, who swore to be a monk only if he could become invincible in Jiaodi.

Ranged weapons

The bow and arrow

Before Li Yuan (later Emperor Gaozu of Tang, 566–635) launched his rebellion against the Sui dynasty, he was in charge of defending against the Kok Turks people in Mayi County in the north with another general of Sui dynasty, Wang Rengong. Li Yuan shared his viewpoint with Wang that the Kok Turks people were skilful in horseback archery. And with the addition of their nomadic habits, their armies were able to use their strong mobility to their advantage in war. Therefore, he made up a cavalry of more than 2,000 soldiers. These horseback archers learnt from the Kok Turks not only archery but also their nomadic habits.[53] Li Yuan's cavalry later played an important role in the battles overthrowing the Sui dynasty and other hostile military forces and later in the establishment of the Tang dynasty. For instance, in the battle with the peasant insurgent army led by Wei Dao'er[54] of late Sui (?–618), when Li Yuan's cavalry broke up Wei Dao'er's army and led the infantry onto the field, as recorded in *The Making of Emperor Gaozu of Tang*. Despite *Old Book of Tang* stating that it was Li Shimin (son of Li Yuan and later Emperor Taizong, 598–649) who commanded the cavalry in this battle, the contribution of the cavalry and horseback archers is incontrovertible. During the Tang dynasty, horseback archery remained a long-term project for the emperors and officials because they had to defend against the northern peoples, namely the Kok Turks people (see Figure 4.2).

There emerged a great number of skilful archers during the Sui, Tang, and Five Dynasties and Ten Kingdoms periods – for example, Du Junmo of the late Sui dynasty. According to *Extensive Records of the Taiping Era*, Du was good at shooting and could hit any target accurately with his eyes closed. When he wanted to hit the target's eyes, he did; if the mouth, he did again. There is a story of Wang Lingzhi learning archery from Du. Wang thought he had learnt all

Figure 4.2 A Dunhuang mural of archery during the Tang dynasty, number 346 mural in Dunhuang, Gansu Province.

the archery skills from Du and planned to shoot Du so as to earn his own fame. Du succeeded in cutting up all but one of the incoming arrows with a short sabre. Then he gripped the final arrow with his teeth, bit it off, and said to Wang: 'you've learnt archery from me for a couple of years, but luckily I have never taught you the way to bite off an arrow'.[55] The description of hitting the target with closed eyes and biting off an arrow is certainly exaggerated, but Du was undoubtedly adept in archery. General Zhang Sunsheng of the Sui dynasty[56] and Gao Pian (military strategist) of the Tang dynasty[57] were both said to have once shot two flying vultures with one arrow. The famous Chinese idiom *Yijian Shuangdiao* (kill two birds with one arrow)[58] stems from Gao's legend. Other skilful archers include Xue Rengui[59] and Wang Qiyao[60]; both were famous military officials in Tang. In the historical writings of the Tang dynasty, there are a great many words and expressions of praise for the superb shooting skills of the archers.

In fact, there were also skilful archers beyond the military domain. Indeed, even a poet like Du Fu (712–770) was said to 'ride a horse with a long bow, hit the birds in the sky without a miss' during his outdoor trips.[61] During the Tang and Five Dynasties periods, even the maids in the palace often entertained themselves by hunting with the bow and arrow. In Du Fu's poem *Sorrows on the Qu River*,[62] Wang Jian's poem *The Palace*,[63] and Lu Lun's poem *Everlasting*,[64] there are descriptions of maids shooting with the bow and arrow. Although the character *She* (射, shoot) does not appear in Zhang Ji's *The Palace* (same title, but different from Wang Jian's works), the poem vividly depicts a hunting scene with the maids[65] (see Figure 4.3). Albeit the sentence 'the arrow flies into the sky, the two birds flying wing to wing fall down to the earth' is a metaphor for the death of Yang Yuhuan, consort of Emperor Xuanzong of Tang and one of

Figure 4.3 A silk flower with shooting pattern from the Tang dynasty, excavated in Turpan, Xinjiang.

the Four Beauties of ancient China, in Du Fu's *Sorrows on the Qu River*, but it reveals the fact that the maids were treating shooting as a game, and their archery skills seem to have been good as well.[66] Also, *Literatures of Tang, Five Dynasties and Song*,[67] and *The Palace*[68] record that the games of rice-ball-shooting and duck-shooting were also popular in the palace.

There are also many works on the theories of archery from the Tang dynasty, notably Wang Ju's *Scripture of Archery*, Zhang Shouzhong's *Records on Archery*, and Ren Quan's *On the Bow and Arrow*, as recorded in *New Book of Tang*.[69] However, the works by Zhang and Ren are now lost. Wang's *Scripture of Archery* contains 14 pieces of writing. They are informative, with details of training methods for archery, and they are still referred to by some archers today.

The crossbow

The crossbow underwent rapid development during the Tang dynasty. The Tang armies were equipped with many kinds of crossbows. According to *Six Codes of Tang*, there were the Fuyuan Crossbow, Bizhang Crossbow, Jiaogong Crossbow, Mudan Crossbow, Da Mudan Crossbow, Zhugan Crossbow, and Da Zhugan Crossbow.[70] *New Book of Tang* says the Fuyuan Crossbow could fire 300 steps.[71] Wang Ju's *Scripture of Archery* notes that there was the Jiaoche Crossbow with a 700-step range, employed as a siege-weapon; the Bizhang Crossbow with a 300-step range, used by infantry in battle; and the Ma Crossbow with a 200-step range, used by cavalry in battle.[72]

The soldiers in the Tang armies were required to take crossbow shooting exams. To pass the exams, the candidates had to successfully shoot two times out of four a Fuyuan Crossbow to a distance of more than 300 steps, shoot two times out of four a Bizhang Crossbow to more than 230 steps; shoot three times out of four a Jiaogong Crossbow to more than 200 steps; and shoot two times out of four a Dangong Crossbow to more than 160 steps.[73]

The crossbow was advantageous in its long shooting range and impact force. But it was big and heavy to carry and some of them needed several or even dozens of men to get it notched. Therefore, it could hardly be used on horseback or in the changing circumstance of the battlefield where the soldiers fight each other at close quarters.

Arrows were used both in the bow and crossbow. The arrows of the Tang dynasty were classified into many categories according to their usage. For example, the Toujia Zhui Arrow could shoot through leather armour; Langshe Arrows were good for shooting horses; Liuye Arrows were good for shooting both horses and men; and Chuan'er Arrows, on which the arrowhead was as small as a needle, were specially made for shooting enemies wearing armour.[74] There was also the poisonous arrow used in the Sui and Tang dynasties – for example, those used by the Mohe people in the north-east.[75] In the Tang dynasty, the fire arrow was employed, for instance, in the battle where Emperor Taizong conquered the land to the east of the River Liao (now in the east and south parts of Liaoning Province) in 645.[76] This kind of fire arrow was produced by binding some inflammable materials around the arrow, then setting it on fire before shooting it (see Figure 4.4).

The projectile

People in the Sui and Tang dynasties used the bow and ball as a ranged shooting weapon. General Zhangsun Sheng was famous for this martial skill. *Book of Sui* notes that Zhangsun succeeded in shooting ten flying birds at the request of Emperor Wen.[77] Novelist Duan Chengshi of Tang says in his *Miscellaneous Morsels from Youyang* that a monk named Lingjian was also adept at the bow and ball, and that he made the ball by himself with some mud, carbon powder, porcelain powder, elm bark, starch water, butea, sand, rattan paper, and sugarcane wax. These nine ingredients were mixed and ground 3,000 times, then kneaded into a ball form, and air-dried in the shade.[78]

The trebuchet

Trebuchets prevailed during the Sui, Tang, and Five Dynasties and Ten Kingdoms periods. *New Book of Tang* notes the trebuchet was used to take a castle in the late

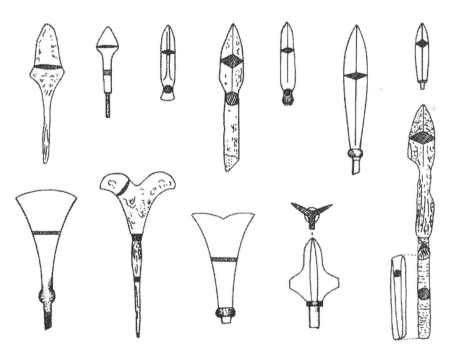

Figure 4.4 Various iron arrowheads from the Sui and Tang dynasties.

Sui dynasty.[79] Employing a trebuchet to destroy a castle is also recorded in *New Book of Tang* and *Old Book of Tang*.[80] The trebuchet was also employed against enemy soldiers, as seen in battle when General Li Guangbi suppressed the insurgent troops during the An Lushan Rebellion,[81] and when Emperor Shizong of Later Zhou (921–959) of the Five Dynasties conquered Huainan County in 956.[82]

Melee weapon skills

By the time of the Sui and Tang dynasties, a rich variety of martial skills with melee weapons had emerged. This section takes a brief look at them from the perspectives of long weapons and short weapons.

Spear skills

The Chinese characters of '枪' (Qiang), '矟' (Shuo), and '槊' (Shuo) often appear in the classics of the Sui, Tang, and Five Dynasties periods, but they refer to the same kind of weapon, the spear. The spear was one of the main weapons used by both infantry and cavalry during the Sui, Tang, and Five Dynasties periods. In specification, the spears used by the cavalry were slightly longer than those of the infantry.

The brick painting of Sui in Lu'an City of Anhui province shows a scene of soldiers on the move with spears and shields (see Figure 4.5). In the Tang dynasty, a certain number of infantry were provided with the following weapons: 12,500 spears, 2,500 cowhide shields, 2,500 crossbows, 12,500 bows, 700,000 arrows of all types, 10,000 sabres, 2,500 long sabres, and 2,500 cudgels. The quantity of spears was the largest of all the melee weapons.[83] *The Records of Origin on Things and Affairs* says that the Baigan Spear in the Tang dynasty was a wooden stick with an iron head and adorned with a red tassel,[84] which is quite similar to what it is in modern times.

Many generals were proficient with the spear in the Tang dynasty, for example, the senior general Yuchi Jingde. When Emperor Taizong led the army to fight against Dou Jiande, leader of the insurgent troops, he said to Yuchi that 'when I am holding the bow and arrow while you are holding your long spear to fight, we will be invincible, even though faced with millions of enemies'. Thus, they rode to Dou's barrack and he shouted, 'I am the emperor of Tang! Those who think they can fight come forward and challenge me!' Although many horsemen of Dou chased them, none dared to get too close.[85] Yuchi mastered not only fighting with the spear, but also dodging and grabbing his opponent's spear. *New Book of Tang* records that he was able to ride into his enemies without being killed and grabbed the enemies' spears to fight back, and he even, at one time, easily grabbed a spear three times from Li Yuanji (fourth son of Emperor Gaozu) who intended to stab him on his horse.[86] Many historical records can also be found about the skilful spear masters of the Tang dynasty, namely, General Qin Shubao[87] and General Ge Shuhan.[88]

Figure 4.5 A brick painting of soldiers walking with spears and shields from the Sui dynasty excavated in Lu'an, Anhui Province.

During the Five Dynasties period there were warriors using iron spears. General Wang Jingyao and Wang Yanzheng of the Later Liang dynasty, stood out among them. Wang Jingyao was said to hold an iron spear of more than 19.9 kg in battle,[89] while Wang Yanzhang's iron spear was said to be nearly 66.1 kg.[90] *Spring and Autumn Annals of the Sixteen Kingdoms* mentions another warrior named Wang Chengxie who was able to wield an 9.9 kg iron spear.[91] Obviously, the employment of the iron spear was in consideration of its weight for piercing the enemy's helmet and armour.

There are also records of short spears in the Five Dynasties.[92] The length of the spear was not specifically recorded. Perhaps it was short relative to the long spear.

Cudgel skills

The *New Book of Tang* notes that General Li Siye often used a large cudgel to disperse his enemies.[93] In the Tang dynasty, cudgels were not only used by the generals, they were a regular weapon in the army.

Halberd skills

During the Sui, Tang, and Five Dynasties periods, the halberd was rarely used on the battlefield; they are only mentioned on a few occasions. In most cases, the halberd was used for the purpose of rites or ceremonies. They were kept standing at the front door as a symbol of identity for the nobility. Several classics, such as *Book of Sui*, *New Book of Tang*, and *Comprehensive Statutes* have recorded the rules about the number of halberds representing different ranks of officials. According to *Six Codes of Tang*, only the officials above the third rank and the regional administration offices above prefectural level were allowed to stand a halberd at the front door.[94] *New Book of Tang* says that the imperial temples, imperial adoratories, and palaces were allowed to stand 24 halberds at their front door.[95] There is a wall painting of halberd-standing in the tomb of Li Chongrun (first son of Emperor Zhongzong of Tang). It shows 24 halberds in total were standing respectively on the east and west sides with 12 along each.

Swordsmanship

During the Sui, Tang and Five Dynasties periods, the sword was no longer included in conventional military equipment, yet the sabre was. The sword had, to a great extent, stepped down from the stage of war.

Wearing a sword remained symbolical in this period. *Book of Sui* writes that the swords the Sui officials wore were made with different kinds of materials, such as jade, gold and silver, and different kinds of decorative stones and silk ribbons, according to the officials' different ranks. When called in by the emperors, the officials were required to remove these swords before they entered the imperial court. The only exception was for the emperors' guards. However, *Book of Sui* also has some records of Sui officials wearing wooden swords in the imperial court.[96] Since many rules and regulations of the Tang dynasty were inherited from the Sui dynasty, the rules on wearing the sword were probably similar. The wooden sword was certainly only worn for rites and ceremonies. The sword had become a symbol of social status for those officials in the court. The real swords (originally made of iron or bronze) as a weapon were replaced by the ornamental swords, made of jade, gold, silver or wood, and worn as an accessory. It can be seen how the sword in court had lost its application as a practical weapon.

Nevertheless, swordsmanship was well developed among the people during the Tang dynasty, in an age when wuxia spirit prevailed. The wuxia used the sword in most circumstances. It was by the power of thousands of swordsmen that Emperor Taizong seized the throne.[97] Poet Li Bai had a Longquan Sword himself.[98] Also, judging from the incident when Li Bai killed several people on Chang'an Street, the sword in his hand was very much a real one and Li was good at swordsmanship.

Coinciding with its demilitarization, the sword became imbued with mystery and sanctity. A Taoist in Eastern Jin dynasty named Ge Hong wrote that the sword was able to behead demons and to ward off back luck. Li Chuo in Tang dynasty wrote that all Taoists should wear a sword.[99] Since then, the sword has become a conjuring tool of the Taoist.

While the sword was mystical, it was also sacred. Some poets in the Tang dynasty regarded it as a metaphor for friendship, as can be seen in many poems, such as *Sharp Sword*,[100] *A Poem for Zhuangyuan Yi*,[101] and *A Poem for Li Zhao*.[102] A Japanese student named Abe Nakamaro had established a deep friendship with Li Bai and Wang Wei, also a famous poet. When Abe returned to Japan, he gave his sword to Wang Wei.[103] Additionally, the poets often expressed their ambitions with the sword. To take Li Bai's poems as an example, his ambition is demonstrated in many works, for instance, 'How I wish to drive off the invaders and keep the border safe for my country with my treasured sword in my hand!'[104]

Most notably, the sword of the Tang dynasty was significantly improved on that of the Sui dynasty, and had taken the shape and specification still in use today, as Zhou Wei notes.[105]

Sabre skills

There were four types of sabres in the Tang dynasty: the Yi Sabre, the Zhang Sabre, the Heng Sabre, and the Mo Sabre. According to *Six Codes of Tang*: the Yi Sabre was often decorated with silver and gold, with a ring of an interlaced dragon and phoenix, and was worn by the bodyguards of the emperors; the Zhang Sabre was often used for close-quarters self-defence; the Heng Sabre was given the name in the Sui dynasty and was carried by soldiers; and the Mo Sabre was a type of long sabre often carried by the infantry.[106] There are few records remaining of the Zhang Sabre (see Figure 4.6).

In *Taibai Yinjing*, it is said that the Tang army had 12,500 soldiers, with 10,000 carrying the Heng Sabre and 2,500 wearing the Mo Sabre.[107] So it may be seen that the Heng Sabre and Mo Sabre were the most widely used sabres in the army, with the Heng Sabre being more common. *Old Book of Tang* tells that the Mo Sabre was first used in the armies of Tang dynasty.[108] However, it is still not known what the Mo Sabre looked like since no documentary or archaeological evidence survives. But we can speculate on its shape and structure from other historical records. The Mo Sabre is also named the horse-cutting sword as it was said to be sharp enough to cut horseflesh and was used as early as the Han dynasty.[109] As such, the Mo Sabre was probably a two-handed sword. It was also known as the long sabre. Therefore, the Mo Sabre had either a long handle or a long blade, and it took both hands to hold it. *Records of Spear and Sabre Skills* says the Mo Sabre was a lethal weapon when employed in the battles of the Tang dynasty.[110] *Cefu Yuangui*[111] and *New Book of Tang*[112] add that there were special troops trained in using the Mo Sabre and that perhaps some special general or officials were appointed to command the Mo Sabre troops.

Not only the imperial armies but also the insurrectionary armies widely employed the sabre in the Sui and Tan dynasties. According to *New Book of Tang* and *Old Book of Tang*, in the late Sui there was a leader of a peasant uprising named Wang Bo based in Changbai Mountain with his followers, who composed a song named *Wuxiang Liaodong Langsi Ge* in order to influence the masses and inspire loyalty in his followers.[113] The lyrics of this song tell how the main weapon they used was the sabre, and that they used the sabre to kill animals for food and to defend against the imperial army. The Lun Sabre they used is probably a type of ring-headed sabre.[114]

Figure 4.6 A image of officials standing with walking sabre from the tomb of the Tang dynasty, excavated in Xianyang, Shaanxi Province.

Iron claw

Old History of the Five Dynasties has recorded two brave generals who were skilled at using the iron claw (with a long handle): Li Cunxiao, wearing heavy armour and riding two horses, was able to change from one horse to another, wielding an iron claw to break the enemy's array;[115] General Zhou Dewei, used an iron claw to unhorse general Chen Zhang. Zhou then captured Chen alive.[116]

Dagger skills

In the novels about the Tang dynasty, there are some descriptions of the Tang people using daggers. *Yuanhuaji* writes that the wife of Cui Shensi came down from the housetop, her body wrapped in white silk, holding a dagger in her right hand and the head of the man who killed her father in her left hand.[117] *The Legend* describes Kunlun Slave Mo Le[118] flying over a high wall with a dagger in hand.[119] *Beimeng Suoyan* says that 'Lu Sheng took a dagger in his hand to cut the sadiron on the stove. The dagger was so sharp that cutting the sadiron was just like cutting a wooden piece'.[120] To some extent, these literary descriptions of the dagger in novels mirror the facts in the development of martial arts in the Tang dynasty.

Other martial skills

The rope lasso

The northern peoples during the Tang dynasty were adept at using the rope lasso. *Anecdotes of the Sui and Tang* notes that General Li Kaigu of Khitan captured two senior generals of Tang in the battlefield by using his rope lasso. Even though he lost the war, when he surrendered to the Tang dynasty, he was spared the death penalty and, instead, was appointed as a general by Empress Wu Zetian due to his superior martial skills.[121]

The meteor hammer

The meteor hammer was a type of soft weapon. From ancient times, people tied stones to rattans for hunting, which was an early form of the meteor hammer. *The Legends*, a collection of short stories, document that a Kunlun slave Mo Le killed vicious dogs with the meteor hammer for his master in the Tang dynasty.[122] Another similar type of these soft weapons in this period was the rope-dart, a sharp metal head tied to a rope.

Unarmed combat

There are some records of the use of unarmed combat skills in the Sui, Tang, and Five Dynasties and Ten Kingdoms periods. For example, the Sui soldiers are said to have killed thousands of Kok Turks enemies with their bare hands when they ran out of weapons in a war in 582.[123]

In this period, there were also recorded some other unarmed martial skills, such as the Yinggong, Dali, Shanzou, Qinggong. However, some of these skills are outside the scope of martial arts, being only anecdotes without supporting historical records, or are unnatural, superstitions, or folk stories.

Martial dances and the forms of martial arts

The opening of the Silk Road facilitated the introduction of some cultures and arts from China's western neighbours. Their engagement with China's indigenous dancing arts affected the development of Chinese dances to an unprecedented degree in the Tang dynasty. The dances of Tang were generally classified into two categories, the Jian dances with faster rhythms and the Ruan dances with slower rhythms. Both categories of dances were more popular among the higher classes. To a great degree, the Jian dances were martial dances. At least, a large number of them can be categorized as martial dances.[124]

Among the martial dances, the development of the spear dance was notable in this period. The wonderful performance of the spear dance in this period was presented in *The Ba Man Holding a Spear*.[125] The dance of *Breaking the Battle Array* is a very famous dance of the Tang dynasty, which eulogizes Emperor Taizong's defeat of the rebel forces led by Liu Wuzhou. This martial dance was probably performed with the halberd and the dagger-axe[126] (see Figure 4.7). Apart from these, the Jianqi dance, sword dance, and lion dance are also worth addressing.

Jianqi dance

Jianqi dance was popular in the Tang dynasty. However, what the Jianqi dancers performed with is still unknown. In general, three arguments have been made so far. First, it was performed with the sword, as Zheng Yu of the Tang dynasty suggested in the poem *Gate of Jinyang*,[127] Song Xiangfeng of the Qing dynasty in *Dynastic Records*,[128] and most recently, Chen Yinke in *Yuanbai Shi Jianzheng*.[129] Second, it was a dance with bare hands, as suggested in *Comprehensive Studies in Administration* by Ma Duanlin, a historian of the Song and Yuan dynasties.[130] Third, it was performed with symbolic meteors made from coloured silks with two heads knotted, as described in Gui Fu's *Zhapu* from the Qing dynasty.[131]

In response to the above arguments, the author considers that the Jianqi dance was performed not only with the sword, bare hands, and silks, but also with the sabre, white flag, red flag and more.[132] Furthermore, the Jianqi dance should be regarded as a kind of martial dance as noted by *Records of the Music Bureaus* where the Jianqi dance was classed as Jian Dance.[133]

Figure 4.7 A Dunhuang mural of martial skills practicing during the Tang dynasty, number 217 mural in Dunhuang, Gansu Province.

Sword dance

In *Miscellaneous Morsels from Youyang* written by Duan Chengshi of the Tang dynasty, there is a depiction of an old man from Lanling County who was good at the sword dance. He wore a purple gown and danced with seven swords of different lengths at the same time.[134] In *Records of the Odds* by Li Kang of the

Tang dynasty, it says that Wu Daozi, a well-known painter of Tang, was invited by General Pei Min to draw several murals of supernatural images in Tiangong Temple of Dongdu (now in Luoyang City of Henan Province). Pei's mother had recently died and Pei wished that she would be taken good care of by the immortals in her afterlife. Wu replied that he had given up painting for a long time but suggested that Pei perform a sword dance to inspire him. At this, Pei took off his mourning apparel and danced a sword dance. He wielded the sword while riding a fast-running horse. Then he threw the sword high in the air. When the sword began to fall down, he raised his scabbard and the sword slid into the scabbard precisely. Pei's spectacular sword-wielding skills greatly inspired Wu and he immediately drew a great mural, one of the most competent of his career.[135]

Lion dance

The lion dance is still very popular among the Chinese people. It is closely related to martial arts and other martial activities even in modern China. The moves included are so complicated that they can only be practiced by those good at martial arts. The competition of a lion dance is virtually a martial competition.

The exact time and place of the lion dance's birth lacks specific records. But the first literary record of the lion dance appears in *New Book of Tang* on the Tang dynasty.[136] Bai Juyi, a famous poet of Tang dynasty also described the costume and performance of the lion dance in his poem *Arts of Western Liang*. He also mentioned that the lion dance was a popular pastime among soldiers.

Martial dances and the forms of martial arts shared the same form in the early days. But since the Tang dynasty, they have detached from each other. The aforementioned figures, such as Pei Min, were skilful swordsmen rather than dancing artists. Yet for quite a long time, until recently, martial dances and martial arts were still closely related and influenced each other. The major difference was that martial dances contain certain plots and emphasis on the thoughts and feelings of the characters while the martial art forms aim to showcase martial skills. In any case, they are still related to each other, as both of them are based on martial skills.

Notes

1 (Tang) Wei Zheng. Suishu•Gazu Ji (隋书•高祖记).
2 *Institutional History of Tang*. (Song) Wang Bo. Tang Huiyao•Fuming (唐会要•府名).
3 *An Armless Old Man in Xinfeng County*. (Tang) Bai Juyi. Xinfeng Zhebiwong (新丰折臂翁).
4 *Penal Code of Tang*. (Tang) Zhangsun Wuji. Tanglv Shuyi• Shanxing (唐律疏议•擅兴).
5 *Old Book of Tang*. (Later Jin) Liu Xu. Jiu Tangshu• Zhiguan Zhi (旧唐书•职官志).

6 The regular task of the soldiers was to serve as guards in the Forbidden City. Soldiers also needed to go to other places to fight and defend.
7 (Song) Wang Yinglin. Yuhai •Juan 139 (玉海•卷139).
8 (Song) Sima Guang. Zizhi Tongjian •Tangji (资治通鉴•唐记).
9 The Nine-rank Official System meant dividing the officials into nine levels, an important approach to appointing officials during the Wei, Jin, and Southern and Northern Dynasties.
10 (Song) Song Qi, Ouyang Xiu et al. Xin Tangshu•Bingzhi (新唐书•兵志).
11 Tongdian. (Tang) Du You. Tongdian •Xuanju San• Lidaizhi Xia (通典•选举三•历代志下).
12 (Song) Song Qi, Ouyang Xiu et al. Xin Tangshu• Xuanju Zhi (新唐书•选举制).
13 (Later Jin) Zhao Ying. Jiu Tangshu•Chai Shao Zhuan (旧唐书•柴绍传).
14 (Tang) Wei Zheng. Suishu •Yangdi Ji (隋书•炀帝记).
15 (Song) Song Qi, Ouyang Xiu et al. Xin Tangshu•Bingzhi (新唐书•兵志); (Tang) Wei Zheng. Suishu•Duan Lun Zhuan (隋书•段纶传).
16 (Song) Song Qi, Ouyang Xiu et al. Xin Tangshu•Shentong Zhuan (新唐书•神通传).
17 (Later Jin) Liu Xu. Jiu Tangshu• Liu Hongji Zhuan (旧唐书•刘弘基传).
18 (Tang) Wei Zheng. Suishu•Liu Quan Zhuan (隋书•刘权传).
19 (Tang) Wei Zheng. Suishu•Wang Kui Zhuan (隋书•王頍传).
20 (Ming) Mao Yuanyi. Wubeizhi• Shuangshou Jianpu (武备志•双手剑谱).
21 Kasaya, a term for the traditional robes of Buddhist monks. In the Tang dynasty, only officials above the third rank were eligible to wear purple cloth. Therefore, only very few monks were given a purple kasaya.
22 (Tang) Tang Pei. Shaolin Sibei (少林寺碑).
23 (Tang) Du You. Tongdian• Xuanju San •Lidaizhi Xia (通典•选举三•历代志下).
24 (Tang) Li Bai. Xiakexing (侠客行).
25 (Tang) Wei Zheng. Suishu• Liu Yu Zhuan (隋书•柳彧传).
26 (Tang) Wei Zheng. Suishu• Yangdi Ji (隋书•炀帝记).
27 A dance imitating boating in the river, but performed on the land.
28 A man holding or heading a long stick, other men made performance on the stick.
29 A Miscellaneous Record of the Emperor Xuanzong Era. (Tang) Zheng Chuhui. Minghuang Zalu •Juan Shang (明皇杂录•卷上).
30 Jiju (击鞠) was a Chinese form of polo which was most prevalent in the Tang dynasty.
31 (Song) Wang Qinruo, Yang Yi et al. Cefu Yuangui• Diwang Bu •Yanxiang (册府元龟•帝王部•宴享).
32 (Later Jin) Liu Xu. Jiu Tangshu• Muzong Ji (旧唐书•穆宗纪).
33 (Later Jin) Liu Xu. Jiu Tangshu• Wenzong Ji (旧唐书•文宗纪).
34 (Song) Sima Guang. Zizhi Tongjian• Wuzong Ji (资治通鉴•武宗纪).
35 Old History of Five Dynasties. (Song) Xue Juzheng, Li Jiuling et al. Jiu Wudai Shi•Qian Liu Zhuan (旧五代史•钱镠传).
36 (Song) Tiao Luzi. Jiaoli Ji (角力记).
37 (Song) Tiao Luzi. Jiaoli Ji (角力记).
38 (Song) Xue Juzheng, Li Jiuling et al. Jiu Wudai Shi•Li Cunxian Zhuan (旧五代史•李存贤传); (Song) Tiao Luzi. Jiaoli Ji (角力记).
39 (Tang) Wei Zheng. Suishu •Liu Yu Zhuan (隋书•柳彧传).
40 (Song) Tiao Luzi. Jiaoli Ji (角力记).
41 (Song) Tiao Luzi. Jiaoli Ji (角力记).
42 (Qing) Wuxing Zalu (吴兴杂录).
43 (Tang) Wei Zheng. Suishu ·Liu Yu Zhuan (隋书•柳彧传).
44 (Song) Tiao Luzi. Jiaoli Ji (角力记); (Qing) Wuxing Zalu (吴兴杂录); (Tang) Wei Zheng. Suishu•Liu Yu Zhuan (隋书•柳彧传).
45 (Ming) Wang Qi. Xu Wenxian Tongkao•Yuekao (续文献通考•乐考).

46 (Song) Tiao Luzi. Jiaoli Ji (角力记).
47 Ibid.
48 (Song) Sima Guang. Zizhi Tongjian•Houtang Ji •Zhuangzong (资治通鉴•后唐纪•庄宗).
49 (Song) Song Qi, Ouyang Xiu et al. Xin Tangshu• Huanzhe Liezhuan (新唐书•宦者列传).
50 (Song) Song Qi, Ouyang Xiu et al. Xin Tangshu•Bingzhi (新唐书•兵志); (Northern Song) Wang Dang. Tang Yulin•Haoshuang (唐语林•豪爽).
51 (Qing) Wuxing Zalu (吴兴杂录). Miasma, a noxious atmosphere originating in mountains, forests, and swamps in the southern and south-western regions which can cause disease.
52 (Song) Tiao Luzi. Jiaoli Ji (角力记). Wanying, literally undefeatable.
53 (Tang) Wen Daya. Datang Chuangye Qiju Zhu•Juan Yi (大唐创业起居注•卷一).
54 Wei Dao'er, claiming to be Li Feishan.
55 (Song) Li Fang, Li Mu et al. Taiping Guangji•Juan 227 (太平广记•卷二百二十七).
56 (Tang) Wei Zheng. Suishu• Zhangsun Sheng Zhuan (隋书•长孙晟传).
57 (Song) Song Qi, Ouyang Xiu et al. Xin Tangshu•Gao Pian Zhuan (新唐书•高骈传).
58 Yijian Shuangdiao (一箭双雕), means killing two vultures with one arrow, later refers to do one task and finish two or more goals.
59 (Song) Song Qi, Ouyang Xiu et al. Xin Tangshu•Xue Rengui Zhuan (新唐书•薛仁贵传).
60 (Song) Song Qi, Ouyang Xiu et al. Xin Tangshu• Wang Qiyao Zhuan (新唐书•王栖曜传).
61 (Later Jin) Liu Xu. Jiu Tangshu•Du Fu Zhuan (旧唐书•杜甫传).
62 (Tang) Du Fu. Aijiangtou (哀江头).
63 (Tang) Wang Jian. Gongci (宫词).
64 (Tang) Lu Lun. Zaqu Geci•Tianchang Dijiu Ci (杂曲歌辞•天长地久词).
65 (Tang) Zhang Ji. Gongci (宫词).
66 (Tang) Du Fu. Aijiangtou (哀江头).
67 (Qing) Chen Shixi. Tangren Shuihui• Shewei (唐人说荟•射围).
68 (Tang) Huarui Furen. Gongci (宫词).
69 (Song) Song Qi, Ouyang Xiu et al. Xin Tangshu•Yiwen Zhi (新唐书•艺文志).
70 (Tang) Zhang Yue, Zhang Jiuling et al. Tang Liudian•Wuku Ling (唐六典•武库令).
71 (Later Jin) Liu Xu. Jiu Tangshu• Bing Zhi (旧唐书•兵志).
72 (Song) Li Fang, Li Mu et al. Taiping Yulan•Juan Sansiba (太平御览•卷三四八); (Tang) Wang Ju. Shejing (射经).
73 (Song) Song Qi, Ouyang Xiu et al. Xin Tangshu• Bing Zhi (新唐书•兵志).
74 (Tang) Zhang Yue, Zhang Jiuling et al. Tang Liudian•Wuku Dian (唐六典•武库典).
75 (Tang) Wei Zheng. Suishu•Mo He Zhuan (隋书•靺鞨传).
76 (Later Jin) Liu Xu. Jiu Tangshu•Taizong Ji (旧唐书•太宗纪).
77 (Tang) Wei Zheng. Suishu•Zhangsun Sheng Zhuan (隋书•长孙晟传).
78 (Tang) Duan Chengshi. Youyang Zazu•Guang Zhi (酉阳杂俎•广知).
79 (Song) Song Qi, Ouyang Xiu et al. Xin Tangshu• Li Mi Zhuan (新唐书•李密传).
80 (Song) Song Qi, Ouyang Xiu et al. Xin Tangshu• Gaoli Zhuan (新唐书•高丽传); (Later Jin) Liu Xu. Jiu Tangshu•Houjun Jizhuan (旧唐书•侯君集传).
81 (Song) Song Qi, Ouyang Xiu et al. Xin Tangshu•Li Guangbi Zhuan (新唐书•李光弼传).
82 (Song) Sima Guang. Zizhi Tongjian•Juan 293 (资治通鉴•293卷).
83 (Tang) Li Quan. Shenji Zhidi Taibai Yinjing•Zhan Ju (神机制敌太白阴经•战具).

84 (Song) Gao Cheng. Shiwu Jiyuan• Juan San (事物纪原•卷三).
85 (Tang) Liu Su. Suitang Jiahua•Juan Shang (隋唐嘉话•卷上).
86 (Song) Song Qi, Ouyang Xiu et al. Xin Tangshu•Qin Qiong Zhuan (新唐书•秦琼传).
87 (Song) Song Qi, Ouyang Xiu et al. Xin Tangshu•Qin Qiong Zhuan (新唐书•秦琼传); (Tang) Liu Su. Suitang Jiahua•Juan Shang (隋唐嘉话•卷上).
88 (Song) Song Qi, Ouyang Xiu et al. Xin Tangshu•Geshu Han Zhuan (新唐书•哥舒翰传).
89 (Song). Xue Juzheng. Jiu Wudai Shi•Wang Jingyao Zhuan (旧五代史•王敬尧传).
90 (Song) Ouyang Xiu. Xin Wudai Shi• Wang Yanzhang Zhuan (新五代史•王彦章传); (Northern Song) Wang Qinruo, Yang Yi et al. Cefu Yuangui•Juan Sanjiuliu (册府元龟•卷三九六). (Later Jin) Liu Xu. Jiu Tangshu•Bai Xiaode Zhuan (旧唐书•白孝德传).
91 (Northern Wei) Cui Hong. Shiliuguo Chunqiu• Qianshu (十六国春秋•前蜀).
92 A Collection of Yutang Novels. (Five Dynasties) Wang Renyu. Yutang Xianhua• Juan Yi (玉堂闲话•卷一).
93 (Song) Song Qi, Ouyang Xiu et al. Xin Tangshu •Li Siye Zhuan (新唐书•李嗣业传).
94 (Tang) Zhang Yue, Zhang Jiuling et al. Tang Liudian•Shangshu Libu (唐六典•尚书礼部).
95 (Song) Song Qi, Ouyang Xiu et al. Xin Tangshu•Baiguan Zhi (新唐书•百官志).
96 (Tang) Wei Zheng. Suishu•Liyi Zhi (隋书•礼仪志).
97 (Ming) Mao Yuanyi. Wubeizhi•Juan 86 (武备志•卷八十六).
98 Ode to the Military Officials. (Tang) Li Bai. Zai Shuijun Yanzeng Mufu Zhu Shiyu (在水军宴赠幕府诸侍御).
99 Anecdotes of Master Zhang. (Tang) Li Chuo. Shangshu Gushi (尚书故实).
100 (Tang) Han Yu. Lijian (利剑).
101 (Tang) Li Bai. Zeng Yi Xiucai (赠易秀才).
102 (Tang) Li Bai. Zeng Congdi Xuanzhou Zhangshi Zhao (赠从弟宣州长史昭).
103 Farewell to my Chinese Friends. (Tang) Chao Heng. Xianming Huanguo Zuo (衔命还国作).
104 Frontier Fortress. (Tang) Li Bai. Si Xia Qu (塞下曲).
105 Zhou Wei, The History of Chinese Weapons (Tianjin: Baihua Literature and Art Publishing House, 2015), 147.
106 (Tang) Zhang Yue, Zhang Jiuling et al. Tangliudian•Modao (唐六典•陌刀).
107 (Tang) Li Quan. Shenji Zhidi Taibai Yinjing•Juan Si (神机制敌太白阴经•卷四).
108 (Later Jin) Liu Xu. Jiu Tangshu•Li Siye Zhuan (旧唐书•李嗣业传).
109 (Eastern Han) Ban Gu. Hanshu•Zhu Yun Zhuan (汉书•朱云传), annotated by Yan Shigu (581–645) in the Tang dynasty.
110 Records of Spear and Saber Skills. (Ming) Wu Shu. Shoubilu•Dandao Tushuo Xu (手臂录•单刀图说序).
111 (Song) Wang Qinruo, Yang Yi et al. Cefu Yuangui• Juan 396 (册府元龟•卷三九六).
112 (Song) Song Qi, Ouyang Xiu et al. Xin Tangshu• Geshu Han Zhuan (新唐书•哥舒翰传).
113 (Song) Sima Guang. Zizhi Tongjian •Suiji (资治通鉴•隋记).
114 A Collection of Ballads. (Ming) Yang Shen. Gujin Fengyao (古今风谣).
115 (Song) Xue Juzheng, Li Jiuling et al. Jiu Wudai Shi•Li Cunxiao Zhuan (旧五代史•李存孝传).
116 (Song) Xue Juzheng, Li Jiuling et al. Jiu Wudai Shi•Zhou Dewei Zhuan (旧五代史•周德威传).
117 (Tang) Huangpu Shi. Yuanhuaji (原化记). A collection of legendary novels of ancient China.

118 Slaves from Southeast Asia during the Tang dynasty.
119 (Tang) Pei Xing. Chuanqi (传奇).
120 (Song) Sun Guangxian. Beimeng Suoyan (北梦锁言).
121 (Tang) Zhang Zhuo. Chaoye Qianzai•Juan Liu (朝野佥载•卷六).
122 (Tang) Pei Xing. Chuanqi (传奇).
123 (Song) Wang Qinruo, Yang Yi *et al.* Cefu Yuangui • Juan 395 (册府元龟•卷395).
124 (Tang) Duan Anjie. Yuefu Zalu•Wugong (乐府杂录•舞工).
125 (Tang) Lu Guimeng. Wuqu Geci•Wu Yu'er Wuge•Maoyu (舞曲歌辞•吴俞儿舞歌•矛俞).
126 (Tang) Su E. Duyang Zabian • Juan Zhong (杜阳杂编•卷中).
127 (Tang) Zheng Yu. Jingyangmen (津阳门).
128 (Song) Fan Gongcheng. Guotinglu (过庭录).
129 Chen Yinke. Yuanbai Shi Jianzheng Gao (元白诗笺证稿).
130 (Yuan) Ma Duanlin. Wenxian Tongkao•Wubu (文献通考•舞部).
131 (Qing) Gui Fu. Zhapu• Jianqi (札朴•剑器).
132 *Three Poems on the Jianqi.* (Tang) Yao Heyou. Jianqi Ci Sanshou (剑器词三首).
133 (Tang) Duan Anjie. Yuefu Zalu• Wugong (乐府杂录•舞工).
134 (Tang) Duan Chengshi. Youyang Zazu• Daoxia (酉阳杂俎•盗侠).
135 (Tang) Li Kang. Duyizhi • Juan Zhong (独异志•卷中).
136 (Song) Song Qi, Ouyang Xiu *et al.* Xin Tangshu• Liyue Zhi (新唐书•礼乐志).

Chapter 5
Martial arts in the Song dynasty (960–1279)

In 960, Zhao Kuangyin (927–976, later Emperor Taizu of Song) launched the Chenqiao Mutiny and seized power from the Later Zhou dynasty, establishing the Northern Song dynasty (960–1127) and making Bianliang (now Kaifeng City of Henan Province) the capital.

From then on, the Song dynasty reinforced the centralization of its power. With the 'From the South to the North' military strategy, Northern Song unified the territories of the central plains and the small states in the south. At that time, there were other political regimes in power based on the non-Han peoples around the frontiers of the Northern Song, namely, the Liao dynasty (916–1125), the Jin dynasty (1115–1234), and the Western Xia dynasty (1038–1227). After the Jurchen people defeated the Liao dynasty in the northeast and set up the Jin dynasty in 1115 they kept invading the Northern Song. With the frequent offensives by the Jin dynasty, the Northern Song dynasty was forced to relocate its capital to Lin'an (now Hangzhou City, Zhejiang Province) beginning the period of the Southern Song dynasty (1127–1279).

Conflicts with the Liao, Jin, and Western Xia dynasties persisted throughout the 320-year reign of the Song dynasty. Hence, the Song emperors laid much stress on military development. In Song, the Mubing system[1] was adopted to select and enroll martial talents into the armies. Additionally, uniform military codes and standards of assessment for military training were regulated. Such normalization and systemization of military training promoted the development of martial skills. Moreover, the variety of weapons and the skills in using them increased dramatically in this period.

During the Song dynasty, the prosperity of commerce and the expansion of the civil class accelerated the development of urban culture. Some societies which used martial arts as a form of fitness and entertainment emerged in the urban areas. There also emerged specialized venues to accommodate the citizens' demand for recreation, which were called Washe and Goulan.[2] Various martial skills were performed in these venues. Furthermore, a great number of stories about martial skills can also be found in the Chinese operas, dramas, and novels of Song.

With the rapid development of popular martial skills, some societies for martial arts were set up in the rural areas with the Xiangshe[3] as the basic unit.

People in a Xiangshe voluntarily formed a society who often farmed and practiced martial arts together. Popular martial skills were developed in these rural societies.

The system of Chinese martial arts took its substantial shape during the Song dynasty. Besides the competitive martial arts, such as Jiaodi and unarmed combat, the performance-oriented martial arts were also promoted. During the Song dynasty, Chinese martial arts gained momentum among the public.

The development of military martial skills

The normalization of military training

The emperors of the Song dynasty took military training seriously. Emperor Taizu set out to strengthen the imperial barracks in the second year of his reign (961). He set up imperial barracks in the capital, inspecting and training them strictly by himself. Those offensive and defensive fighting skills which were widely used in war were the main subjects for the barracks training. The bow and arrow, the crossbow, the sabre, and the spear were the main weapons, so there were strict rules about training in the use of these weapons.[4]

During the two political reforms initiated by Emperor Renzong (1010–1063) and Emperor Shenzong (1048–1085), two codes were issued to regulate the programs, methods, and weapons within military training. For example, *Illustrated Codes for Military Training* issued by Emperor Renzong in 1079 contained illustrations of the training methods for certain military martial skills, such as foot archery, bow-drawing, horseback archery, horseback spearing and so on. All military officials and soldiers had to learn these formulas by heart.[5]

Within the military training system of the Song dynasty, regulations covered not only the normalized training codes but also explicit and detailed rules for the assessment of proficiency in the martial arts skills. There were two major indicators for assessing the standards of archery, the weight of a bow or crossbow the soldiers could draw, and the soldiers' shooting accuracy. For example, in 1068, Emperor Shenzong regulated that those who could draw a bow of 50.54 kg were ranked in the first class, 44.93 kg in the second, and 39.31 kg in the third; those who could draw a crossbow of 151.63 kg were ranked in the first class, 134.78 kg in the second, and 117.94 kg in the third.[6] A similar set of criteria was adopted in assessing ability with the spear, the iron whip, the iron mace,[7] the double swords, the broadax, and the flail on horseback. The soldiers had to try to hit a wooden target ten times from the left side and ten times from the right side. They had to hit the target at least five times to pass the exam.[8] *Regulations of Military Skills Test in the Capital* notes that the assessment results were divided into three classes for archery: the superior, the average, and the inferior. The soldiers had six chances in all. Those who could hit the target three times or more were regarded as the superior class, those who could hit the target twice were regarded as the average class, and those who could hit the target only once were regarded as the inferior class.⁹ *History of Song* records that if a soldier beat three soldiers in the spear and sabre competitions, he was regarded as outstanding.¹⁰ In order to meet the assessment standard, the imperial barracks practiced martial arts day and night, which greatly advanced the military training.

The emperors of Song dynasty also made an effort to summarize, generalize, and promote the experience of military training. For example, a set of archery training codes were introduced into military training in 1044 and a set of crossbow training codes in 1078 and again in 1085. Since a number of soldiers were required to promote and implement the military training regulations, the profession of military instructor was born. *History of Song* notes that in 1044, some instructors from Shaanxi were sent to Hebei by the central government.¹¹ Wang Anshi even institutionalized this strategy in his *Reformation of the Military System* so that the central government would send martial arts masters to the armies to train the soldiers.¹² To achieve this, the central government also conducted short-term or rotational camps to train the instructors at a grassroots level.

In 1079, Emperor Shenzong issued the *Regulations of Assembling the Secondary Bao Supervisors for Military Training in the Capital*, which ordered that a training ground be set up in every second county; the supervisors of the secondary baos¹³ were convened regularly for training in military skills. Ten of them would be assembled for training in one martial skill, and an instructor was appointed to them. The training lasted for three years and the cost was covered by the government. After graduation, they returned to their own districts to act as the local instructor. Five days were taken as a session for each martial skill. Ten local instructors were responsible for 100 households. In this way, a top-down military training network was formed, within which the military officials could examine the effects of the training every year. The powers of the instructors were restricted to military training separate from military command. Therefore, they could concentrate on training and studying martial skills, which was beneficial in improving the military training and weapon skills.

The unified and specific criteria for selecting, training, and examining soldiers in the Song dynasty upheld the normalization and institutionalization of military training and the development of military martial skills to an unprecedented high level, as Shen Kuo (statesman, 1031–1095) of Northern Song argues in *Dream Pool Essays*.¹⁴

The publication of the military classics

Apart from the strengthening of military training, the Song dynasty also encouraged the compilation of the classic ancient military texts. The *Complete Essentials for the Military Classic* was completed by the Northern Song imperial officials in 1044, which covered various fields of military development, including military organization, military institutions, infantry and cavalry training, troop marching, camp-based battles, weapons manufacturing, and other strategies and skills, as well as military geography. In particular, various kinds of ranged and melee weapons used in the Northern Song were well illustrated in this work. In addition, it also compiled the details of military strategies and tactics used before the Song dynasty.

The *Seven Military Classics* was also published during the Song dynasty; it was compiled and revised on the instructions of Emperor Shenzong. The works included were Sunzi's *The Art of War*; Sima Rangju's *Simafa*, and *Wei Liaozi*; Jiang Ziya's *Six Secret Teachings*; and Wu Qi's *Wuzi*, *Three Strategies of Huang Shigong*, and *Questions and Replies between Emperor Taizong of Tang and Li Weigong*. The *Seven Military Classics* were later made compulsory reading for the Imperial Martial Examination. During the Southern Song, it was ordered that the questions for the Imperial Martial Exams come from the *Seven Military Classics*. The *Seven Military Classics* had become the fundamental textbook for the training of martial talents in ancient China, and the first ever book series among all ancient military classics in China.

The diverse development of weapons

The manufacture of weapons was the subject of extensive attention in the Song dynasty. In the capital, there were the South Arsenal, the North Arsenal, and an Archery Wing directly under the jurisdiction of the central government. Additionally, the local governments of each province or prefecture built their own arsenals. Within the local arsenal, there was a clear assignment of roles. Wang Dechen, scholar-official of Northern Song, notes in his *Zhu Shi* that there were 11 subordinate departments working on the manufacture of weapons. This weapons manufacturing system was established under the reign of Emperor Shenzong. In order to improve the quality of the weapons, elite craftsmen throughout the country were brought to the arsenals where they could share their experiences in making fine weapons. New military inventions would be promoted and the inventors would be rewarded.[15] These strategies not only positively improved the quality of weapons, but also increased the scale of production. According to *History of Song*, the South and North Arsenal made around 32,000 fine armours annually, the Archery Wing made more than 1,650,000 fine bows and arrows annually, and the local arsenals made more than 620,000 fine crossbows annually.[16] This demonstrates the success of the institutionalization of weapon production in the Song dynasty.

The bow and crossbow

The concept of 'Eighteen Martial Skills' is a significant concept in the history of Chinese martial arts. As far as can be seen from the historical records, it was first mentioned in *The Bow*, the 7th volume of *The Political and Military Thoughts of Hua Yue*. The author, poet Hua Yue of the Southern Song dynasty, argues that the bow took first place among the Eighteen Martial Skills.[17] As ranged shooting weapons, the bow and the crossbow played an important role in the Song armies. According to *History of Song*, crossbow skills accounted for 60 per cent of the contents of the weapon skill training of the imperial barracks, while bow skills accounted for 20 per cent, and all other weapon skills accounted for 20 per cent. Most of the bows used in the Song dynasty were composite bows (see Figure 5.1). The Shenbi Bow was a lethal weapon made in the reign of Emperor Shenzong, which had a range of up to 240 steps with a strong impact force. The Shenbi Bow was not as heavy as the Chuangzi Crossbow (a stationary windlass device with a triple-bow) and could be held by one man, so it was widely used in the Song armies. In the Southern Song, the Shenbi Bow was further developed into the Kedi Bow which not only had a range of up to 360 steps,[18] but was also capable of penetrating strong armour and armoured horses.[19]

There were many types of crossbow in use in the Song dynasty. *Complete Essentials for the Military Classics* refers to the Chuang Crossbow with two bows, Chuang Crossbow with three bows, Xiao Hechan Crossbow, and Da Hechan Crossbow. To use these crossbows, it required anything from several to more

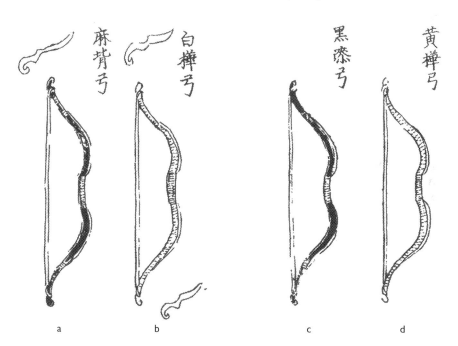

Figure 5.1 Bows from the Song dynasty.
Source: Complete Essentials for the Military Classics.
Notes
a   Mabei Bow;
b   Baihua Bow;
c   Heiqi Bow;
d   Huanghua Bow.

than 100 men to draw the string. The mallets were often used as arrows. They could shoot to a distance of up to 120 steps. The Chuang Crossbow with three bows, also named Ba'niu Crossbow, was the most powerful one. The arrow of it was flat with a triangular shaped head, a wooden or iron shaft, and iron fins. This kind of crossbow could fire three arrows at one time and reached an unprecedented distance of up to 300 steps[20] (see Figure 5.2).

The sabre

Despite the indispensable role the bow and crossbow played in Song warfare, the Song armies regarded other weapons as an important supplement. The cavalry and infantry were required to master various weapons besides the bow and crossbow, such as the sabre, sword, iron whip, and short spear. As a type of short weapon, the sabre was improved in the Song dynasty, witnessing the change from a long and narrow shape to a shape with a sharp front-edge and a wide blade. In addition, a hand guard was fitted, but the big oval ring and the decorations, such as drawings of birds and beasts, of earlier styles were removed. Meanwhile, various types of long-handled sabres emerged, as found in *Complete Essentials for the Military Classics*: the Zhao Sabre, Qu Sabre, Huan'er Sabre, Yanyue Sabre, Ji Sabre, Meijian Sabre, Fengzui Sabre and more[21] (see Figure 5.3).

The Northern Song saw great economic and cultural development. Mutually beneficial marine trade was underway between the Song and Japan. Therefore, a

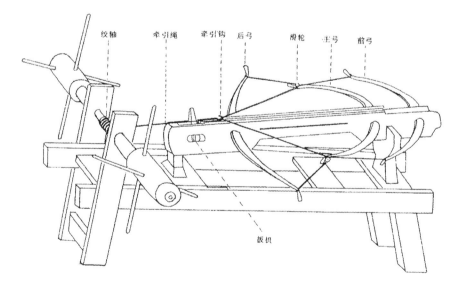

Figure 5.2 Chuang Crossbow with three bows.

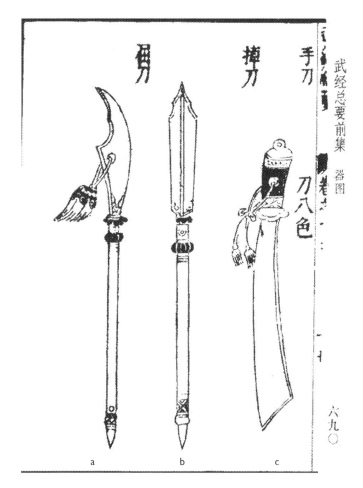

Figure 5.3 Sabres from the Song dynasty.

Notes
a   Qu Sabre;
b   Zhao Sabre;
c   Shou Sabre.

large number of sabres were imported from Japanese merchants. The number of these imported sabres might have come to 30,000 annually.

In the Song dynasty, there were a great number of masters of the sabre, notably, Generals Guan Sheng[22] and Mi Xin.[23] *History of Jin* also writes that Xu Wen, a navy lieutenant general of Song, was good at using the sabre and carried a 30.5 kg sabre in battle[24]; while *Huichenlu* notes that Military Director of Taiyuan Wang Bing was adept in using the sabre on horseback[25]; and *Anecdote of Southern Song* notes that the insurrectionary leader Yang Miaozhen could use two sabres to fight on horseback when she was 20 years old.[26]

The spear

The spear was still an important weapon in the Song dynasty. *Complete Essentials for the Military Classics* records that the cavalry and infantry mainly employed nine types of spears; these were: the Yaxiang Spear, Sumu Spear, Huanzi Spear, Dangou Spear, Shuanggou Spear, Tai'ning Bi Spear, Chui Spear, Suo Spear, and Zhui Spear (see Figure 5.4). In the Song dynasty, the spear was made from a wooden handle, an iron spearhead, and an iron butt. The spears employed by the cavalry were equipped with side barbs on the spearheads and a ring on the handle, such as the Shuanggou Spear and Dangou Spear; while the infantry used spears without any barbs, such as the Sumu Spear and Yaxiang Spear. The Zhui Spear had a rhombic head which was sharp but could not be used to cut. The Tai'ning Bi Spear had a blade-surrounding iron plate several centimetres below the spearhead, so that a defending enemy was not able to grab the spear. The short-head spears were

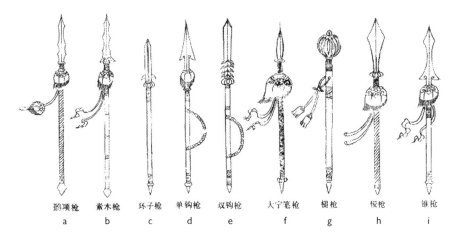

Figure 5.4 Various spears used by infantry and cavalry.

Source: Complete Essentials for the Military Classics.

Notes
a   Yaxiang Spear;
b   Sumu Spear;
c   Huanzi Spear;
d   Dangou Spear:
e   Shuanggou Spear;
f   Tai'ning Bi Spear;
g   Chui Spear;
h   Suo Spear;
i   Zhui Spear.

specialized for storming a castle, such as the Duanren Spear, Duanzhui Spear, Zhua Spear, Jili Spear, and Guai Spear. They were short (1.24 m–1.87 m) and mainly used at close quarters. Those spears specialized for defending a castle were the Guaitu Spear, Zhua Spear, Guairen Spear, and Boathook. Their handles were long, about 7.8 m, so as to be able to reach enemies who were climbing up a castle wall.[27]

Remarkable masters of the spear in the Song dynasty include Song General Yue Fei (1103–1142) who was known to hold a spear (around 6.3 m) to fight,[28] and Li Quan (?–1231) who was good at fighting with the spear on horseback.[29] There were also masters who fought with two spears, such as the famous anti-Jin general, Zhao Li.[30]

Other weapons

Dozens of miscellaneous weapons of the Song dynasty are also recorded in the *Complete Essentials for the Military Classics*.

1. Jili (Tribulus shaped weapon) and Suantou (Garlic shaped weapon), were hammer-like attacking weapons which were assembled from a long wooden stick and an iron head. The iron mace had a square section, while the iron whip resembled bamboo. The shape and length of these weapons could be adjusted according to the needs of the user.
2. Keli Mace, Gou Mace, Gan Mace, Chu Mace, Bai Mace, Zhuazi Mace, and Wolf-tooth Mace were developed from the lance of ancient times. They were made of hardwood, about 1.25 m–1.56 m in length. Some of them were wrapped with iron at both ends; some were fixed with a hook and a butt; and some were equipped with nails at the head. They were generally named after their shapes.
3. The Flail was a kind of flexible weapon first used by the non-Han people and later adopted by the Han People. It was made from long and short sticks chained together by iron rings. In using the Flail, one held the long stick and waved the short stick, which could produce a strong attacking force.
4. Axes of the Song dynasty were of different shapes and sizes. *Complete Essentials for the Military Classics* records that there were many kinds of axe, such as the Kaishan Axe, Jingyan Axe, Rihua Axe, Wudi Axe, and Changke Axe. In addition to the common axes, there were also the castle-storming Fengtou Axe, which had a 24.96 cm blade and a 78 cm handle; the Emei Axe, the blade of which was 15.6 cm in width, the handle 93.6 cm in length; and the Cuowang Axe, which was used to cut down enemies climbing up castle walls, with a blade 21.84 cm in width and a handle 1.09 m in length (see Figure 5.5).

116 Song dynasty

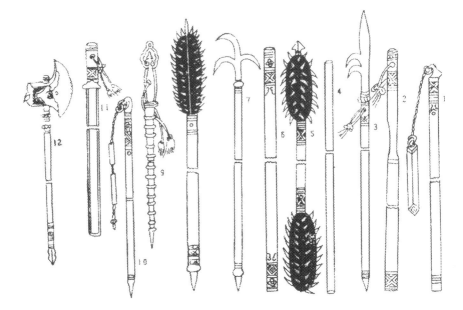

Figure 5.5 Miscellaneous weapons (part) in the Song dynasty.
Source: Complete Essentials for the Military Classics.

Notes
 1 Flail;
 2 Keli Mace;
 3 Gou Mace;
 4 Gan Mace;
 5 Chu Mace;
 6 Bai Mace;
 7 Zhuzi Mace;
 8 Wolf-tooth Mace;
 9 Iron Whip;
10 Lianzhu Iron Whip;
11 Iron Mace;
12 Broad Axe.

The performance of martial skills in the army

In the Northern Song dynasty, the imperial barracks drafted a number of entertainers who were good at martial skills and Hundred Skills from the local armies and the populace. These entertainers were registered with and supported by the army system. Meng Yuanlao, a writer of the Song dynasty, depicted scenes of martial arts performances for the emperor by these entertainers. There were both one-on-one and team-on-team fighting performances. The use of real weapons made these performances breathtaking; the weapons involved included the sword, the sabre, the axe, and the cudgel.[31]

There were also group martial arts performances. More than 100 people would stand in lines or other arrays, each of them holding a wooden Zhao Sabre in hand. The performers moved in patterns and then formed a straight line. Then they took turns to fight each other in pairs. One acted being stabbed, throwing down his sabre and falling to the ground.[32] Extra movements could be put into the performance to increase its impressiveness.

There were some other martial arts performed in the Song armies, such as the sword dance and Jiaodi. *Sequel to Comprehensive Mirror in Aid of Governance* writes that during the reign of Emperor Taizong (939–997), hundreds of selected warriors were trained in the sword dance. All of them were able to throw the sword in the air and then catch the falling sword with the scabbard while flexibly moving their body.[33] In the Southern Song dynasty, the popularity of sword dance remained, as depicted in *Records of Capital Lin'an*.[34] In the Southern Song dynasty, a Jiaodi team of 120 soldiers was made up to perform during the royal fairs, festivals, and banquets, who were selected through special exams.[35]

The Imperial Martial Examination and the martial academy

The Imperial Martial Examination

The Imperial Martial Examination was first introduced in the early Tang dynasty but abolished in the late Tang. It was resumed by Emperor Renzong of Song in 1029. From then on, the examination was organized without a fixed schedule until Emperor Yingzong (1032–1067) decided in 1075 to have it held every three years. However, the Imperial Martial Examination faded away during the reign of Emperor Duzong (1240–1274).

The Imperial Martial Examination was composed of the provincial exam, the national exam, and the final imperial exam, as well as a qualification exam. The qualification exams were chaired by the Ministry of War when the exams were held in the capital, but chaired by the local officials when they were held outside the capital. It included the martial skills and literacy tests. The quota for the candidates was generally restricted to 200, but could be adjusted according to the needs of war in the border regions.

The provincial exam was chaired by the Ministry of War, through which 70–80 candidates would be promoted to the national exam. As in the qualification exam, the provincial exam was also divided into the martial skills and literacy tests. In the literacy test, the candidates would be examined on the *Seven Military Classics* in a paper exam or interviewed on military strategies. The candidates would then be ranked as excellent or average.[36]

The composition of the national exam was similar to the qualification test and the provincial exam, and included martial skills and literacy tests organized by the Ministry of War. Archery skills were an important element in the martial skills test together with other skills with melee weapons. These archery skills not only included using the bow and arrow on foot or on the horse, but also firing the crossbow. During the national exam, archery skills were the first subject to be tested. Those without proficient archery skills would be rejected immediately. The exams in archery skills were held in the armouries from 1030 in the Northern Song dynasty. From 1128, the venue was changed to the imperial barracks in the Southern Song dynasty.[37] The literacy test examined the candidates' command of the *Seven Military Classics* through questions and answers, along with their insights on practical military strategy and tactics through completing a paper of no more than 700 words.

The first imperial exam of the Imperial Martial Examination of the Song dynasty was held in 1030, when Emperor Renzong personally chaired the examination of 12 candidates. Although martial skills tests were also included, military strategy and tactics was the major subject to be tested in the imperial exam.

The martial academy

The martial academy system of the Song dynasty was first established in 1043 but was abolished after only three months. In 1072, the central martial academy was rebuilt in Prince Wucheng Temple with a twin-track entrance system. That is, for the low-grade military officials (outside of the nine ranks) and the descendants of meritorious officials and other civilians residing in the capital, they had to be recommended by the officials of the central government as well as take an entrance exam; for those residing outside the capital, who had passed the provincial martial exam but failed in the national martial exam, they had to be recommended by local officials but had the entrance exam waived.

The central martial academy was divided into three grades with 200 students enrolled; 30 were in the shangshe (first grade), 70 were in the neishe (second grade), and 100 in the waishe (third grade). The students in shangshe were also ranked into three classes. The first class students could be granted an official position, while the second class students were waived of the national exam, and the third class students were waived of the provincial exam for the imperial martial examination. An official who was both adept in literary and martial knowledge was appointed to take charge of the academy, titled 'Jiaoshou'. In 1082, the title of 'Jiaoshou' was changed to 'Boshi', and an additional official titled 'Xueyu' was appointed. The courses included in the central martial academy were not only about practical martial skills, but also the study of military strategies, as well as moral education in subjects such as loyalty. Therefore, the posts of Boshi and Xueyu were generally taken by one martial official and one civil official respectively.

When it came to the reign of Emperor Huizong (1182–1135), local martial academies were established in the prefectures. Most of the students of the central martial academy were selected from the local academies through an entrance examination. Those who had passed the provincial martial exam but failed in the national martial exam could also be considered for admission as long as they were recommended by local officials as well as an extra examination for waishe recruitment.[38]

However, all local martial academies were abolished in 1120, and the twin-track entry system returned. In the reign of Emperor Gaozong (1107–1187), the total number in the school was reduced to 100, with ten in shangshe, 20 in neishe, and 70 in waishe. The waishe students, non-school candidates, and other students from the former local martial academies could be promoted or admitted to neishe or shangshe level through special examinations.[39]

With the establishment of the Southern Song dynasty, the central martial academy was relocated to Lin'an in 1146. In the same year and later in 1149, all waivers of entrance to the central martial academy were cancelled. Instead, all candidates had to take part in the entrance examination to be recruited to the central martial academy.

Martial arts societies among the general population

The rural martial arts societies

Natural economy played a dominant role in the Song dynasty. This 'unshared housing and unshared farming' production model imposed restrictions on regional communication. In the meantime, people in different xiangshe tended to share a family name under the influence of the feudal patriarchal clan system, which gave rise to a strong regional cohesion in the rural society. Therefore, the rural martial arts societies often used the xiangshe as the basic unit.

The Archery Society was a rural martial arts society with a long history based in Hebei. Su Shi, famous poet and governor of Ding Prefecture of Hebei, said in 1093 that the Archery Society was voluntary and well organized. Taking the xiangshe as the basic unit, one man of every household in the xiangshe was chosen as a member of the society. They selected the wealthy or elite martial masters as their leaders. The members were provided with certain weapons. They brought the bow and arrow when farming, and the sword when they went into the forest. The society developed rapidly and its membership covered a vast territory in the north of Hebei with more than 30,000 members.[40] From the reign of Emperor Renzong (1010–1063), the Archery Society was administrated by the government.

Besides the Archery Society, people formed the Loyalty Society to resist the invasion by the Jurchen people. The Loyalty Society was also a militia supported by the Song government. Members were provided with weapons and trained in martial skills. It was a large-scale martial arts society covering wide territories of Shanxi, Hebei, Henan, and Shandong Province.[41]

Under normal circumstances, the rural martial arts societies were inactive in war, but kept farming and practicing martial arts, and sometimes acted as the intercessor when disputes occurred within or between xiangshes. However, they sometimes gathered revolutionary force and launched large-scale peasant uprisings. For example, the Dare-to-Die Society (Meiming She) during the reign of Emperor Renzong,[42] the Overlord Society during the reign of Emperor Shenzong, and the Dare-to-Die Society (Wangming She) during the reign of Emperor Huizong. In addition, Zhong Xiang also gathered his military force by organizing a martial arts society before he launched the peasant uprising in the Dongting Lake areas of Hunan.[43] The Yang's Society rose to occupy a couple of prefectures in the east of Shandong with tens of thousands of members.[44]

In summary, the activities carried out by these rural martial arts societies had different aims, scopes, and scales. Some gathered together for self-defence or to defend their homeland from being invaded by other peoples, while some aimed to resist the government. But all of these societies stressed the utility of military training. The bow and arrow, crossbow, sabre, and spear were most used in these societies. The emergence of these rural martial arts societies greatly promoted the development of Chinese martial arts in the public society.

The urban martial arts societies

Alongside the development of the rural martial arts societies, urban ones also developed but in a different way. During the Han and Tang dynasties, the cities were composed of various 'fangs'.[45] However, the boundaries of the fangs were broken and the city began to be interconnected with various streets during the Song dynasty. This transformation led to commercial prosperity and the expansion of the urban populace. The citizens tended to seek fitness and recreation through joining martial arts societies in their leisure time.

There were a number of martial arts societies in Lin'an in the Southern Song dynasty, in particular for the practice of Jiaodi, archery, and the cudgel.[46] According to *Records of Entertainment in Lin'an*, each of these societies had more than 100 members. Membership of these societies differed in their aims and objectives. For example, some societies only accepted those of advanced skills; while other societies accepted members of all levels who participated only for fitness and entertainment rather than to make a living.[47]

The societies organized their activities in various sites, namely in the Washe, Goulan, temple squares, and other playing fields. These activities were mostly held during festivals. They were performance-oriented with a stress on entertainment, so it was very different from the rural martial arts societies in the north which aimed to defend against their enemies by practicing martial arts.

The emergence of various kinds of societies in Song also resulted from the development of industry and commerce. During the Song, a significant number of vocations were developed, as *Records of Entertainment in Lin'an* suggests that there were 440 vocations in the capital. Every vocation had their own activities and their own festivals.[48] Various types of associations, including martial arts societies, were set up in this way. It greatly drove the development of Chinese martial arts in the urban society.

Martial arts activities of the civil class

Commercial prosperity and the martial arts performers

The prosperous commodity-based economy of the Song made both Bianliang (capital of the Northern Song) and Lin'an (capital of the Southern Song) large cities with well-developed industry and commerce. Bianliang was the commercial centre of the Northern Song containing about 6,400 stores. *Along the River during the Qingming Festival* vividly depicts the scene of the serried stores along the two sides of the Bian River and the crowded streets. The commodity economy of the Southern Song surpassed that of the Northern Song. The total number of households in Lin'an was 390,000 compared to 260,000 in Bianliang. In the cities, the number of merchants increased dramatically. Furthermore, there was a large number of people flowing into the city to fill the middle and lower classes, many being bankrupt farmers and professional performers.

The prosperity of the commercial economy and the expansion of the civil class stimulated the rise of an urban culture. It witnessed a booming industry in commercialized performances of martial skills, as well as an increasing number of professional martial art performers in the public society. *Records of Bianliang* records more than 70 famous professional performers in the capital of the Northern Song, among whom there were some famous martial arts performers good at Jiaodi and Zhao Sabre, and so on.[49] *The Past of Lin'an* says that there were more than 800 professional performers in the capital of the Southern Song: 49 were Jiaodi performers; and at least six of the professional martial arts performers were women. There were also professional martial arts performers of cudgel skills, weightlifting, and the crossbow recorded in *The Past of Lin'an*. These peoples lived by performing martial arts, which promoted the specialization, professionalization, and commercialization of Chinese martial arts. They entertained the crowds by performing martial arts, which also required skills in the arts of entertainment.[50] This social context of the Song dynasty contributed greatly to the development of Chinese performance-oriented martial arts.

Martial arts in the Washe and Goulan

Washe were the recreational places for the masses in the Song dynasty and were generally located within the city. Goulan were the sites for performing various skills within the Washe, which were encircled by fences with floral designs or rope nets. There were many Washe in Bianliang of the Northern Song dynasty. The large Washe could be found in the main streets and around the city gates. Each of these large Washe included about 50 Goulan with a total audience capacity in the thousands.[51] Many people would come to watch the performances, no matter whether it rained or shone, or whether it was hot or cold. The Washe were filled by audiences every day.[52]

It was similar in Lin'an of the Southern Song dynasty. According to the classics, such as *Records of Capital Lin'an* and *Records of Entertainment in Lin'an*, there were more than 20 famous Washe in or surrounding the capital. Among them, the North Washe in Lin'an was the largest, containing 13 Goulan.[53]

Many skills were performed in the Washe, including some unarmed martial performances such as Jiaodi and quans, as well as various performances with weapons such as the cudgel, sabre, spear, shield, and sword. *The Past of Lin'an* records that women martial performers were invited to showcase the paired fighting forms before the main competition started so as to draw larger audiences.[54]

The Washe provided regular opportunities for the large cohort of professional performers in the Song dynasty. The contents and categories of martial skills performed in the Washe had never been seen before. However, some performers also exhibited their skills at open sites rather than in the Goulan.[55] According to *A Dream Tour of Lin'an*, sites such as the squares outside government buildings were filled with people performing different sports. Even some drug vendors made their own circles with ropes, inside which they performed sword and spear shows to attract customers.[56]

The development of Jiaodi

Jiaodi was very popular among all classes in the Song dynasty, and *Records of Capital Lin'an* indicates that women and children were also keen on Jiaodi.[57] The costume of Jiaodi followed the tradition of the Han and Tang dynasties. The participants were naked to the waist, wearing shorts, in bare feet (although sometimes they wore boots), and with their hair in a bun rather than wearing a hat on their head. It is also worthwhile to note that the women participants were also naked to the waist in most circumstances.[58]

There were two kinds of Jiaodi in the Song, one was the performance or exhibition for the masses in the Washe, the other was the formal competition, a form of challenge competition, as shown in *Records of Capital Lin'an*.[59] The Jiaodi competitions in the Song dynasty emphasized courage, tactics, and skills, so that the contestants of different weights were not divided into different groups, as suggested in *History of Jiaodi*.[60] As in previous ages, formal rules and referees were employed for the Jiaodi competitions of the Song dynasty.

Martial arts in Chinese operas, dramas, and novels

The development of martial arts during the Song dynasty was deeply connected with the development of the arts. Themes around martial arts can be found in the thriving literary and artistic works of the Song dynasty, including in dramas, novels, historical tales, puppet shows, and shadow plays.

In the Northern Song dynasty, drama broadly referred to many kinds of skilled performance, from puppet shows to Jiaodi competitions. *Mulian Saves His Mother* was probably the most popular drama in Bianliang. The drama was full of acrobatic fighting skills which attracted the audience, for example, the famous spear fighting scene. The entire play would last for about seven or eight days.[61] It can also be found in *Records of Bianliang* that the dramas at the end of the Northern Song encompassed many kinds of martial skills, such as Zhao Sabre, children's Jiaodi, and more.[62]

Before the Southern Song dynasty, drama had become the most important of the performing arts, within which certain martial skills could also be found. For instance, *The Zhuangyuan Zhang Xie*, which is collected in *Yongle Encyclopedia*, has records of the Eighteen Martial Skills. The Song drama *A Flying Saber to the Arrow* also describes scenes of fighting with martial skills.[63]

Apart from drama, the puppet show was another popular performing art in the Song dynasty. It used different kinds of puppets to play out different themes or stories. According to *A Dream Tour of Lin'an*, the puppet shows at that time tended to involve supernatural fighting plots.[64] The novels in the Song dynasty were also full of attractive fighting scenes involving all kinds of weapons. For example, one of the great works of Chinese literature, *The Water Margin*, depicts 250 fighting scenes vividly, including the Eighteen Martial Skills and many other unarmed fighting skills.[65] Although the book was written during the Yuan dynasty, it mainly describes the martial arts of the Song dynasty.

Notes

1 The *Mubing* system, one of the major military systems in ancient China, which refers to recruiting soldiers in the form of employment.
2 Washe and Washe, a kind of pleasure house in the Song and Yuan dynasties.
3 Xiangshe, a form of social organization in rural areas. In ancient times, a Xiangshe was often divided into a certain number of acres or households.
4 *Complete Essentials for the Military Classics*. (Northern Song) Ding Lu and Zeng Gongliang. Wujing Zongyao•Juan Er (武经总要•卷二).
5 *History of Song*. (Yuan) Tuotuo Tiemuer and A Lu Tu. Songshi•Bingzhi (宋史•兵志).
6 (Song) Yuan Jiong and Yuan Yi. Fengchuang Xiaodu• Juan Xia (枫窗小牍•卷下).
7 Iron Jian, a weapon similar to a mace in ancient China. It looks like a straight sword with four edges, without a blade.
8 *A History of the Eras of Emperor Gaozong and Xiaozong*. (Song) Huansong Zhongxing Liangchao Shengzheng•Juan 195 (皇宋中兴两朝圣政•卷195).
9 (Yuan) Tuotuo Tiemuer and A Lu Tu. Songshi• Bingzhi (宋史•兵志).
10 (Yuan) Tuotuo Tiemuer and A Lu Tu. Songshi•Bingzhi (宋史•兵志).
11 (Yuan) Tuotuo Tiemuer and A Lu Tu. Songshi•Bingzhi (宋史•兵志).
12 *Reformation of the Military System* changed the organization of the Imperial Guards to three levels of command, unit, and group. It is an important measure in the *Wang Anshi Reform*.
13 Bao, a basic unit of the public military system in the Song dynasty. Every 10 households made up a bao, every 50 households made up a secondary bao, and 10 secondary baos made up a premier bao. All baos were supervised by the wealthiest person

among the households. This system aimed to save military expenditure and prevent peasant uprisings.
14 (Northern Song) Shen Kuo. Mengxi Bitan•Bianzheng Yi (梦溪笔谈·辨证一).
15 (Northern Song) Wang Dechen. Zhushi• Juan Shang (麈史•卷上).
16 (Yuan) Tuotuo Tiemuer and A Lu Tu. Songshi• Bingzhi (宋史•兵志).
17 (Southern Song) Hua Yue. Cuiwei Xiansheng Bezheng Lu• Gongzhi (翠微先生北征录•弓制).
18 (Yuan) Tuotuo Tiemuer and A Lu Tu. Songshi•Zeng Sanpin Zhuan (宋史•曾三聘传).
19 (Song) Hong Mai. Rongzhai Sanbi•Shenbigong (容斋三笔•神臂弓).
20 (Northern Song) Ding Lu and Zeng Gongliang. Wujing Zongyao•Qitu (武经总要•器图).
21 (Northern Song) Ding Lu and Zeng Gongliang. Wujing Zongyao•Qitu (武经总要•器图).
22 (Yuan) Tuotuo Tiemuer. Jinshi•Liu Yu Zhuan (金史•刘豫传); (Qing) Wang Xiangchun. Qiyin (齐音).
23 (Yuan) Tuotuo Tiemuer and A Lu Tu. Songshi•Liezhuan (宋史•列传).
24 (Yuan) Tuotuo Tiemuer. Jinshi•Xu Wen Zhuan (金史•徐文传).
25 (Song) Wang Mingqing. Huichen Lu•Juan Er (挥尘录•卷二).
26 (Southern Song) Zhou Mi. Qidong Yeyu•Li Quan (齐东野语•李全).
27 (Northern Song) Ding Lu and Zeng Gongliang. Wujing Zongyao•Qitu (武经总要•器图).
28 (Yuan) Tuo Tuo Tiemuer and A Lu Tu. Songshi•Yue Fei Zhuan (宋史•岳飞传).
29 (Yuan) Tuo Tuo Tiemuer and A Lu Tu. Songshi•Li Quan Zhuan (宋史•李全传).
30 (Song) Wang Mingqing. Huichen Houlu •Juan Jiu (挥尘后录•卷九).
31 (Song) Meng Yuanlao. Dongjing Menghua Lu •Jiadeng Baojin Lou Zhujun Cheng Baixi (东京梦华录•驾登宝津楼诸军呈百戏). 东京梦华录, 东京是开封的意思, 当时的首都.
32 (Song) Meng Yuanlao. Dongjing Menghua Lu•Jiadeng Baojin Lou Zhujun Cheng Baixi (东京梦华录•驾登宝津楼诸军呈百戏).
33 (Song) Li Tao. Xu Zizhi Tongjian Changbian• Juan Er (续资治通鉴长编•卷二).
34 (Southern Song) Wu Zimu. Mengjiang Lu• Juan Er (梦梁录•卷二).
35 (Southern Song) Wu Zimu. Mengliang Lu•Juan Er (梦梁录•卷二).
36 (Yuan) Ma Duanlin. Wenxian Tongkao•Xuanju Qi (文献通考•选举七).
37 *A Miscellaneous Records of Emperor Era.* (Song) Li Xinchuan. Jianyan Yilai Chaoye Zaji•Juan 13 (建炎以来朝野杂记•卷13).
38 (Yuan) Tuo Tuo Tiemuer and A Lu Tu. Songshi•Xuanju San (宋史•选举三).
39 (Yuan) Tuo Tuo Tiemuer and A Lu Tu. Songshi•Xuanju San (宋史•选举三).
40 (Song) Su Shi. Qi Zengxiu Gongjian She Tiaoyue Zhuang (乞增修弓箭社条约状).
41 *Selections of Codes of the Song Dynasty.* (Qing) Xu Song. Song Huiyao Jigao•Bing Er (宋会要辑稿•兵二).
42 (Song) Li Tao. Xu Zizhi Tongjian Changbian•Juan 117 (续资治通鉴长编•卷117).
43 (Song) Xiong Ke. Zhongxing Xiaoji•Juan Ba (中兴小纪•卷八).
44 (Yuan) Tuo Tuo and A Lu Tu. Qidong Yeyu•Li Quan (齐东野语•李全); (Yuan) Tuo Tuo Tiemuer and A Lu Tu. Songshi•Li Quan (宋史•李全).
45 The largest division within a city in ancient China was a fang (坊), equivalent to a modern-day precinct.
46 *The Past of Lin'an.* (Southern Song) Zhou Mi. Wulin Jiushi•Shehui (武林旧事•社会); (Southern Song) Wu Zimu. Mengliang Lu•Shehui (梦梁录•社会); *A Dream Tour of Lin'an.* (Southern Song) Nai Deweng. Ducheng Jisheng•She Hui (都城纪胜•社会); *Records of Entertainment in Lin'an.* (Southern Song) Xihu Laoren. Xihu Laoren Fansheng Lu (西湖老人繁胜录).
47 (Southern Song) Xihu Laoren. Xihu Laoren Fansheng Lu (西湖老人繁胜录).

48 (Southern Song) Xihu Laoren. Xihu Laoren Fansheng Lu (西湖老人繁胜录).
49 (Song) Meng Yuanlao. Dongjing Menghua Lu• Jingwa Jiyi (东京梦华录•京瓦技艺).
50 (Southern Song) Zhou Mi. Wulin Jiushi• Zhuse Jiyi Ren (武林旧事•诸色伎艺人).
51 (Song) Meng Yuanlao. Dongjing Menghua Lu• Dongjiaolou Jiexiang (东京梦华录•东角楼街巷).
52 (Song) Meng Yuanlao. Dongjing Menghua Lu• Dongjiaolou Jiexiang (东京梦华录•东角楼街巷).
53 (Song) Zhou Mi. Wulin Jiushi •Washe Goulan (武林旧事•瓦舍勾栏); (Song) Xihu Laoren. Xihu Laoren Fansheng Lu (西湖老人繁胜录).
54 (Song) Zhou Mi. Wulin Jiushi •Washe Goulan (武林旧事•瓦舍勾栏).
55 (Song) Zhou Mi. Wulin Jiushi •Washe Goulan (武林旧事•瓦舍勾栏).
56 (Song) Nai Deweng. Ducheng Jisheng •Shijing (都城纪胜•市井).
57 (Song) Wu Zimu. Mengliang Lu• Jiaodi (梦梁录•角抵).
58 *Women Xiangpu on the Lantern Festival.* (Song) Sima Guang. Lun Shangyuan Ling Funv Xiangpu Zhuang (论上元令妇女相扑状).
59 (Song) Wu Zimu. Mengliang Lu• Jiaodi (梦梁录•角抵).
60 (Song) Tiao Luzi. Jiaoli Ji•Shuzhi (角力记•述旨).
61 (Song) Meng Yuanlao. Dongjing Menghua Lu•Zhongyuan Jie (东京梦华录•中元节).
62 (Song) Meng Yuanlao. Dongjing Menghua Lu•Jingwa Jiyi (东京梦华录•京瓦技艺).
63 (Ming) Xie Jin, Xie Jin *et al.* Yongle Dadian•Xiwen (永乐大典•戏文).
64 (Southern Song) Nai Deweng. Ducheng•Jisheng•Washe Zhongji (都城纪胜•瓦舍众伎).
65 (Ming) Shi Naian. Shuihuzhuan•Di-er Hui (水浒传•第二回).

Chapter 6
Martial arts in the Liao, Jin, Western Xia, and Yuan dynasties (916–1368)

China is a country with one of the most ancient civilizations in the world, and its history has been written by many diverse ethnic groups. The non-Han people have made a great contribution to the development of Chinese martial arts with the infusion of their characteristic martial arts. The most notable influences have come from the Khitan, Jurchen, Tangut, and Mongolian peoples, who established the Liao (916–1125), Jin (1115–1234), Western Xia (1038–1227), and Yuan (1271–1368) dynasties. These dynasties coincided with the Song dynasty of the Han people between 916 and 1368.

The Liao dynasty of the ancient Khitan people, who inhabited areas of the Inner Mongolia Autonomous Region of contemporary China, had contended with the Northern Song dynasty for more than 200 years. To the west of Northern Song's borderland (now around the Gansu and Ningxia provinces) was where the Tangut people[1] founded the Western Xia dynasty, which lasted for approximately 200 years and formed their splendid national culture. The Jurchen people, who were the descendants of the Heishui Mohe people, inhabited the present-day north-eastern area of China. The Jurchen people established the Jin dynasty in 1115 and overthrew the Liao dynasty in 1125. Two years later, the Jin dynasty conquered the Northern Song dynasty, resulting in the Northern Song dynasty moving southwards to Lin'an and subsequently becoming the Southern Song dynasty. The Jin dynasty made Yanjing (now Beijing) their capital city, and this brought a period of flourishing economy and active ethnic fusion in what is today north China. In the early thirteenth century, Genghis Khan (1162–1227) leader of the growing Mongolian population, conquered the Western Xia and Jin dynasties. He then began to invade other states and areas in Eurasia, eventually establishing the Mongol Empire. The Yuan dynasty, a khanate of the Mongol Empire established by Kublai Khan (1215–1294), conquered the Southern Song dynasty in 1279. From that time, the territory of present-day China was ruled by the Yuan dynasty of the Mongolian people in Chinese history. The non-Han peoples from all of these regimes by contributed significantly to the development of Chinese martial arts in the ancient days.

The advocacy and prohibition of martial arts

There was a major emphasis on the military for the Khitan, Tangut, Jurchen and Mongolian peoples of this period. Martial affairs played a very important role in their nomadic lives on the broad deserts and grasslands. Any male aged 15–50 had to serve in the army according to the Khitan's conscription system. The Tangut peoples were accomplished horse riders. Most of the ordinary people aged 15–60 were trained to be soldiers, who would support themselves with armour and weapons and were prepared to fight if a war occurred. Along with the well-trained cavalries and infantries, the Tangut armies also contained female soldiers who were skilful in martial arts. Gallantry and unity were two prominent characters of the Jurchen people who merged the basic army structure and household register system. Three hundred families generally formed a 'Mouke' military unit, while ten 'Mouke' made up a 'Meng'an'. The family names of these people followed those of the military units. All able-bodied men were trained to be soldiers. This well-trained Jurchen military force defeated the Liao dynasty, even though the Liao had more soldiers, and went on to establish the Jin dynasty. The Mongolian people gained their power by resisting the oppression from the Jin dynasty in the early thirteenth century. All men aged 15–70 were trained as soldiers. Similar to the Jin dynasty, Genghis Khan framed the household register system of the Mongolian people as different scales of military units with the divisions of ten households, 100 households, 1,000 households and 10,000 households. The well-equipped Mongol armies were particularly adept at horseback archery, so that they succeeded in conquering a wide region of Eurasia as a stronghold for the Mongol Empire.

In order to consolidate their sovereignties, these non-Han dynasties also adapted some rules and regulations from the Han people to improve their military training and warlike spirits, for example, by employing the martial exams to select martial talents. Imitating the Song dynasty, the Jin dynasty adopted the provincial exam, the national exam and the final imperial exam in their martial exams. There were three subjects included in the outfield exams for the candidates:

> Foot archery: the target was usually set 150 steps away in the fixed-point shooting; for long-distance shooting, however, the target was set 220 steps away. The result depended on the number of the arrows that successfully hit the target.

> Horseback archery: within a total area of 150 steps, two deer targets about 15.6 cm in length and 24.96 cm in width were fixed on the ground at 50-step intervals. The candidates were required to shoot the targets by using the big iron arrows with a large chisel-shaped arrowhead while riding the horse. The candidates were required to hit the target two to three times to pass the exam.

Horseback spearing: within a total area of 150 steps, four puppets of approximately 93.6cm in height, each wearing a square plank with a side length of about 15.6cm, were settled as targets at 30-step intervals. The candidates were required to stab the planks down without knocking down the puppets, and the result was based on the number of planks dropped.[2]

Military strategies and tactics made up the main content in the written exams. The Jin dynasty put so much stress on military knowledge that the candidates with poor military knowledge would have their results in martial skills deducted; the superior labelled as average and the average as superior. Qualified candidates were appointed governmental posts according to their abilities. Moreover, some martial talents could be appointed governmental posts through recommendation, as revealed in the order given by Emperor Zhangzong of Jin (1168–1208): those who were excellent in military strategies and tactics or other related talent, superior in martial arts and military skills would be encouraged to be recommended.[3]

The non-Han dynasties had tried to prohibit martial arts in the public society in order to consolidate their sovereignties. For instance, the Jin dynasty prohibited the public practiced martial arts, such as Jiaodi and spears. The violators would be punished.[4] In addition, some of the Yuan rulers also issued decrees prohibiting the Han people from practicing martial arts and regularly confiscated their weapons between 1263 and 1345. In 1285, the Yuan ruler categorized the weapons confiscated from the Han people into three classes. The inferior weapons were destroyed, the moderate granted to the nearby Mongolian people and the superior stored in the Yuan arsenals. Those Han people who were found in possession of military weapons such as armour and bows and arrows would be put to death immediately. They were also prohibited from non-military martial arts, such as hunting. According to *History of Yuan*, the Han people, whether they were teachers or learners, who practiced Jiaodi or other martial skills, would be clubbed 77 times.[5] There is no doubt that the rulers' prohibition, in the name of resolving ethnic disputes, delayed the development of Chinese martial arts to a certain extent. However, such a prohibition can't eliminate ethnic disputes. Apart from its military application, martial arts can also be used for fitness and entertainment. Therefore, the masses continued to practice martial arts in secret.

Horseback archery

Historians often claim that the Jin and Yuan dynasties were established through horseback archery[6] (see Figure 6.1). The chieftains of the northern peoples were often excellent archers. For instance, Aguda (Emperor Taizu of Jin, 1068–1123) had great command of archery since he was young. When Aguda was a child, he was asked to perform his archery skills for the ambassadors from the Liao dynasty by shooting a flock of birds in the sky with his bow and arrows. None of his

Figure 6.1 Battle picture of the Yuan army.

three arrows in a row missed his target. The ambassadors praised him and said he was a talented boy. Aguda was also good at ranged shooting. It was impossible for others to shooting a target over 320 steps away, but he could manage it. Aguda established remarkable merits repeatedly in the battlefield for his amazing archery.[7]

Soldiers of the Yuan dynasty did better than those of the Jin dynasty. Genghis Khan (1162–1227) enjoyed a good reputation on account of his excellence in both horseback archery and Jiaodi, so that his army triumphed across the course of their military expedition from Asia to Europe (see Figure 6.2). According to *The Travels of Marco Polo*, the Yuan army, led by Temür Khan (Emperor Chengzong, 1265–1307) subdued the enormous elephant army of India with their excellent archery skills. According to the book, there were

Figure 6.2 Archery picture of Emperor Shizu of Yuan and his followers, National Palace Museum.

2,000 war elephants carrying towers on their backs with more than ten soldiers standing on each tower, along with over 60,000 cavalries and infantries of the Indian army. At this sight, the horses of the Yuan army were frightened by the elephants. Then the Yuan soldiers got off their horses and planned an ambush by waiting for the elephant troop in the woods. When the troop arrived, hundreds of thousands of arrows suddenly rained in the air, and the elephants either died or quickly withdrew. The Indian army was defeated completely. This record demonstrates the mighty power of archery of the Yuan army.[8]

The Khitan, Tangut and Mongolian peoples were all well versed in horseback archery. Apart from holding archery contests, hunting was seen as an important aspect of practicing horseback archery skills. Both the Liao and Jin dynasties enacted different rules and methods of hunting for each season. Through hunting, the soldiers could be trained at riding, shooting and jumping, as well as developing other fighting and killing abilities. In addition, large-scale hunting competitions were also adopted to select martial talents.

During the Liao, Jin and Yuan dynasties, a variety of horseback shooting games prevailed in the public society; notably, willow-shooting, wooden-rabbit shooting and straw-dog shooting. Willow-shooting was derived from the worship ceremonies of the ancient peoples, which had been very popular in the Northern Zhou dynasty in the Southern and Northern dynasties. As the successors of the Xianbei people,[9] the Khitan people inherited and carried forward this ancient archery game. It should be noted that this game was not only prevalent in the Liao, Jin and Yuan dynasties, but also in the later Ming and Qing dynasties.

Despite willow-shooting having originated from ancient religious activities, it had close ties with archery and other martial skills, and had developed into a kind of recreational game. Therefore, the cultural connotations of willow-shooting were multiple, encompassing religion, warlike spirits, rites and entertainment. Moreover, with the close cultural communication since the Jin and Southern and Northern dynasties, willow-shooting was also welcomed by the Han people in the central plains as an important recreational game. Willow-shooting and Jiju competitions were often held together, and became important military sports in ancient sports history.

During the Liao and Jin dynasties, willow-shooting was employed to pray for the rain, which made this archery game a kind of rite.[10] However, praying for the rain was not the only function of willow-shooting. *History of Jin* notes that during the reign of Emperor Zhangzong, the royal family carried out willow-shooting in their resorts or worship ceremonies on the festival-dates in May, July, and September.[11] According to *History of Jin*, the purpose of willow-shooting was not only to pray for the rain, but also as a recreational exercise, as the games were held on fixed dates.

The willow shooters had special costumes, instruments and horses.[12] Originally, the game was performed in the willow forest; then it developed into an activity performed at squares. Willow branches were inserted into the ground, which were shot by arrows with a fan-shaped arrowhead.[13] This kind of arrow was found in a tomb of the Liao dynasty in the Beipiao County of Liaoning Province. They were probably not for military use or hunting, but more likely for shooting the willows. Willow branches were thin, soft and round, and it was hard to break the branches by ordinary arrows, so these kind of fan-shaped arrows were used.[14]

The rules of the willow-shooting contest in the Liao and Jin dynasties were detailed in *History of Jin*: one man rode a horse to lead the participants, who were required to follow on their own horses and shoot the willow branches; those who succeeded in hitting down the branch and who rode on to catch the falling branch in hand were ranked as outstanding, those hitting the branch but failing to catch it were ranked as average, while those who succeeded in hitting the branch where the branch remained intact, or those who failed to hit the branch at all, were ranked as the losers. During each round of shooting, the drummers would beat the drums to cheer the shooters on. It's evident that it was very difficult to complete a willow-shooting game without certain martial skills. In Khanbaliq (now Beijing), willow-shooting was held annually during the Dragon Boat Festival. The military officials had to take part in the event, and there were rewards and punishment meted out. It was also an opportunity for military officials to show their extraordinary martial skills.[15]

There were also other similar shooting games. For example, wooden-rabbit shooting was warmly welcomed by the Khitan people of the Liao dynasty during their festivals. The Liao dynasty and the Song dynasty shared a historic period of more than 200 years, during which the Liao had adopted some cultural forms from the Song, such as having the Double Third Festival[16] and the Double Ninth Festival. However, the Khitan people celebrated these festivals with their own ethnic traditions. The wooden-rabbit shooting on the Double Third Festival and the tiger-shooting on the Double Ninth Festival were some of their own festival martial activities.

Both of these horseback shooting games required proficient horse-riding and archery skills.[17] And the games reflected the hunting life of the Khitan people. In addition, the Khitan people, as well as other northern non-Han peoples, tended to use hunting to practice their horseback archery skills. This is a tradition that continued into the Qing dynasty.

The Mongolian straw-dog shooting game was more of a religious activity in an attempt to pray for good life and to safeguard against disaster. The game was held in a clean place on one of the last ten days of December. Materials for making the targets, such as thread, needle and satin, and instruments for shooting, such as bows and arrows, were supplied by certain imperial office. The straw targets were composed of one staw man and one straw dog. The straw man and the straw dog were dressed with pieces of colourful silks to symbolise their internal organs. The elites of the noble class took turns to shoot the straw targets. A sacrifice was made to the heavens with sheep and wine when the straw dog or straw man was shot into pieces.[18]

Among the northern non-Han peoples, there were many archery competitions held to advance archery skills and warlike spirits. During the Nadam Fair, a traditional festival of the Mongolian peoples, archery accounted for one major competition alongside horse-riding and Jiaodi. This fair was held frequently since the establishment of the Yuan dynasty. Till now, Nadam Fair represents a typical activity for advocating martial arts in the Mongols.

Unarmed combat and Jiaodi

Unarmed combat and Jiaodi were popular martial arts in the Liao, Jin, Western Xia and Yuan dynasties. There were no systematic and official records about unarmed combat in the historical documents of the Khitan, Jurchen and Mongolian peoples. But there are some historical records that imply a fairly high level in combat skills. In 1016, when a tiger was rushing at Emperor Shengzong of Liao (972–1031) during a hunting expedition, Chen Zhaogun, an official in charging of hunting affairs, jumped from his horse; he hopped on the tiger's back and grasped the tiger's ears tightly. Although the tiger flailed around in a rage, Chen finally managed to kill it.[19] By taking on a tiger solely with his bare hands, he truly displayed his superb unarmed combat skills. There were also plenty of soldiers of the Jin dynasty who were proficient at hand combat. For instance, Pucha Shijie was able to kill a four-year-old bull by breaking its ribs with his bare hands.[20] Although the description that he killed the bull with one punch was much exaggerated, it still implied his powerful strength and excellent martial skill.

The Chinese character '白打' (Baida) was referred to a kind of unarmed combat skill in the Yuan dynasty. *General Yuchi Challenging Ageing*, a popular folk opera of the Yuan dynasty, sings of Yuchi Jingde who had learnt the Eighteen Martial Skills, and that baida was also included in the Eighteen Martial Skills as the only unarmed skill.[21] This indicates that unarmed combat was regarded as one of the Eighteen Martial Skills as early as during the Yuan dynasty, and that the standard of unarmed combat skills at that time had reached a high level.

According to some historical records that describe the scenes of Jiaodi, such as the *Two Poems of Xiangpu* written by Hu Zhiyu of the Yuan dynasty, Jiaodi in the Jin and Yuan dynasties were mixed with unarmed combat skills besides tumbling.[22]

Jiaodi was a traditional martial art of the northern peoples. It became popular and widespread because of both its significance in practicing martial arts and its function in competitive games for recreation. Jiaodi was one of the most important performances in the banquets and celebrations in the Han and Tang dynasties, and this tradition continued with the Song dynasty. In the Liao and Jin dynasties, Jiaodi was also part of the loyal rites and performances of birthdays or weddings of emperors, or on diplomatic occasions.[23] There are also records of Jiaodi competitions between the Khitan and Han peoples, such as the one during a banquet to celebrate the birth of a son of Emperor Xingzong of Liao in 1041.[24] These Jiaodi competitions suggest a cultural communication and close relationship between the Khitan and Han peoples. Jiaodi performances could also be seen in the fairs in Shangjing (one of the capital cities of Liao), where all sorts of skills were shown.[25] This phenomenon was probably influenced by the Washe culture of the Northern Song dynasty, but it also highlights the popularity of Jiaodi among the common people during the Liao dynasty.

As mentioned above, the Jin and Yuan dynasties had prohibited the Han people from learning and practicing martial arts, which had a negative effect on the development of Jiaodi. Nevertheless, Jiaodi was popular and advocated as a military activity by the Jurchen and Mongolian peoples. There were plenty of skilful Jiaodi fighters in the Jin armies, such as Pucha Shijie. Besides, Jiaodi was listed as one of the compulsory martial arts that the noble families of Jin had to practice from a very early age. Prince Wanyan Ang, for example, started learning and practicing Jiaodi when he was 15 years old, and he was able to defeat six rivals at that age. The Emperor Taizu awarded him a gold medal as a reward for his excellent performance. Later, he became a famous general and became known as the 'Man with a Gold Medal'.[26]

As a traditional martial art in Mongol, Jiaodi was quite popular in the Yuan dynasty. *History of Yuan* has documented that the emperors of Yuan often rewarded winners of the Jiaodi. For instance, Emperor Wuzong (1281–1311) appointed Ma Shamou a position as a high official (equal to a provincial governor) for winning the Jiaodi.[27] In 1310, he awarded Ali silver of more than 1,000 taels.[28] In 1321, Emperor Yingzong (1303–1323) offered a large sum of money for each of the 120 Jiaodi winners. This suggests the popularity and large scale of the Jiaodi event.[29] The Jiaodi contest was also popular among the general public, and had attracted a large audience. After the establishment of the Yuan dynasty, the Mongolian people imitated the Tang and Song dynasties by setting up a special bureau in charge of Jiaodi affairs in 1319.[30] Most of the Mongolian Jiaodi fighters wore the professional leather clothes without sleeves, which differed from those of the Tang and Song dynasties who wore fewer clothes and left parts of their bodies were naked. After the establishment of the Mongol Empire, the emperors organized some Jiaodi contests. The competitors for these events came from diverse ancient Asian countries and cultures. For instance, Emperor Taizong (1186–1241) convened a number of Mongol, Golden Horde, Han and Persian men to compete in Jiaodi.[31] It was rare to see so many Jiaodi masters in Eurasia compete together. Such events displayed the distinct Jiaodi skills of different peoples in Eurasia, and there is no doubt that both the competition and lines of communication between these Asian countries and states would have been enhanced by them.

Having lived in the broad deserts and grasslands for generations, the Mongolian people were physically very strong, and there were also some women with excellent martial skills. *The Travels of Marco Polo* tells the story of a Mongolian heroine who selected her husband by Jiaodi. The King of Haidu, the nephew of

Kublai Khan, had a healthy, strong daughter named Eiji Amr (referring to the moon in the Mongolian language). Proficient in martial arts, she told her father that she would only marry a man with brilliant martial skills who could defeat her. Her father promised to find such a man for his daughter, so she announced that whoever could defeat her would be her husband or else he must give her 100 nice horses. Many young men tried, but all of them failed. That is until 1280, when a rich and handsome prince of Pammal came in the hopes of winning the princess's heart by outdoing her in the contest. The King of Haidu quite favoured this prince and persuaded his daughter to make a concession in the match, but the princess refused to make any concessions. When the competition started, both the king and the queen expected the prince to win, but their daughter was so strong that the prince was thrown on the ground and lost his chance.[32] This story not only shows the valiant and heroic bearing of Mongolian women and their noble spirits in pursuit of triumph, but also indicates their high level in Jiaodi.

Nadam Fair was a military competitive meeting used to train and select soldiers in ancient Mongol, and the winner could receive an honorary title, 'Warrior of Mongolia'. According to *Badu*, when Badu, a grandson of Genghis Khan, started a military expedition towards the west, he held a Nadam Fair on the grassland under the foothills of Mountain Ulker in Russia. In the final competition of Jiaodi, a warrior named Ge Rule defeated his opponent in a violent match. The defeated warrior was so miserable about his failure that he wanted nothing but to end his life. Just at this very moment, a messenger brought an order to them: the kind and generous Badu appreciated their bravery and fearlessness, so he decided to recruit both of them as guards in the Mongolian army. At this news, the two Jiaodi fighters immediately thanked the king for his generosity.[33] The story suggests that the Nadam Fair was a way to select martial talents and the Mongolian warriors viewed mastering superb Jiaodi skills as an honour. Furthermore, the popularity of this activity continues to stimulate the emergence of outstanding Mongolian wrestlers in the present day.

The armed martial skills

Weapons of all shapes and different sizes had been well developed from the primitive ages to the Song dynasty. *Complete Essentials for the Military Classics*, by Ding Du and Zeng Gongliang of the Song dynasty, illustrates various types of weapons, including almost 20 types of long weapons (e.g. the long iron-head spear), almost ten types of long-handled sabres and more than 20 types of short weapons such as the sabre, sword, axe, cudgel, and hammer.[34]

The weapons of the Liao, Jin and Song dynasties had inevitably influenced each other during their long-term warfare. Zhou Wei, a famous expert on the history of weapons, points out that the long weapons of the Song dynasty resembled those of the Sui and Tang dynasties. The spear was the dominant weapon and the long-handled sabre came later, along with other long weapons such as boathook and fork rod. These long weapons were influenced by the Hu people. In addition, the specification of some long spears followed those of the ethnic peoples, such as the Khitan, Jurchen and Mongolian peoples.[35] This indicates that the Song weapons were much affected by those of the Liao, Jin, and Western Xia dynasties. The Khitan, Jurchen and Mongolian peoples excelled in horseback archery, as we have discussed, but they were also experts at manufacturing sharp and fine weapons. With the military system of the Liao dynasty, every regular soldier was provided with a full set of military equipment, including three horses and nine iron weapons (namely, four bows, 400 arrows, the long spear, the short spear, the short pole lance, the broadax, the hammer, the banderole and the fire stone).

During the Liao and Jin dynasties, the cavalries mostly used the long spear to fight, but they were also equipped with the short spear. In most circumstances, they used the spear, but occasionally they used the spear and the sabre together. The well-known general, Wanyan Talan, was famous for his proficiency in martial arts, in particular the long spear skills, and it was said that he easily killed seven enemies with a long spear and beat down nine on-horse enemies with his bare hands when the spear broke.[36] There were many other famous generals who excelled at using the long spear in the Jin dynasty, such as general Mou Yan,[37] Wanyan Haili,[38] to name a few. Besides, there were many generals of the Jin dynasty skilled at using the sabre, such as General Pucha Shijie[39] and Wanyan Gouying,[40] who were said to chop their enemies' incoming spears off with their sabres.

During the Western Xia dynasty, the Tangut culture was to a great extent influenced by the Han culture owing to their communication. Farming was the major economy of the Western Xia dynasty, while metallurgy was also very common. According to *Collections of Tangut Script*, a rarely extant dictionary written in the Tangut language, there were various types of metallic tools and weapons in the social life of the Tangut people, including the sabre, the sword, the halberd, the arrow and the axe.[41] The Western Xia was famous for producing the crossbow, which was sometimes offered as a present to the Northern Song dynasty. *Dream Pool Essays*, written by Shen Kuo during the Song dynasty, records that General Li Ding of the Western Xia (who later surrendered and paid allegiance to the Song) once presented a Shenbi Bow to the Song dynasty. The arrows of this Shenbi Bow could reach 300 steps and stick into the earth with force.[42] The armours made in the Western Xia were also famous for their great quality, so that normal arrows could hardly penetrate them. Of all the weapons made by the people in the Western Xia dynasty, however, the sword had earned enormous fame. The emperors of the Song dynasty, such as Emperor Qinzong of Song (1100–1156), loved to wear the sword,[43] Chao Buzhi of the Song dynasty praised the exquisite craftsmanship and decorative design of the sword of the Western Xia in his poem *Sword of the Western Xia*.[44] In 1975, an exquisite iron sword approximately one metre long was unearthed from an imperial tomb of the Western Xia in Ningxia, which serves as good evidence that this was the location of a high-level sword manufacturer.

During the Yuan dynasty, the Mongolian people's overwhelming military power over Eurasia relied not only on their proficient horse-riding and archery skills, but also on the skills in production and use of a wide range of weapons. Regarding short weapons, the sword, the sabre, the axe and the hammer were mostly used, the main long weapon was the spear and occasionally the cudgel, as noted by Marco Polo[45] and Zhou Wei.[46] But it is also worth noting that such weapons of the Mongolians were different from those of the Han people. Deeply influenced by Europe and West Asia, most of the Mongolian weapons were sharp and well crafted. It is also recorded in Zhou Wei's works that the Mongolian emperor used to gather a number of famous craftsmen from Persia and India to make and decorate various weapons, which made the standard of the manufacture of weapons in Mongolia unprecedented at the time. The most remarkable weapons were the Shashpar melon-shaped hammer, thrown spear (similar to javelin), small axe, and broad axe and so on. In addition, each of the emperor's weapons had a name; for example, one Yuan emperor's favorite short swords were called 'Ganjiang', and he owned about 30 Ganjiang Swords. Every month a new one would be made to be hung in his palace. For his own use, he also had around 40 Kemaier Heteromorphy Swords, around 40 short and broad swords, 40 small but broad swords. There was a large amount of other types of weapons such as the hammer, the axe, the spear and the sabre, and they were carried by the emperor's military officials while on military expedition. Long spears were rarely used by Mongolian people: *The History of Chinese Weapons* only records three types of them. The first type, named Qihuda, was relatively long; the front head was fixed with a triangular blade, while the back head had a petal-shape blade. This meant that both heads could be used to stab, and the spear could also be a throwing weapon. The second type, named Barchah, was also a long spear and could stab with both heads and used a throwing weapon. The front head was fixed with a rhombus blade, while the back head had a round-headed-nail-shaped blade. The third type, named three-bladed thrown spear had three sharp blades fixed at the end of the spear. Although it could be used to stab from the horse, most of the time it was used merely as a throwing weapon.[47] Thus, Mongolian people usually made the most of their long weapons by throwing them, which was different from the ways of Han people who tended to use them in a fight on horseback.

Further in Zhou Wei's works, we learn of a lethal Mongolian weapon named the 'Wheel'. The Mongolian called this weapon Chacarari or Chakram in their language, but it was called Yin-Yang Blades Wheel (Yinyang Cilun) or Universe Ring (Qiankun Quan) in Chinese. The wheel was small and had blades outside the wheel. The Mongolia soldiers often ringed up to eight wheels on the left wrist, and then used the fingers of the right hand to circle inside the Wheel and threw the Wheel away to attack the enemy. The enemy's head and neck would be badly hurt once they got hit.[48] It was a legendary weapon among the Han people, but it was used in the battlefield by the Mongolian armies. In the history of martial arts of the Han people, there were the Sun-Moon Universe Ring (Riyue Qiankun Quan), Sun-Moon Wind-Fire Wheel (Riyue Fenghuo Lun), Sun-Moon Yanchi Wheel (Riyue Yanchi Lun), which were made when the iron rims were equipped with different shapes of sharp blades. These types of lethal hidden weapons were widely used in the Song and Yuan dynasties. Whether or not they originated from the Mongolian people requires further study.

In general, the Mongolian people were excellent at martial arts and producing weapons. However, they had prohibited the public, especially the Han people, from practicing martial arts after the establishment of the Yuan dynasty. In the early Yuan, the rulers had prohibited common people from possessing weapons. As a result, the development of martial arts among ordinary people was largely limited. Nevertheless, martial arts in the public society had developed and disseminated to some extent with the rapid development of the Yuan drama. A few of plots of martial arts could be found in the Yuan dramas, such as in *Guan Yu Attending the Banquet Alone with only A Sabre*, *Yuchi Jingde Used a Long Whip against with the Spear* and *Lv Bu against with Three Men*. According to *Taihe Music Scores*, the dramas of the Yuan dynasty could be categorized into 12 types, among which there was a special type themed on acrobatic fighting actions.[49] At that time, one of the most famous theatrical troupes, called *Lan Caihe*, was always equipped with spears, sabres, swords, halberds, tamtam, drums and flutes and these weapons were commonly used on the stage. Another type of drama, known as 'forest outlaws drama', which mainly highlighted stories of the brigand and wuxia outlaws, also contained many plots concerning martial arts. This shows that the development of on-stage martial arts had come into a new stage, which underpinned the great progress of on-stage martial arts in the later Ming and Qing dynasties.

Notes

1. The Tangut people were one of the ancient northern ethnic minority groups derived from the Qiang ethnic minority group.
2. (Yuan) Tuotuo Tiemuer. Jinshi•Xuanju Zhi (金史•选举制).
3. (Yuan) Tuotuo Tiemuer. Jinshi•Xuanju Zhi (金史•选举制).
4. (Yuan) Tuotuo Tiemuer. Jinshi•Zhangzong Benji (金史•章宗本纪).
5. (Ming) Song Lian and Wang Hui. Yuanshi•Xingfa Zhi (元史•刑法志).
6. (Ming) Song Lian and Wang Hui.Yuanshi•Bingzhi (元史•兵志).
7. (Yuan) Tuotuo Tiemuer. Jinshi•Zongxiong Zhuan (金史•宗雄传).
8. Marco Polo, translated by Liang Shengzhi. *The Travels of Marco Polo* (Beijing: Chinese Literature and History Press, 1998), 175–176.
9. The Xianbei people, an ancient nomadic people on the Mongolian plateau, which rose in the Greater Khingan Range.
10. History of Liao. (Yuan) Tuotuo Tiemuer, He Weiyi *et al.* Liaoshi•Guojie (辽史•国解); (Yuan) Tuotuo Tiemuer, He Weiyi *et al.* Liaoshi •Yiwei Zhi (辽史•仪卫志); (Yuan) Tuotuo Tiemuer, He Weiyi *et al.* Liaoshi•Muzong Ji (辽史•穆宗纪).
11. (Yuan) Tuotuo Tiemuer. Jinshi•Taizu Benji (金史•太祖本纪).
12. (Yuan) Tuotuo Tiemuer, He Weiyi *et al.* Liaoshi•Taizong Ji (辽史•太宗纪).
13. (Yuan) Tuotuo Tiemuer. Jinshi•Lizhi (金史•礼志).

138 Liao, Jin, Western Xia, and Yuan dynasties

14 Chaoyang Cultural Relics Organization, 'A Brief Report on the Excavation of the Liao Tomb at Koubu Yingzi Village,' in *Cultural Relic Information Series (Volume 2)*, ed. Cultural Relic Committee (Beijing: Cultural Relics Publishing House, 1978), 129–134.
15 (Yuan) Tuotuo Tiemuer. Jinshi•Lizhi (金史•礼志).
16 Shangsi Festival, commonly known as Double Third Festival, is a holiday to commemorate Huangdi.
17 (Yuan) Tuotuo Tiemuer, He Weiyi *et al.* Liaoshi• Lizhi (辽史•礼志).
18 (Ming) Song Lian and Wang Hui. Yuanshi•Jisi Zhi (元史•祭祀志).
19 (Yuan) Tuotuo Tiemuer, He Weiyi *et al.* Liaoshi•Shengzong Benji (辽史•圣宗本纪).
20 (Yuan) Tuotuo Tiemuer. Jinshi•Pucha Shijie (金史•蒲察世杰).
21 (Ming) Zhu Guozhen. Yongzhuang Xiaopin•Bingqi (涌幢小品•兵器).
22 (Yuan) Hu Zhiyu. Zijinshan Da Quanji•Xiangpu Ershou (紫金山大全集•相扑二首).
23 (Yuan) Tuotuo Tiemuer, He Weiyi *et al.* Liaoshi•Lizhi (辽史•礼志).
24 (Yuan) Tuotuo Tiemuer, He Weiyi *et al.* Liaoshi•Xingzong Benji (辽史•兴宗本纪).
25 (Yuan) Tuotuo Tiemuer, He Weiyi *et al.* Liaoshi•Dili Zhi (辽史•地理志).
26 (Yuan) Tuotuo Tiemuer. Jinshi•Bendu Zhuan (金史•奔睹传).
27 (Ming) Song Lian and Wang Hui.Yuanshi•Wuzong Benji (元史•武宗本纪).
28 (Ming) Song Lian and Wang Hui.Yuanshi•Wuzong Benji (元史•武宗本纪).
29 (Ming) Song Lian and Wang Hui.Yuanshi•Yingzong Benji (元史•英宗本纪).
30 (Ming) Song Lian and Wang Hui.Yuanshi•Renzong Benji (元史•仁宗本纪).
31 Duo Sang, translated by Feng Chengjun. *History of Mongolia* (Beijing: Zhonghua Book Company, 2004), 231.
32 Marco Polo, translated by Liang Shengzhi. *The Travels of Marco Polo* (Beijing: Chinese Literature and History Press, 1998), 285–286.
33 Baduhan•Menggu Jun Zhi Nadamu (巴都罕•蒙古军之那达慕).
34 (Northern Song) Ding Du and Zeng Gongliang. Wujing Zongyao (武经总要).
35 Zhou Wei, *The History of Chinese Weapons* (Tianjin: Baihua Literature and Art Publishing House, 2015), 157–158.
36 (Yuan) Tuotuo Tiemuer. Jinshi•Talan Zhuan (金史•挞懒传).
37 (Yuan) Tuotuo Tiemuer. Jinshi•Mouyan Zhuan (金史•谋衍传).
38 (Yuan) Tuotuo Tiemuer. Jinshi•Haili Zhuan (金史•海里传).
39 (Yuan) Tuotuo Tiemuer. Jinshi•Pucha Shijie Zhuan (金史•蒲察世杰传).
40 (Yuan) Tuotuo Tiemuer. Jinshi•Wanyan Gouying Zhuan (金史•完颜彀英传).
41 *Collections of Tangut Script*. Wen Hai (文海).
42 (Northern Song) Shen Kuo. Mengxi Bitan•Qiyong (梦溪笔谈•器用).
43 (Yuan) Tuo Tuo and A Lu Tu. Songshi•Wang Lun Zhuan (宋史•王伦传).
44 (Song) Chao Bu. Xiaren Jian (夏人剑).
45 Marco Polo, translated by Liang Shengzhi. *The Travels of Marco Polo* (Beijing: Chinese Literature and History Press, 1998), 284.
46 Zhou Wei, *The History of Chinese Weapons* (Tianjin: Baihua Literature and Art Publishing House, 2015), 159.
47 Zhou Wei, *The History of Chinese Weapons* (Tianjin: Baihua Literature and Art Publishing House, 2015), 159–160.
48 Zhou Wei, *The History of Chinese Weapons* (Tianjin: Baihua Literature and Art Publishing House, 2015), 161.
49 (Ming) Zhu Quan. Taihezheng Yinpu (太和正音谱).

Chapter 7

Martial arts in the Ming dynasty (1368–1644)

The Yuan dynasty was overthrown by the peasant revolts of the mid-fourteenth century. Zhu Yuanzhang (Emperor Hongwu, 1328–1398) established the Ming dynasty (1368–1644) and made Nanjing the capital city in 1368. With the founding of the dynasty, China again entered a long stable historical phase. During this period, Chinese martial arts made remarkable improvements and entered a new stage.

After the establishment of the Ming dynasty, the Wala tribe of Mongolia continued warring with the Ming dynasty for a long time. Even Emperor Zhengtong (1427–1464) was captured by the Wala during the Tumupu Crisis in 1449. Throughout the entire Ming dynasty, the northern peoples posed a constant military threat. Additionally, many feudal lords, warriors, ronin, and merchants living in western Japan and supported by the Japanese feudal dukes raided the south central coastal areas of China as pirates. They are called *Wokou* in Chinese history. How to defend against these Japanese pirates was a serious military issue for the Ming dynasty. The priority given to military development would spur the development of martial arts. It was in this context that a great number of martial and military classics were written based on people's experience of military training and practice, including, *A Collection of Military Martial Arts*[1] written by Tang Shunzhi (1507–1560); *Righteousness Hall Military Martial Arts Compilation*[2] written by Yu Dayou (1503–1579); *New Treatise on Military Efficiency*[3] and *Record of Military Training*[4] written by Qi Jiguang (1528–1588); *Array of Discipline*[5] written by He Liangchen; and *Jiangnan Military Defense Strategies and Plans*[6] written by Zheng Ruozeng (1503–1570). Qi Jiguang and Yu Dayou, the two national heroes of China and outstanding military leaders, were also pioneers in the development of martial arts practice and theory. In short, a phenomenon that can be observed in the history of martial arts of the Ming dynasty was the emergence not only of a great number of martial and military classics, many of which are still read today, but also a large number of generals who made a remarkable contribution to the development of martial arts.

Beyond the military domain, there were many developments within popular Chinese martial arts. First, they were no longer categorized according to the weapon employed, such as the sabre, the spear, or the cudgel. Instead, a variety of martial arts sects had formed throughout the country, including the Kongtong Sect, Wudang Sect, Shaolin Sect, Emei Sect, and Kunlun Sect. Moreover, the exact names and weapons of the Eighteen Martial Skills were further clarified, which marks the formal systemization of Chinese martial arts. Second, China and Japan were involved in extensive and frequent cultural exchange during the Ming dynasty. The Chinese sabre masters were deeply influenced by the Japanese, while the creation of Japanese judo and karate were much influenced by Chinese martial arts. Third, since the beginning of the Ming dynasty, Shaolin martial arts had been much promoted and celebrated.

The Imperial Martial Examination and the martial academy

Although Emperor Hongwu had clearly rejected the proposal for reestablishing the Imperial Martial Examination and martial academy systems of the previous dynasties in 1387, he did not deny the importance of developing armaments and martial skills. What he wanted was all-round talents with both literary and martial capability rather than separating the literary talents from the martial talents.[7] Therefore, both the school system and imperial examination system contained literary and martial education throughout the reign of Emperor Hongwu.

In 1369, Emperor Hongwu set up an extensive school system and all students in those schools had to choose one of the 'Six Arts' as their major subject. The 'Six Arts' were rites, music, archery, riding, calligraphy, and mathematics.[8] In May 1370, the emperor issued a law which required all students to practice archery skills. He believed that while the special martial talents were expert at archery, the civil officials had only learned a little about it. So he ordered the Ministry of Rites to design sets of archery rites and demanded that all students in government schools practice archery on the 1st and 15th of every month.[9] Later in August of the same year, he made an order to add a martial skills test into the imperial examination system so that all promoted candidates from the provincial exam were required to take part in an extra qualification test, which included riding and archery skills. How fast they rode and how many targets they shot would decide their grades on riding and archery.[10] Emperor Hongwu also realized that later generations of military officials knew little about literature. So he sent them to the national academy to improve their literary ability.[11] Consequently, there were many examples of civil officials who were good at martial skills in the Ming dynasty. For instance, Jinshi[12] Lu Xiangsheng was able to precisely hit a flower target from 50 steps away.[13] This can, to some extent, be attributed to Emperor Hongwu's taking both liberal arts and martial arts seriously.

The Imperial Martial Examination of the Ming dynasty was launched during the reign of Emperor Zhengtong when he ordered that some reserve military officials should be selected directly through the national exam in 1464.[14] From then on, the Imperial Martial Examination system continued until the late Ming dynasty. The exams included three levels: the provincial exam, the national exam, and the final imperial exam. The provincial exam was held in the capital city every three years. The national exam was held in the capital every three years; it was first organized by the Ministry of War but later by the Hanlin Academy (an academic and administrative institution.). Only those who passed the provincial exam qualified to sit the national exam. The best candidates of the national exam made up the Wujinshi class. It was not until 1631 that the final imperial exam was first organized, and Wang Laipin was selected as the first Wuzhuangyuan of the Ming dynasty.[15]

Those who passed the provincial examination would be given an official position. In 1464, those who passed the national exam were divided into two classes. For those candidates who had been military officials, the first-class ones would be promoted by two ranks (there was a total of nine ranks in the civil service hierarchy), while the second-class were promoted by one rank. With regard to the soldier candidates, the first-class ones would be given a Zhenfu (secondary class, Sixth Rank) position, the secondary class given a Zongqi (leader of five teams, with ten soldiers in each team) position. For the civil candidates, the first-class candidates would be given a Jingli (secondary class, Seventh Rank) position and the second-class ones would be given a Zhishi (standard class, Eighth Rank) position. Up to 1622, Emperor Tianqi (1605–1627) divided the examinees into three classes according to their exam results. The first class had three candidates who would be given a Qianshi (standard class, Third Rank) position. The second class had 30 candidates that would be given a Shoubei (standard class, Fifth Rank) position. The third class had more than 100 candidates who would be given different official positions within three years according to their exam results.[16] During Emperor Chongzhen's reign, the best candidate of the first class would be given the position of deputy commander-in-chief.[17]

The method of organizing the Imperial Martial Examination remained roughly the same during the Ming dynasty. From 1487, the provincial exam and the national exam for martial examinations were arranged in the same manner as the literary examination. From 1493, the military examination was held every six years and only those who passed the military strategies test were qualified to take part in the next stage of archery and riding tests. From 1504, the military examination was changed to be held every three years again and the final results were opened to the public.[18] In general, the Imperial Martial Examination balanced military knowledge with practical martial skills for most of the Ming dynasty. However, a relatively significant change was made during the reigns of Emperor Longqing (1537–1572) and Emperor Wanli (1563–1620) in that practical martial skills began to outweigh military knowledge in the martial examination.[19] This tendency probably resulted from the increasing military threat on the borders so that more soldiers were needed.

The martial academies had been set up in the early Ming dynasty. In February 1399, for the first time, a martial official was commissioned to deal with the routine affairs of the martial academies. In 1441, two martial academies were set up in the two capitals of the Ming, Beijing and Nanjing. Fifty-one coaches were appointed to train the approximately 100 junior officials in these two academies. Later, all the male children over ten years of age of the local martial officials were required to attend local martial academies, or a Wei Academy or Confucianism Academy if there was no martial academy available.[20] The examination in the martial academy was very strict. Between 1465 and 1487, students who had not passed the examination after ten years' study would be sent to the army for further training and asked to compensate the cost of the martial academy.[21]

Martial training in the army

The Ming dynasty employed a *Weisuo* military system. The Wei and Suo were set up as the basic military units throughout the country, with the Weis generally located in the important garrison towns. There were two types of Suo according to their size. The smaller Suo were made up of approximately 112 men, while the larger Suo were of 1,120 men. Every Wei contained about 5,600 men. The total number of soldiers in the Weis and Suos was about two million which accounted for all the soldiers in the Ming army.

The Ming emperors paid much attention to military training. Emperor Hongwu often ordered his experienced generals or veterans to train the armies. He also enacted the training rules for the armies.[22] Many records about the Ming emperors supervising military training themselves can be found; for instance, Emperor Jianwen (1377–?) inspected the army six times as soon as he was enthroned.[23] Records of the arrangement of military training in the Ming armies still exist. For example, records from 1527 say that within a battalion, one or two soldiers skilful in each martial skill, namely the spear, the sabre, the sword, the shield, or the hand cannon, were selected as coaches; a battalion was divided into 30 units with 30 generals, and each general was in charge of the military training of 3,000 soldiers; the best soldiers were chosen as the elites; and every month, the viceroy spent four days supervising the training camp and the generals supervised the rest of the time.[24]

Firearms were initially used in the Song dynasty and became more common in the Ming dynasty. *History of Ming* notes that the army of Emperor Yongle (1360–1424) used more than ten different types of firearms in battle. In addition, he set up a special firearms division. However, the early firearms did not replace cold arms or challenge the status of cold arms in the Ming army. Instead, firearms were used with cold arms on the basis of their respective characteristics in battles.[25] Since cold arms were more useful in battles fought in close quarters, the Ming soldiers were expected to put practicing cold arms skills first, as Qi Jiguang stressed in his *Record of Military Training*.[26] Qi also encouraged the soldiers to practice martial skills for self-defence and to win honour and glory in battle.[27]

Besides routine martial training, martial competitions were also conducted with a clear system of reward and punishment to improve military training in the Ming armies.[28] Pragmatism was important in military training in this period, so many performance-oriented martial activities were excluded.[29] In the Ming dynasty, emperors also attached great importance to the development of paramilitary forces and militia.[30] The emphasis on martial arts training undoubtedly promoted the development of the martial arts in the military. The attention given to martial arts training of militiamen promoted a martial spirit in the public and increased the connection between military martial arts and popular martial arts.

The generals of the Ming dynasty observed the dialectical relationship between the training of martial skills and bravery. In *Array of Discipline*, He Liangchen addressed the idea that training in martial skills led to the cultivation of bravery.[31] Qi Jiguang, however, believed that the braver soldiers would show higher levels of martial skills than the ordinary soldiers. He also believed that brave soldiers could defeat any enemies with courage even if only part of their martial capability was exploited. Unfortunately, he claimed, without courage they would forget how to act when fighting an enemy. Therefore, he believed that bravery underpinned the practice of martial skills.[32]

The formation of martial arts systems

Chinese martial arts were mainly categorized by weapon before the Song dynasty, but during the Ming dynasty they began to be categorized by school. That is to say, there were different schools with different styles, features, and contents for one martial skill or weapon, or there were different featured martial skills or weapons for one school.

Zheng Ruozeng (1503–1570), a senior official in charge of defending against the Japanese Wokou in Zhejiang, mentioned that there were at least 11 schools for the quan, 31 schools for cudgel skills, 16 schools for spear skill, 15 schools for sabre skills, six schools for swordsmanship, ten schools for miscellaneous weapons, five schools for rake skills, and 16 schools for horseback weapons and so forth.[33]

The 11 schools for quan skills included: the Zhaojia Quan, Nan Quan, Bei Quan, Xijia Quan, Wen Gougua Quan, Sun Pigua Quan, Zhangfei Shen Quan, Bawang Quan, Hou Quan, Tongzi Baiguanyin Shen Quan and Jiugun Shiba Die Dazhua Quan.

The 31 schools for cudgel skills included: Zuoshou Shaolin, Youshou Shaolin, Da Xunhai Yecha, Xiao Xunhai Yecha, Da Huolin, Xiao Huolin, Tongxu Zhangjia Cudgel, Guanyin Danao Nanhai Shen Cudgel, Shaozi Cudgel, Lianhuan Cudgel, Shuangtou Cudgel, Yinshou Duangun Shierlu, Xuebang Soushan Cudgel, Da Babang Fengmo, Xiao Babang Fengmo, Erlang Cudgel, Wulang Cudgel, Shibaxia Wolf-tooth Cudgel, Zhaotaizu Tengshe Cudgel, Anhou Sun Cudgel, Da Liubang Jinchanshen, Shibamian Maifu Ziweishan Tiaozi, Zuoshou Tiaozi, Youshou Tiaozi, Bianlan Tiaozi, Xuecha Liutiaozi, Kuahu Tiaozi, Gunshou Tiaozi, Hetu Boathook and Xishan (see Figure 7.1).

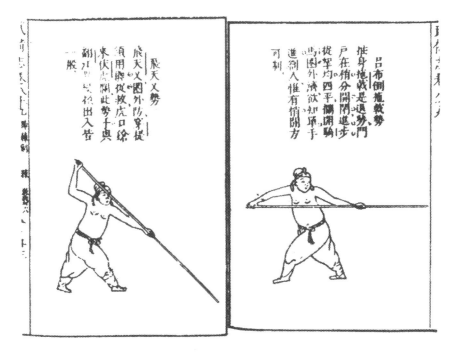

Figure 7.1 Shaolin Cudgel Skills from the Ming dynasty.

The 15 schools for sabre skills included: Yanyue Sabre, Double Sabre, Gou Sabre, Shou Sabre, Ju Sabre, Zhao Sabre, Taiping Sabre, Dingjie Sabre, Chaotian Sabre, Kaitian Sabre, Kaizheng Sabre, Huazheng Sabre, Pian Sabre, Che Sabre, and Dagger.

The 16 schools for spear skills included: Yang Lihua Spear, Sha Spear, Neijia Spear, Ma Spear, Li Short Spear, Henan Li Kefu Long Spear, Liuhe Spear, Baqiangmu, Guandong Yang Jiaoshi Spear, Jin Spear, Zhangfei Shen Spear, Xianshen Spear, Shi Spear, Han Spear, Emei Spear, and Shandong Fanqiang Shifa.

The six schools for swordsmanship included: Bian Zhuang Fenjiaofa, Wang Juzhi Qiluofa, Liu Xianzhu Guyingfa, Ma Mingwang Shandianfa, Ma Chao Chushoufa, and Bianche Houji Duanshenfa.

The division between internal quan and external quan dates back to the late Ming dynasty, as noted in Huang Zongxi's *The Epitaph for Wang Zhengnan* and Cao Bingren's *Prefectural Annals of Ningbo*. They argued that the external quan focused on initiative attack, with Shaolin quan as a typical example; while the internal quan stressed making an attack with the practitioner's internal exercises after being attacked, with Zhang Songxi's quan the most representative. Zhang's internal quan also placed emphasis on attacking acupoints. He had also developed some formulas to help practice this skill. It is said that the internal quan had inundant power so that it was more useful than the external quan.[34]

Huang's work was the first to claim that it was Zhang Sanfeng[35] who created the internal quan. Cao's work repeats this claim. Some other works, such as *Choreography of Shaanxi*, *Choreography of Shanxi*, and *History of Ming*, also mention Zhang Sanfen. However, the birthplace of Zhang is ambiguous in these works, and some did not even mention Zhang practicing martial arts at all. Therefore, the relationship between the origin of the internal quan and Zhang Sanfeng needs further study.

Nevertheless, the inherited system of internal quan was quite clear in the Ming dynasty. According to the literature, the internal quan was first popularized in Shaanxi Province and Wang Zong was the most well-known master. Chen Zhoutong, a native of Wenzhou, Zhejiang Province, learned the internal quan from Wang Zong and later popularized it in Wenzhou. Between 1522 and 1566, Zhang Songxi, another native of Zhejiang Province, became the leading master and had three or four disciples. Ye Jimei and Ye Jinquan were the best of Zhang's disciples. Because they were from Siming, the internal quan became popular in that place. Later, Ye Jinquan took some disciples to pass on the skills.[36]

The emergence of various martial arts schools demonstrates the systemization of Chinese martial arts and the further development of martial arts during the Ming dynasty.

The Eighteen Martial Skills

In the Ming dynasty, Xie Zhaozhi said that the Eighteen Martial Skills were the bow, crossbow, spear, sabre, sword, ancient-style spear, shield, axe, broadax, halberd, round bar mace or iron whip, bar mace, pole-pick, lance, trident, rake, rope, and baida in his *Wuzazu*.[37] According to another work of the Ming dynasty, *Yongzhuang Xiaopin* written by Zhu Guozhen, similar martial skills were included, but the cudgel rather than the lance and the claw rather than the pole-pick.[38] Although *The Water Margin* was completed in the Ming dynasty, it was about the stories of Song. Therefore, this novel might reflect, to some extent, what the Eighteen Martial Skills referred to in the Song dynasty. It refers to the ancient-style spear, hammer, bow, crossbow, hand canoe, round bar mace or iron whip, bar mace, sword, chain, claw, axe, broadax, dagger-axe, halberd, shield, mace, spear, and trident.[39] Although there are different records of the Eighteen Martial Skills, these different opinions reflect the wide range of weapons used in the Ming dynasty since they include both the unarmed and armed martial skills. The armed martial skills included long weapons, short weapons, long-ranged weapons, and soft weapons.

Quan skill was an essential martial skill for practicing other martial arts.[40] Most of the basic movements in the quan of the Ming dynasty were close to those of today, including the footwork, stances, striking, and other balancing and jumping movements. Furthermore, the quans in the Ming dynasty placed stress on theories and methods of practice. *A Collection of Military Martial Arts*, written by Tang Shunzhi, states that the movements of quans in Ming dynasty were ever-changing both in attack and defence.[41]

Similarly, most movements in cudgel skills were fundamental to other martial arts, a view agreed on by many martial arts masters of the Ming dynasty.[42] It was for this reason that cudgel skills were regarded as important by the Ming martial artists. There were a variety of cudgel skills in the Ming dynasty. Among the tens of schools of cudgel skills in Ming, Yu Dayou's techniques, most of which were included in his *Cudgel Treatise*, were the most representative and outstanding, as argued by He Liangchen and Qi Jiguang.[43]

As mentioned above, there were many well-known schools of different styles of spear skills during the Ming dynasty, including the Sha, Ma, Shi, Shaolin, and Emei. However, the Yang school was the most prominent among them, famous for its excellence in using the (long) spear with the application of close quarters weapon techniques.[44] He Liangchen summarized some of his experiences of learning and teaching spear skills. For instance, the learner first needed to practice bodywork, footwork, and hand techniques, and only then should they learn the attacking techniques and practice again and again until they commanded the skills proficiently. He also suggested periodic contests should be conducted to examine the learner's progress. The contests generally included a show of individual skills and actual combat, sometimes fought against another student and sometimes fought against a wooden target.[45] The theories of the spear arts saw great improvement during the Ming dynasty. First, there were elaborations on the specification, function, and technique of the spear; as well as detailed manuals, training methods, and test criteria for practicing spear skills. Second, some songs and rhymes were created in order to help the learner remember the movements. Third, there were many illustrations in the spear treatises to aid visualization of the movements for practicing spear skills, and the names of these movements were also picturesque: 'the azure dragon stretching out its claws', 'ambush on all sides', 'the blue dragon swinging its tail', and 'Jiang Taigong fishing' (waving the spear as if fishing).

The bow and the crossbow were still significant weapons for both military and non-military use in the Ming dynasty. *Records of Armaments and Military Provisions* ranks them the first among all weapons.[46] *On Archery Techniques*, a noted work about archery skills, was written by Li Chengfen in the Ming dynasty. This work consisted of 14 chapters and had a detailed account of shooting weapons and specific techniques.[47] The 25 sections in *New Treatise on Military Efficiency* were on archery theory and illustrated how to hit a long-distance target, and explained the process, requirements, and key points of bow shooting in detail. It also described the common mistakes of bow shooting in detail, detailing how the mistakes occurred and how to correct them.[48] In regard to the crossbow, the *Experience and Methods of Using Crossbow* written by Cheng Zongyou is worth mentioning. The work contains various illustrations of methods for drawing the crossbow, including the treadle shooting crossbow, lap shooting crossbow, ordinary crossbow, and shooting crossbow in sequence.[49]

In the Ming dynasty, the sword still prevailed among the general populace even though it was rarely found in the army. *History of Ming* says that Xu Fang, one of the renowned recluses of Ming in Tonglu County of Zhejiang Province, was a wuxia who used his sword in doing justice for people.[50] *Records of Spear Skills*, authored by Wu Shu, says that he learned swordsmanship from an old man who was a master of traditional swordsmanship.[51] *Thesis of Mr Fu Ting* also says that Shi Jingyan, who was famous for his spear skills, had learned swordsmanship from Geng Ju.[52] Moreover, judging from the spectacular performance of the sword dance in Song Cunbiao's *Ode to Sword Dance*,[53] swordsmanship had reached a considerably higher level in the Ming dynasty.

There was a great variety of techniques for using the sabre in the Ming dynasty, which had been influenced by the skills of the Japanese during China's wars against the wokou pirates.

Apart from the schools for the major weapons such as the cudgel, sword and sabre, there were also other schools of martial arts in the Ming dynasty. For example, there were some schools known for using different minor weapons, such as the iron whip, clamp sticks, iron chain, Jili, Suantou, Jin'gang ring, manzhang iron ruler, steel trident, wolf spear, bladed trident and others; some schools for using different rakes with different methods; and some schools for using various weapons on the horse, such as the whip, chain, hammer, meteor hammer, fangtian halberd, spear, guan sabre, chopping horse sabre, yue spear and more.[54] It is apparent that the number of weapons or martial skills utilized was far greater than 18, and that the Eighteen Martial Skills referred to broad categories of weapons or martial skills in the Ming dynasty.

The variety of weapons in use and the popularity of certain weapons varied from region to region in the Ming dynasty. Taking Guangdong Province as an example, people in the eastern regions tended to practice the shield and the sabre, while people in the central regions practiced the spade.

The rise of Shaolin martial arts

Since the Shaolin Temple was built in 495, eminent monks had come to the temple to practice martial arts, including Huiguang, Sengchou, and Yuanjing. By the time of the Ming dynasty, the Shaolin Temple had become very famous. Wang Shixing, a renowned scholar of Ming, wrote in his *Journey to Mountain Song* that there were more than 400 monks in the temple, all of whom were excellent in martial arts, such as quan skills and cudgel skills.[55]

The Shaolin martial arts were characterized by the use of cudgels, which involved different individual and paired skills. All of these skills were illustrated. Some argue that Shaolin cudgeling was created by the legendary Kinnara when he defeated the Turban Rebellion in the late Yuan dynasty. However, the fact is, the Shaolin cudgel skills came from the traditional folk society. It says in *Righteousness Hall Military Martial Arts Compilation* that during the reign of Emperor Jiajing (1507–1567), when General Yu Dayou was sent to conquer the south, he paid a visit to the Shaolin Temple but only to find that the illustrious Shaolin cudgel skills had, in reality, failed to be handed down. Therefore, he brought two monks with potential martial skills, Zongqing and Pucong, to the south with him. After three years, Zongqing and Pucong became masters in the cudgel through Yu's personal training. Additionally, Yu imparted his *Cudgel Treatise* to Zongqing, who later returned to the Shaolin Temple and began to teach cudgel skills. Almost 100 monks were trained and influenced. Since Yu Dayou's cudgel skills came from the Jingchu[56] area, it can be seen that the Shaolin cudgel skills should be regarded as originating in the traditional folk society.

Another proof can be found in the words of Cheng Zongyou, a remarkable martial artist of Ming, when he said that his martial arts were learned from the Shaolin monk Hongzhuan, while Hongzhuan was a disciple of the Shaolin monk Hongji.[57] In addition, *Records of Spear Skills* informs us that Hongji learned his martial arts from famous master of Liu Dechang.[58] These historical materials indicate that the Shaolin martial arts began to take shape by making use of the essence of folk martial arts.

The Shaolin monks of the Ming dynasty and their cudgel skills made a great contribution to the fight against the Japanese pirates. As depicted in *Wusong Jiayi Wobianzhi*, *Yunjian Jottings*, and *Wokou Incidents*, the Shaolin monks were able to carry an iron cudgel of about 2.24 m and 17.7 kg in battle, and they could use their cudgels so skilfully that they easily defeated their enemies.[59] At the end of the Ming dynasty, the Shaolin monks began to mainly practice the quan instead of the cudgel. In brief, the emergence of Shaolin martial arts in the Northern Wei period (386–534) and their rise in the Ming dynasty is a significant page in the history of Chinese martial arts.

Individual and paired martial arts forms

The forms of Chinese martial arts were developed considerably during the Ming dynasty. For instance, Cheng Zongyou adapted the sabre skills taught by Master Liu Yunfeng into a set of sabre forms. While recognizing the practical functions of Liu's sabre skills, he suggested that the stylization of these skills would be an indispensable approach for training. Therefore, he arranged all movements into certain fixed sequences. In performing the form, the odd sequences started with a circle from right to left, while the even sequences circled from left to right, with the sequences including the slash, arc, straight, eight-shape and more[60] (see Figure 7.2). The layout of this sabre form is straightforward and rational.

Qi Jiguang also composed a set of quan forms, which emphasized the interconnection of the strikes and the tactics of using fixed forms or sequences flexibly.[61] Cheng's sabre form and Qi's quan form are the earliest recorded martial arts forms of China that were detailed and illustrated. Additionally, the poem *Ode to the Quan by a Taoist in Mount Emei* contains a lively description of the quan form. The description covers the full course of the quan form from the beginning to ending movements, including strength, body movements, strikes,

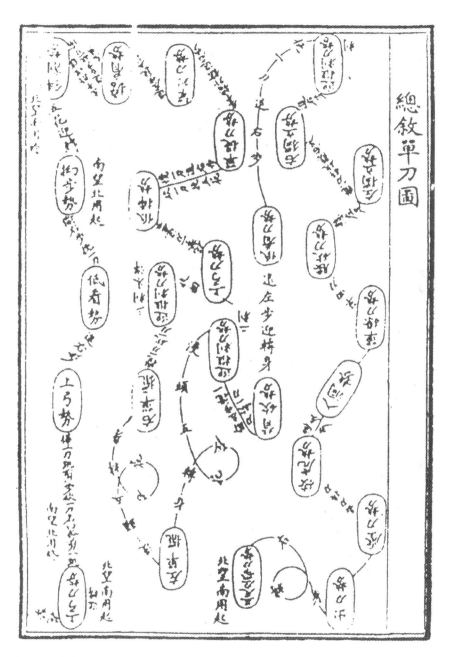

Figure 7.2 Practicing sabres displayed by Cheng Zongyou in the Ming dynasty.

breath, rhythm, and posture.[62] The emergence of these martial arts forms indicates the fully fledged development of Chinese martial arts.

The paired martial arts forms were practiced by two or more people who attacked and defended within certain prescribed sequences. In the Ming dynasty, the criteria for examining the paired martial arts forms consisted of nine ranks based on the participants' strength, strikes, speed, and proficiency of matching-up. This shows the normalization of the paired martial arts forms in the Ming dynasty.[63]

There are some records of martial arts contests of the Ming dynasty to be found in the historical classics. For instance, Yuan Hongdao, scholar-offical and writer of Ming, wrote in his *Journey to Mountain Song* that he saw the Shaolin monks practicing unarmed combat.[64] Jie Xuan, strategist and astronomer of Ming, suggested different sequences and tactics should be employed in different circumstances during Jiaodi.[65] *The Water Margin* also presents a spear contest between Yang Zhi and Zhou Jin.[66]

Jiaodi

Jiaodi in the Ming dynasty does not seem to have thrived as it did in the Song and Yuan dynasties, but it was still practiced widely in the palaces, among the general population, and in the army. For instance, Emperor Zhengde (1491–1521) loved watching Jiaodi. In order to flatter the emperor, Liu Jin often arranged Jiaodi performances outside the palace and helped the emperor to secretly watch them. Consequently, the emperor gradually grew to trust Liu and later appointed him to an official position. Liu Jin himself was a good Jiaodi practitioner.[67]

According to the *Major Events in the Ming Dynasty*, Jiaodi was also employed in military training in the Ming dynasty.[68] Another writer, He Liangjun, adds that Jiaodi talents could be found in both the south and north armies during the reign of Emperor Zhengde. The northern ones were outstanding in strength, while the southern ones were better in applying techniques and tactics.[69]

There are a number of skillful traditional Jiaodi masters to be found in the historical records. For example, Master Zhang, who was said to be able to take advantage of every situation and take great strength from small efforts (四两拨千斤), a concept which was later introduced to the Shaolin Martial Arts[70]; and Master Xu, a street-vendor who made a living by selling shrimps but was bullied by other vendors at times, Xu struck back at them using Jiaodi and thus won his fame.[71] *Taoan Mengyi*, authored by Zhang Dai, a writer of Ming, notes that on the Tomb Sweeping Day, people in Yangzhou would hold a series of outdoor activities, such as horse walking, falcon freeing, Jiaodi, and so forth.[72]

He Liangjun also tells how movements like hitting and pushing were employed in Jiaodi. Moreover, kicking and punching movements were found in the Jiaodi contest between Jiao Ting and Li Kui mentioned in *The Water Margin*.[73] Therefore, it seems the Jiaodi of Ming included not only tumbling skills but also other fighting skills.

The exchange of martial arts between China and Japan

The Ming dynasty witnessed much exchange of martial arts between China and Japan. The inflow of Japanese sabres and sabre skills was celebrated by the Chinese military and martial artists. Meanwhile, the relationship between Japanese karate and judo and Chinese martial arts began in this period.

During the Ming dynasty, Japanese sabres were well known for their excellent quality. The blades of these sabres were about 1.22 m in length, and the handle was about 38.4 cm long. The back edge was thick, getting thinner from hilt to point. There was a ridge along both sides of the Japanese sabre. The cutting edge was thin and sharp. The scabbard was also well made to allow the swordsman to easily withdraw or insert the sabre, being neither too tight nor too loose. These sabres were quite sharp, and were made so meticulously and exquisitely that they became fairly popular with Chinese armies.[74] It has been described how the Japanese sabre was so sharp that it led to death almost as soon as it was unsheathed.[75] Furthermore, Qi Jiguang realized, that when the Japanese pirates invaded China, their sabres had been a fatal weapon on the battlefield.[76]

Chinese martial artists in the Ming dynasty were not conservative. They soon adopted Japanese sabre skills in Chinese martial arts. Qi Jiguang, who claimed to have acquired his Japanese sabre skills during the war against Japanese pirates, compiled details of the Japanese sabre skills in his *New Treatise on Military Efficiency*.[77] Other Chinese martial artists who practiced Japanese sabre skills in the Ming dynasty included Cheng Zongyou, Liu Yunfeng, Wu Shu, and so forth. It is from Liu Yunfeng that Cheng Zongyou began to learn Japanese sabre skills. However, Cheng regarded Liu's sabre skills as difficult to learn by heart although they were rich in movements and tactics. Therefore, Cheng named each of the skills and provided an illustration of them.[78] Many of these skills ceased to be Japanese as they became integrated into the Chinese tradition, such as the Dandao Sabre Skill and Wuhua Sabre Skill. The integration of Japanese sabre skills into Chinese ways of practicing sabre positively spurred the development of Chinese martial arts.

However, Chinese martial arts also had a profound influence on the development of Japanese martial arts in the Ming dynasty. The mutual exchange between the two countries began as early as the establishment of the Ming dynasty. From 1386, 19 years after the establishment of the Ming dynasty, they exchanged ambassadors more than ten times. With the deepening of cultural communication, some Chinese martial arts classics spread into Japan, for example, Qi Jiguang's *Essential Treatise of Quan*, between 1573 and 1619.

In the late Ming dynasty, Master Chen Yuanyun escorted the renowned scholar Zhu Shunshui to Japan in 1619, before the entry of the Qing army into the central plains. Chen, who was accomplished in both literary and martial arts, had, on the one hand, influenced the Japanese writers, and, on the other hand, influenced Japanese martial arts. In 1629, he arrived in the Baoguo Temple to teach quan skills to some Japanese ronin.[79] It was by building on Chen quan skills that the Japanese martial artists created jujutsu (later judo). Since those ronin who learned quan skills from Chen are reputed to be the forefathers of Judo in Japan, there is no denying that Cheng played a significant role in the initial development of Japanese Judo.

The Ryukyu Islands, now known as Okinawa and governed by Japan, served as a bridge for the exchange of martial arts between China and Japan during the Ming dynasty. It was not until 1879, during the Qing dynasty, that Japan claimed sovereignty over the islands, before then the Ryukyu Kingdom was a vassal state of China. It's still unknown when karate (see tangshou[80]) was introduced into the Ryukyu Kingdom from China. But the Japanese generally say it was during the Ming dynasty.[81]

There were two major schools of karate in the Ryukyu Islands, the Shuri-Te and the Naha-Te, two Japanese names given when Okinawa was accepted as a member of the Japanese martial arts federation. It is said that the Shuri-Te, which was popular among the samurais in Japan, was derived from the Jiangxi tangshou of China; while the Naha-Te, which was prevalent among the common people, stemmed from the Fujian tangshou of China. Even today, karate shares many of the same movements with Fujian quans. In the paper *Japanese Karate Originates from Fujian*, the authors quote a report from the 1980s which says that when the Japanese karate delegate visited Fuzhou (capital city of Fujian), they brought with them a *Manual of White Crane Quan* and said that their training methods for karate were from that book. The authors recognized that the book of the Japanese visitors was a handwritten copy of the *White Crane Quan* of Fuzhou. Therefore, it seems that the Japanese karate delegation practiced *White Crane Quan* of Fuzhou.

The Japanese literature has also reported that the Chinese from Fujian generally lived in Kumemura when they arrived in the Ryukyu Islands. They spread their tangshou there. The Cai tangshou and the Zheng tangshou were still practiced there and were types of Naha-Te.

After Chinese tangshou was introduced into the Ryukyu Kingdom, the islanders were prohibited from practicing martial arts twice. Both campaigns strictly prevented people from practicing with any type of weapon. Therefore, they changed the name of Chinese tangshou to karate and the martial arts survived in the Ryukyu Islands.

Distinguished martial arts classics and their authors

New treatise on military efficiency

The author of this book was Qi Jiguang, a famous general and strategist who was honored as a national hero for fighting against the wokou pirates during the

Ming dynasty. Born into a family of generals (with a long military tradition), Qi was soon promoted to be a commander-in-chief, and assigned to defend the Ji County two years after defeating the wokou with General Yu Dayou in Shandong Province. He started compiling his *New Treatise on Military Efficiency* and completed 14 volumes in 1560. The other four volumes were written later. The book was first published in 1562.

The book has been published in many versions, with varying contents. For instance, the Zhou Shi version, published in 1595, included 18 volumes, among which some sections or chapters cover the skills of various martial arts, including long weapons, shield, short weapons, archery and quan; however, sabre skills were excluded from this version. The Wang Xiangquan version contained 14 volumes, covering the martial arts of the spear, the shield, the cudgel, archery, and so on; however, quan skills were excluded from this version.

Qi's *New Treatise on Military Efficiency* include the *Yang Liuhe and Bamu Spear Skills*; and Yu Dayou's *Sword Treatise* and *Thirty-two Forms of Quan Treatise* (see Figure 7.3), which he had invented himself by learning from various schools of folk quans. The book has long been an important work in the study of Chinese martial arts. Some of its content was widely reprinted in the later martial

Figure 7.3 Thirty-two Forms of Quan Treatise (part) from the Ming dynasty.

classics, such as *Records of Armaments and Military Provisions* and *Sancai Tuhui*. The North Korean people edited the *Comprehensive Illustrated Manual of Martial Arts* (무예도보통지)[82] based on it. Moreover, the Japanese reprinted this classic under different titles, such as *Wushu Zaoxue*, *Junfa Bingji*, and *Bingfa Aoyi Shu* (in Chinese).

Record of military training and miscellaneous record of military training

Both of these books were also authored by Qi Jiguang when he was acting as Viceroy of Jiliao, a very important position in the defence of the northern borders. *The Record of Military Training* is a handbook of nine volumes on border defence and military training, covering the training of battle array, soldiers' courage, strength, body, leadership in battles and so on. For generations, this book was not only influential in military studies, but also in practical martial training.

In the six-volume *Miscellaneous Record of Military Training*, Qi systematically expounded on ethics, command of military techniques, strategies, tactics, and training methods for military officials. Notably, the book addressed the dialectical relationship between bravery and martial skills, which is informative for practical military training.

The book has been reprinted in many versions, such as the Ge version in the Ming dynasty, the Guangji Hall (publishing house) version in the Qing dynasty, and the version included in *Complete Library in Four Branches of Literature*.

A collection of Tang Shunzhi's works

The collection was authored by Tang Shunzhi of the Ming dynasty, who was a renowned general during the war against the wokou pirates. The book was a collection of his notes and essays. Much of the collection relates to martial arts, such as *Journey to Shaolin Monastery in Mountain Song*, *Spear of Yang Jiaoshi*, *Quan of Emei Taoist* and *Japanese Sword*.

During the period of the Republic of China, a block-printed edition of this collection was kept in the Yongfen Building (publishing house) in Shanghai, and was later entered into the category of literary works of the *Sibu Congkan* (series of books).

A collection of military martial arts

This book was also compiled by Tang Shunzhi and introduced the training methods in various military weapons and martial arts from before the Ming dynasty. Similar to *New Treatise on Military Efficiency*, this book introduced various schools of martial arts. It was published during the Reign of Emperor Jiajing, and was later included in *Complete Library in Four Branches of Literature*.

Sancai Tuhui

Sancai Tuhui was edited by Wang Xin and Wang Siyi during the Ming dynasty and was published in 1607. It included 106 volumes, covering 14 subjects, such as astronomy, geography, and biography. A number of illustrations of martial arts, such as archery, spear, cudgel, and quan, were included in the *Sancai Tuhui*, which were collected from *New Treatise on Military Efficiency* and *Complete Essentials for the Military Classics*.

Jiangnan military defence strategies and plans

This book was authored by Zheng Ruozeng of the Ming dynasty and published in 1614. The book was made up of eight volumes, with each volume consisting of two parts. Volume 8 related to martial weapons such as the sabre, the cudgel, the bow and arrow, and, in particular, the spear. The content on the schools of quan was largely identical to that in *Sequel of Comprehensive Studies in Administration*, except for the introduction to Zhao's quan. The book has been collected in *Complete Library in Four Branches of Literature*.

Righteousness hall military martial arts compilation

This book was a collection of the works of the famous anti-Japanese pirates general Yu Dayou of the Ming dynasty. Yu, born in Fujian, was competent both in pen and sword, in particular the long sword. The book was published twice, in 1565 and 1569. It included martial arts such as sabre skills and archery skills in the fourth volume. In 1841, during the Qing dynasty, the book was reedited and reprinted under the title *Beilu Jihui*. It contained content on sabre skills and cudgel skills.

Wuzazu

Wuzazu was authored by Xie Zhaozhi, a writer of Ming who was born in Fujian. The book was a collection of Xie's notes. It consisted of 16 volumes, covering five aspects of astronomy, geography, biography, objects, and events. Some of the contents referred to the martial arts of the Ming, such as the Shaolin martial arts and the Eighteen Martial Skills. The book was reprinted by the Zhonghua Book Company in 1959.

Yongzhuang Xiaopin

Yongzhuang Xiaopin was a book about the laws and regulations of the Ming Dynasty written by Zhu Guozhen, a historian born in Zhejiang. This book comprised 32 volumes. Volume 12 recorded the martial artists and weapons of Ming. It referred to the Eighteen Martial Skills as the bow, crossbow, spear, sabre, sword, ancient style spear, shield, axe, broadax, halberd, round bar mace or iron whip, bar mace, claw, lance, trident, rake, rope, and baida. The author also explained that baida was a game of unarmed combat.

Array of discipline

Array of Discipline was written by General He Liangchen in the Ming dynasty. The book was first published in 1591 and was later revised several times. The book had four volumes and 66 articles; all were about military training.

Gengyu Shengji

Gengyu Shengji was compiled by Cheng Zongyou, a famous martial artist of the Ming dynasty who was born in Anhui. Cheng was adept at the cudgel, the sabre, the spear, and the crossbow. The book consisted of three volumes on Shaolin cudgel skills, one volume on long spear skills, one volume on sabre skills, and one volume on *Experience and Methods of Using Crossbow*. In 1929, *Gengyu Shengji*, renamed as *National Four Books on Martial Arts*, was published containing six volumes, mainly giving an account of the techniques of Shaolin cudgel with rich illustrations.

Toubi Futan

Toubi Futan[83] was completed between 1522 and 1619. It is an important military classic of the Ming dynasty. The author did not give his true name but called himself Hermit Xiyuan. The author was, in fact, a Jieyuan (First Laureate in the imperial provincial exam) of Zhejiang named He Shoufa. The book was of two volumes consisting of 13 articles. These articles were deep in philosophy, which served as a good guide to strategies and tactics in single combat or on the battlefield.

Records of Armaments and Military Provisions

This work was authored by Mao Yuanyi (1594–1640), a senior military official of the Ming dynasty. It took Mao 15 years to complete the work. The book contained 204 volumes, many of which were related to martial arts. Many of the martial skills in the book were learned from the older military and martial arts classics, such as *Complete Essentials for the Military Classics* and *New Treatise on Military Efficiency*. The book was later banned during the Qing dynasty. *Records of Armaments and Military Provisions* has been collected into the *History of Ming*.

Techniques of Internal Quan

This book was written by Huang Baijia, a scholar of the early Ming dynasty. The book included techniques of internal quan. It pointed out that in employing the quan, proficiency in a quan outweighed the number of quans used. The book was collected as Volume 33 of *A Collection of Books in the Qing Dynasty*.

Notes

1. (Ming) Tang Shunzhi. Wubian (武编).
2. (Ming) Yu Dayou. Zhengqitang Ji (正气堂集).
3. (Ming) Qi Jiguang. Jixiao Xinshu (纪效新书).
4. (Ming) Qi Jiguang. Lianbing Shiji (练兵实纪).
5. (Ming) He Liangchen. Zhenji (阵纪).
6. (Ming) Zheng Ruozeng. Jiangnan Jinglue (江南经略).
7. (Ming) Wang Qi. Xu Wenxian Tongkao•Xuexiao Yi (续文献通考•学校一).
8. *History of Ming*. (Ming) Zhang Yanyu. Mingshi•Xuanju Yi (明史•选举一).
9. (Ming) Wang Qi. Xu Wenxian Tongkao•Xuexiao Yi (续文献通考•学校一).
10. (Qing) Gu Yanwu. Rizhi Lu•Jingyi Lunce (日知录•经义论策).
11. (Qing) Liu Yong, Ji Huang *et al*. Xu Tongzhi•Xuanju Lue Si (续通志•选举略四).
12. A successful candidate in the final imperial exam in the Ming and Qing dynasties.
13. (Ming) Zhang Yanyu. Mingshi•Lu Xiangsheng Zhuan (明史•卢象升传).
14. *Codes of the Ming Dynasty*. (Qing) Long Wenbin. Ming Huiyao•Xuanju Yi (明会要•选举一).
15. (Ming) Zhang Yanyu. Mingshi•Xuanju Er (明史•选举二).
16. (Qing) Long Wenbin. Ming Huiyao •Xuanju Yi (明会要•选举一).
17. (Ming) Zhang Yanyu. Mingshi•Jiang Mingwu Zhuan (明史•姜名武传).
18. (Ming) Zhang Yanyu. Mingshi•Xuanju Er (明史•选举二).
19. Ibid.
20. (Ming) Wang Qi. Xu Wenxian Tongkao•Xuexiao Yi (续文献通考•学校一).
21. (Ming) Zhang Yanyu. Mingshi•Xuanju Yi (明史•选举一).
22. (Ming) Zhang Yanyu. Mingshi•Bingzhi (明史•兵志).
23. Ibid.
24. Ibid.
25. Ibid.
26. (Ming) Qi Jiguang. Lianbing Shiji • Chulian Tonglun (练兵实纪•储练通论).
27. In the fourth chapter of *New Book on Military Training*. (Ming) Qi Jiguang. Jixiao Xinshu•Jinling (纪效新书•禁令).
28. (Ming) Qi Jiguang. Jixiao Xinshu•Bijiao Wuyi Shangfa Pian. (纪效新书•比较武艺赏罚篇).
29. (Ming) He Liangchen. Zhenji•Qizheng (阵纪•奇正).
30. (Ming) Zhang Yanyu. Mingshi•Shihuo Yi (明史•食货一).
31. (Ming) He Liangchen. Zhenji•Jiaolian (阵纪•教练).
32. (Ming) Qi Jiguang. Jixiao Xinshu•Jinling (纪效新书•禁令).
33. (Ming) Zheng Ruozeng. Jiangnan Jinglue•Zazhu•Bingqi Zonglun (江南经略•杂著•兵器总论).
34. (Qing) Cao Bingren. Ningbo Fuzhi•Zhang Songxi Zhuan (宁波府志•张松溪传).
35. Zhang Sanfeng was an important figure in Taoism during the Ming dynasty.
36. (Qing) Huang Zongxi. Wang Zhengnan Muzhi Ming (王征南墓志铭).
37. (Ming) Xie Zhaozhe. Wuzazu •Renbu Yi (五杂俎•人部一).
38. (Ming) Zhu Guozhen. Zhu Guozhen. Yong Zhuang Xiaopin•Bingqi (涌幢小品•兵器).
39. (Ming) Shi Nai'an. Shuihuzhuan•Di-er Hui (水浒传•第二回).
40. (Ming) He Liangchen. Zhenji•Jiyong (阵纪•技用).
41. (Ming) Tang Shunzhi. Wubian•Quan (武编•拳).

42 (Ming) Cheng Zongyou. Gengyu Shengji•Shaolin Gunfa Chanzong•Wenda (耕余剩技•少林棍法阐宗•问答).
43 (Ming) He Liangchen. Zhenji•Jiyong (阵纪•技用); (Ming) Qi Jiguang. Jixiao Xinshu•Duanbing Changyong Shuo (纪效新书•短兵长用说).
44 (Ming) Qi Jiguang. Jixiao Xinshu•Changbing Duanyong Shuo (纪效新书•长兵短用说); (Ming) He Liangchen. Zhenji•Jiyong (阵纪•技用).
45 (Ming) He Liangchen. Zhenji•Jiyong (阵纪•技用).
46 (Ming) Mao Yuanyi. Wubeizhi • Gongpian (武备志•弓篇).
47 (Tang) Wang Ju. Shejing (射经).
48 (Ming) Qi Jiguang. Jixiao Xinshu•Shefa (纪效新书•射法).
49 (Ming) Cheng Zongyou. Gengyu Shengji•Juezhang Xinfa (耕余剩技•蹶张心法).
50 (Ming) Zhang Yanyu. Mingshi•Yinyi Zhuan (明史•隐逸传).
51 (Ming) Wu Shu. Shoubilu•Yuyang Laoren Jianjue (手臂录•渔阳老人剑诀).
52 (Qing) Lu Shiyi. Futing Xiansheng Wenji•Shi Jingyan Zhuan (桴亭先生文集•石敬岩传).
53 (Ming) Song Cunbiao. Wujianfu (舞剑赋).
54 (Ming) Zheng Ruozeng. Jiangnan Jinglue•Zazhu•Bingqi Zonglun (江南经略•杂著•兵器总论).
55 (Ming) Wang Shixing. Songyou Ji (嵩游记).
56 The territory and cultural area of the former state of Chu, roughly corresponding with present-day Hubei and Henan around the middle Yangtze River.
57 (Ming) Cheng Zongyou. Gengyu Shengji•Shaolin Gunfa Chanzong (耕余剩技•少林棍法阐宗).
58 (Ming) Wu Shu. Shoubilu•Shi Jingyan Qiangfa Ji (手臂录•石敬岩枪法记).
59 (Ming). Zhang Nai. Wusong Jiayi Wobian Zhi (吴淞甲乙倭变志); (Ming) Cai Jiude. Wobian Shilue (倭变事略); (Republic of China). Yunjian Zazhi (云间杂志).
60 (Ming) Cheng Zongyou. Gengyu Shengji•Dandao Faxuan (耕余剩技•单刀法选).
61 (Ming) Qi Jiguang. Jixiao Xinshu•Quanjing Jieyao Pian (纪效新书•拳经捷要篇).
62 *An Essay Collection of Tang Shunzhi.* (Ming) Tang Shunzhi. Tang Jingchuan Xiansheng Wenji•Emei Daoren Quange (唐荆川先生文集•峨眉道人拳歌).
63 (Ming) Mao Yuanyi. Wubeizhi (武备志).
64 (Ming) Wang Shixing. Songyou Ji (嵩游记).
65 (Qing) Jie Xuanzi. Bingfa Yuanji•Fa Bu (兵法圆机•法部).
66 (Ming) Shi Nai'an. Shuihuzhuan •Di Shi-er Hui (水浒传•第十二回).
67 (Ming) Zhang Yanyu. Mingshi•Liu Jin Zhuan (明史•刘瑾传).
68 (Qing) Gu Yingtai. Minshi Jishi Benmo•Jiang Bin Jianning (明史纪事本末•江彬奸佞).
69 (Ming) He Liangjun. Siyouzhai Congshuo (四友斋丛说).
70 (Ming) Qi Jiguang. Jixiao Xinshu•Quanjing (纪效新书•拳经); (Ming) He Liangchen. Zhenji•Jiyong (阵纪•技用).
71 (Republic of China) Chu Hua. Hucheng Beikao•Xu Weng (沪城备考•徐翁).
72 (Ming) Zhang Dai. Taoan Mengyi•Yangzhou Qingming (陶庵梦忆•扬州清明).
73 (Ming) Shi Nai'an. Shuihuzhuan•Di Qi-shi-san Hui (水浒传•第七十三回).
74 (Ming) Cheng Zongyou. Gengyu Shengji•Dandao Faxuan (耕余剩技•单刀法选).
75 *Records of Pyongyang.* (Ming), about the wars between Korea and Japan; (Ming) Cheng Zongyou. Gengyu Shengji•Dandao Faxuan (耕余剩技•单刀法选); (Ming) He Liangchen. Zhenji•Jiyong (阵纪•技用).
76 (Ming) Qi Jiguang. Jixiao Xinshu•Changdao Jie (纪效新书•长刀解).
77 (Ming) Qi Jiguang. Jixiao Xinshu•Xinyou Daofa (纪效新书•辛酉刀法).
78 (Ming) Cheng Zongyou. Gengyu Shengji•Dandao Faxuan (耕余剩技•单刀法选).
79 Mugong Taiyan (木宮泰彦, きみや やすひこ), translated by Chen Jie. *The Transportation History between Japan and China* (Shanghai: Commercial Press, 1935).

80 Tangshou: 唐手, a kind of barehanded combat art in ancient Chinese. Some Chinese scholars argue that karate was formed when the Chinese Tangshou was diffused and adapted in Ryukyu, as well as the infusion of some local Japanese combat arts from other regions.
81 Knacks of Karate (空手道秘诀), a monograph published in Japan.
82 (Ming) Li Demao, Piao Jiaqi and Luo Shangzhi. Wuyi Tupu Tongzhi (武艺图谱通志).
83 (Ming) Xihu Yishi. Toubi Futan (投笔肤谈).

Chapter 8

Martial arts in the Qing dynasty (1644–1911)

Overview

In 1644, the Manchu army of the Qing dynasty conquered Beijing, capital of the Ming dynasty. Later in the same year, the Qing government relocated its capital to Beijing and claimed sovereignty over the central plains. The Qing army, including the firearm troops, was well aware of the importance of martial training, in particular, in archery. Horseback archery was the principal martial skill taught, together with other weapons such as the long spear, the sabre, and the shield. With the outbreak of the Opium Wars, the overwhelming power of the firearm was universally acknowledged. The increasing significance of the firearm in military operations resulted in the marginalization of martial arts, which were more suited to traditional array-oriented battles and close quarters combat. From 1862 to 1874, the Qing government imported a large quantity of guns and cannons. At the same time, they began to construct their own arsenals to manufacture firearms. During the Sino-Japanese War of 1894–1895, these new firearms were provided to the Qing soldiers. Consequently, the Qing government announced the abolition of the Imperial Martial Examination in 1901, which indicates the withdrawal of martial arts from military applications. Conversely, martial arts continued to thrive in civilian society for a number of reasons.

First, increasing conflict between the ruling class and the lower classes, and between the Manchu people and other ethnic peoples, led to the formation of many anti-Qing organizations throughout civil society. Many of these rebel organizations built up their armed forces through practicing martial arts. Cold weapons were widespread in civil society and were important weapons in the anti-Qing rebellions (see Figures 8.1 and 8.2). The rebellions launched by the White Lotus, Qingshui Sect, Tianli Sect or Bagua Sect, the Taiping Heavenly Kingdom, and Yihetuan Movement not only led ordinary people into the anti-Qing campaign, but also popularized Chinese martial arts.

Second, martial arts were practiced by many of the literary class so that there emerged some scholars who were proficient in Chinese quans, such as Chang Naizhou (1724–1783) and Wu Yuxiang (1812–1880). They summarized and

Figure 8.1 Miscellaneous weapons in the Qing dynasty (part one).

Notes
a Erlang Sabre;
b Meijian Sabre;
c Da Spear;
d Wolf-tooth Mace;
e Broad Axe.

generalized the quan skills in their works and thus promoted the development of Chinese martial arts theory. In this period, martial artists commonly integrated martial arts into traditional Chinese culture to enrich the content of their martial arts. The forms in which martial arts were practiced increased, and the cultural connotations of martial arts were deepened. This period also saw a great number, perhaps as many 100, schools of quan emerging in quick succession.

Third, the practice of physical and mental health, and entertainment through Chinese martial arts was further expanded during this period. During

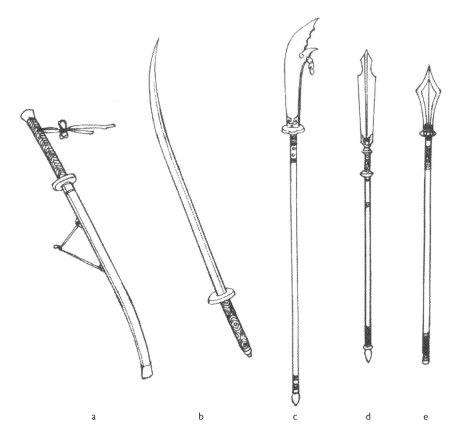

Figure 8.2 Miscellaneous weapons in the Qing dynasty (part two).

Notes
a Zhanma Sabre;
b Miao Sabre;
c Yanyue Sabre;
d Zhao Sabre;
e Huaner Sabre.

the reign of Emperor Xianfeng (1831–1861), the Chinese Taijiquan masters first proposed that the aim of practicing the quan should be for health and fitness so as to extend people's life span. Yang Luchan and Dong Haichuan later adapted their forms of Taijiquan with fewer body movements so as to further popularize Taijiquan. Some traditional quans, such as the Shaolin Quan, also drew on the function of bodybuilding. In the late Qing, the noble class took to martial arts as their main recreation. They hired skillful martial artists to practice or teach various kinds of martial arts in their mansions. It further prompted the development of Chinese martial arts towards healthcare and entertainment among the upper class. The move towards fitness-seeking during the Qing dynasty is a landmark in the sportization process of Chinese martial arts, as well as opening up a new era for Chinese martial arts as a form of sport and physical education.

The martial academy and the Imperial Martial Examination

The decline of the martial academy

The imperial examination of the Qing dynasty aimed to select the best literary and martial talents.[1] Accordingly, the government-run academies did not separate the literary and martial education systems. Martial academies were closed, and all students pursued their studies in the common government-run academies where Confucianism and horseback archery were highly regarded. Teachers of both literary studies and martial training were appointed to these academies, and the number of teachers varied between the different forms of schools.[2]

In order to prevent students form ignoring martial training, the Qing government ordered that all literary-oriented candidates of the imperial exams were required to attend an extra test in horseback archery.[3] For those students who prepared for the Imperial Martial Examinations in the academies, they were required to learn practical martial skills such as horseback archery, foot archery, and the sabre, and additionally study classics such as *Seven Military Classics*, *Biographies of the Eminent Generals*, *Classic of Filial Piety*, and *Four Books*, but traditional martial arts, such as the quan, and other weapons were excluded.

In the late Qing dynasty, these government-run academies underwent significant reformation. The traditional Chinese martial skills included in the schools, such as horseback archery, were replaced by Western forms of physical education, such as military gymnastics. In 1855, Li Hongzhang set up the Tianjin Armament Academy in Hebei. Subsequently, other provinces set up their own military academies one after another. They applied *The Western Ways of Military Training* as a handbook. Instead of practicing and learning the traditional Chinese martial skills and military classics, students were taught the methods of using firearms and cannons, as well as Western military strategies and tactics. The martial academy system, which had originated in the Song dynasty, faded out of the history of Chinese martial arts.

The flowering and decline of the Imperial Martial Examination

As mentioned above, the Qing governors claimed that they would reinforce the state's sovereignty by martial force when they conquered the central plains. In so doing, they highlighted the role of martial exams in selecting martial talents. Shunzhi (1638–1661) was enthroned as the first Qing emperor of China in 1644; the following year, he began to organize the Imperial Martial Examination.

The Imperial Martial Examination of Qing had four levels, the qualification exam, the provincial exam, the national exam, and the final imperial exam, to a great extent following the model of the Ming dynasty.

The qualification exams were held twice every three years. Anyone, regardless of age, who was not studying in the government academies, was eligible to attend. Those who qualified were enrolled as martial students in the local government-run academies.

The provincial exams were held one year after the qualification exams. All the martial students in the government academies and the soldiers from the Green Standard Army[4] were eligible to participate. The total number of candidates was restricted. However, extra quotas of candidates would be accepted in years of imperial celebration. The successful candidates were called Wujuren.

The national exams were held one year after the provincial exams. All the Wujuren and other lower ranks of military officials were eligible to take part in the exams, except for those over 60 years of age. The total number of candidates was restricted. However, an extra quota of candidates would be accepted in those years of imperial celebration. The successful candidates were called Wujinshi.

The final imperial exams were chaired by the emperors and held in the palace a month after the national exams. The results were divided into three ranks: the top three candidates as the first rank, called Wudingjia, and the best of these was selected as the Wuzhuangyuan; more than ten of the candidates made up the second rank, called Wubangyan; and the rest of the candidates were put into the third rank, called Wutanhua.

All the candidates above the level of Wujinshi were appointed as senior military officials. Even the Wujuren who failed to get a promotion to the final imperial exam still had a chance to be appointed provincial military officials.[5] In short, the qualification of Wujuren was the first step to becoming a government official, since the Wujuren also had potential to be promoted to senior military officials. The martial talents selected through the imperial martial examination enjoyed more honour than those promoted by other methods during the Qing dynasty.

The Imperial Martial Examination of Qing included a literary test and a martial test. The first part of the martial test examined the candidates' horseback archery skills, while the second part examined foot archery, bow drawing, sabre skills, and weightlifting. The successful candidates then sat the literary test, which included a section of questions and answers on traditional Chinese classics, such as *Analects* and *Mencius*, and a written thesis on the Chinese military classics, such as *The Art of War* by Sunzi, *Wuzi*, and *The Methods of Sima*. However, most of the candidates performed poorly in the literary test. Therefore, from 1795 onwards, the written test only examined the *Seven Military Classics*. From 1807, the written test in the provincial and national exams only required the candidates to write down more than 100 words from *Seven Military Classics*. Thereafter, the role of the written test in the Imperial Martial Examination was greatly reduced. Although this reformation drew more martial talents to participate in the Imperial Martial Examinations, it reduced the advantages of the literary class.

From the later period of the Qing dynasty, firearms were the primary weapon of war throughout the world. More and more firearms were put into use in the Qing army. Obviously, the purpose of the martial skills being tested in the Imperial Martial Examination was greatly weakened by this development, while the Wujuren and Wujinshi were no longer as competent in giving military training or on the battlefield as before. In 1898, the officials collectively proposed that Emperor Guangxu (1874–1908) reform the Imperial Martial Examination. They believed that firearm skills, rather than traditional martial skills, should be included in the exams. And Kang Youwei, one of the reformers in the Qing dynasty, suggested abolishing the Imperial Martial Examination altogether, and, instead, setting up the armaments schools.[6] In 1901, the Qing government formally announced the abolition of the Imperial Martial Examination.[7]

Martial arts and traditional Chinese culture

The growth of Chinese martial arts was closely connected to traditional Chinese culture. In the Qing dynasty, this connection was further amplified.

Martial arts and holism

The development of martial art theories in the Qing dynasty featured their integration with the traditional holistic ideology of the 'Oneness of Heaven and Men'. Chang Naizhou, a famous quan master of Qing, stressed that harmony of men and nature should be taken into account in practicing quan. He believed that quan practitioners should integrate their internal qi with their external bodily movements.[8]

Wu Shu, of the early Qing dynasty, regarded weapons as an extension of one's arm within the armed martial skills. In this sense, Wu suggested that martial art practitioners should integrate themselves with their weapons. For instance, the Ma Spear was short and tough and was held in the hand with the support of the wrists. However, he said that practitioners should also use their arms to support their wrists, use their bodies to support their arms, and use their feet to support their bodies to achieve this integration of body and spear.[9]

The quan and Chinese philosophy

There were various schools of quan in the Qing dynasty. Some of them were named after traditional Chinese philosophical concepts or used these concepts to elucidate the theories of their quans, such as Taijiquan, Baguazhang, and Xingyiquan.

Taijiquan came to prominence when Yang Luchan began to teach Taijiquan in Beijing between 1850 and 1875. However, Yang quan skills were taught with the Chen quan which took shape in Wen County of Henan Province in the late Ming dynasty and early Qing dynasty. There were many outstanding quan masters in the Chen family, but it is still unknown when they began to use the name of Taiji.[10] In 1852, Wu Yuxiang, who learned quan skills from Yang Luchan and Chen Qingping of the Chen family, said he had received a *Taijiquan Treatise* from his brother which was authored by Wang Zongyue of the Ming dynasty. He found that the quan skills recorded in the book were adapted from the *Taiji Illustrated* by Zhou Dunyi of the Northern Song dynasty, and were complementary of the quan skills he was learning from Yang and Chen. Wu Yuxiang handed down the *Taijiquan Treatise* to his nephew who later further adapted and promoted the philosophy of Taijiquan. Besides, Chen Xin of the Chen family authored the *Illustration of Chen Taijiquan* which also contributed to the spread of the philosophy of Taijiquan.

While Yang Luchan's Taijiquan was celebrated in Beijing, master Dong Haichuan's Baguazhang won its reputation in 1860s. Baguazhang was first called Zhuanzhang (Turning Palms) or Bagua Zhuanzhang because the quan used circling as the basic footwork. The philosophy of The Eight Diagrams theory underlay the practice of Baguazhang, which can be seen in the following cases. First, the practitioner needed to go through each position of the eight trigrams to complete the circling footwork. Second, each part of the body corresponded to a meaning of the trigrams, and these were used to designate the gestures of Baguazhang. For instance, the chest corresponded to the Li trigram which means fire, it required the practitioner to empty the qi from the chest like the hollow at the core of a flame; the abdomen corresponded to the Kan trigram, which means water, and it required the practitioner to fill the abdomen with qi like water. Third, Baguazhang is mainly based on palm skills, and its basic content was the eight skills of the palm, which, again, corresponded to the meaning of the eight trigrams.

Following Baguazhang, Xingyiquan began to be taught in Beijing by Guo Yunshen. Xingyiquan originated in the Xinyi-Liuhe Quan composed by Ji Jike in the early Qing dynasty. It was given the name of Xingyiquan by Li Feiyu in the 1850s. Xingyiquan drew on the Five Elements theory. There were five elementary quans within the Xingyiquan, each of which corresponded to one of the Five Elements in terms of its intrinsic quality. For instance, the Pao Quan (from Pao, meaning cannon) corresponds to fire. In performing the Pao Quan, the practitioner accumulated breath internally and then 'fired' the fist externally. Additionally, the five elementary quans of the Xingyiquan were also stylized according to the interaction of the Five Elements. The individual-form of Wuxing-Xiangsheng Quan stemmed from the positive 'mutually generating' chain of the Five Elements, while the paired-form of Wuxing-Xiangke Quan stemmed from the negative 'mutually overcoming' chain. Additionally, each of the five elementary quans also matched one of the Five Elements in respect of the bodily organs. For example, the Pao Quan corresponded to the heart, as revealed above, through the internal accumulation of breath required in performing the Pao Quan.

Qigong and martial arts

The fusion of qigong with martial arts emerged as early as the Song dynasty, but was recorded in more detail during the Ming dynasty. In the Qing dynasty, almost all masters absorbed qigong and its training methods to improve their practice of martial arts.

From the time of the Qing dynasty, the Shaolin monks not only practiced the quan and cudgel skills, but also neigong.[11] They compiled the *Illustration of Neigong* which included *Yijinjing*, *Baduanjin*, and *Fenxing Neiwaigong*, and took it as a guiding source for practicing martial arts.

During the reign of Emperor Qianlong (1711–1799), Chang Naizhou of Henan Province exemplified the qigong in martial arts with his rich personal exercise experience, as well as taking the principle of Yin and Yang and theory of traditional Chinese Medicine into account. In *Chang's Martial Arts Skills*, he expounded on various aspects of qigong, including the nature, operation, and cultivation of qi. Furthermore, he argued that external body movements and internal qi should also be stressed and combined with each other in practicing martial arts.

The common quans of the Qing, such as Taijiquan, Baguazhang, and Xingyiquan, particularly appreciated the practice of qi. Theoretically, these quans sought for the orderly coordination of the mind, qi, strength, movement, and gesture, so that the mind leads the qi, and the qi controls the strength, movement, and gesture. It was recommended that a practitioner study the qi first, and then the bodily movements and the qi would lead each other. The quans with this training method are called Internal Quan or Neijia Quan.

Martial arts and the populist sects and societies

The Qing government: prohibiting religion but not the quan

From ancient times, it was not uncommon for the masses to form sects or societies for their own benefit. These sects or societies often led the common people to revolt against their rulers. As a result, they were often suppressed by the government from dynasty to dynasty. As soon as the dynasty was established, the Qing government announced all those who participated in heretical activities would be severely punished.[12] The prohibition on the Society of the Heaven and the Earth was even put into the Qing statutes.

Conversely, the Qing government was tolerant of martial arts societies among the populace. In 1649, the Qing government removed the prohibition on ordinary people possessing weapons in consideration of the people's need for self-defence. From then on, except for firearms, all other cold weapons could be held by the ordinary people. Those weapons which had been confiscated by the government were to be returned.[13] Until 1900, when a number of peasant uprisings broke out, Yu Lu, Viceroy of Zhili (Hebei Province) still proposed to the emperor that martial arts should not be banned since they were an important necessity for the peasants to protect their homeland.[14]

Under these circumstances, some popular religious sects and secret societies succeeded in preaching their doctrines through practicing martial arts so as to strengthen their organization and cultivate military force.

The White Lotus and popular martial arts

The White Lotus was originally a sect of Buddhism which gradually developed into a secret anti-feudal religion and resulted in armed uprisings during the Yuan and Ming dynasties. During the Qing dynasty, the White Lotus took 'Opposing the Qing, Restoring the Ming' as its slogan and was active in the rural society of northern China. It had split into various offshoots, such as the Luo Sect, Qingshui Sect, Bagua Sect, Hongyang Sect, Sanyang Sect, Luozu Sect, Hunyuan Sect, and Wuji Sect, in order to escape the oppression of the Qing government. All of them supported 'Opposing the Qing, Restoring the Ming', and obeyed the doctrine of 'Former Heaven, Unborn Venerable Mother'.[15]

In general, the White Lotus made use of martial arts and, in return, spurred on the development of martial arts. First, the White Lotus tried to attract skillful martial artists into their organization, as noted by a proposal to Emperor Qianlong in 1740.[16] In these societies, some elite masters were often elected as leaders in uprisings against the Qing dynasty. For instance, Master Wang Lun led the Qingshui Sect in revolt against Emperor Qianlong in 1774. Meng Can and Zhang Bailu, both masters of Bagua Quan, were also involved in this campaign. In 1813, Master Feng Keshan of Meihua Quan acted as one of the Tianli Sect leaders in the revolt against the Qing dynasty.

Second, the White Lotus tried to secretly spread their doctrines and organize the anti-Qing movements under the cover of practicing martial arts. All of the rebellious leaders mentioned above, Wang Lun,[17] Meng Can, Zhang Bailu,[18] and Feng Keshan[19] conducted their anti-Qing activities in this way.

Third, the White Lotus built their own grounds to teach martial arts. In the case of the Qingshui Sect led by Wang Lun, the students were divided into the civil cohort, who practiced the qi, and the martial cohort, who practiced armed martial arts. The martial cohort had their own grounds, which welcomed non-Qingshui Sect members. In the case of the Bagua Sect, there were two captains each for the civil and martial cohorts. The martial cohort captains were responsible for the development of armed forces.

Within these two White Lotus sects, the members generally practiced quans such as Bagua Quan, Qixing Hong Quan, Meihua Quan, Liutang Quan, Yinyang Quan, and other martial art skills such as Armour of the Golden Bell, Shaozi Cudgel, and Tiger Tail Whip.

From the reign of Emperor Daoguang (1782–1850), the Qing government was challenged by both domestic and foreign military powers. More and more martial art practitioners joined the anti-imperialism and anti-feudalism movements. In this way, the Yihequan, which was subordinate to the White Lotus, rose quickly to prominence.

In Chinese, Yihequan literally means the quan of 'justice and harmony'. Before the reigns of Emperor Daoguang and Xianfeng, this so-called 'justice and harmony' effectively meant 'Opposing the Qing, Restoring the Ming' by the Yihetuan. With the outbreak of the Sino-Japanese War of 1894–1895, however, Yihequan's doctrine of 'justice and harmony' changed to one of support for the Qing government in resisting the foreign invaders. At that time, a large number of patriotic quan practitioners of different schools and levels gathered together in the Yihequan organizations to fight with the Empire against the invaders. In the western Shandong Province alone, there gathered the practitioners of the Meihua Quan, the Hong Quan, the Shen Quan, the Shaolin Quan, the Kunyang Quan, the Qingling Quan, the Yanling Quan, the Wanghu Suoyang Quan, and the Armour of the Golden Bell.

Yihequan's anti-imperial movement had strong support throughout the country. According to the records, there were over 800 grounds for the practice of quans in Chiping County of Shandong Province in 1899; and over 800 in Beijing after 1900. It dramatically pushed the development of martial arts among the masses.

The Heaven and Earth Society and popular martial arts

The Heaven and Earth Society was a secret organization formed by the lower classes in the early Qing dynasty. Although some records of the society can be found from the reigns of Emperor Kangxi (1654–1722) and Emperor Yongzheng (1678–1735), it was not until the reign of Emperor Qianlong (around 1765) that the society was formally established and began to use the name of the Heaven and Earth Society. The members called the society Hongmen. The society was also named Hongjia or Hongbang. Offshoots of the society included the Green Gang, the Dagger Society, the Double-sabre Society, the Cudgel Society, and so forth.

In the early stage, the Heaven and Earth Society mainly gathered along the waterways of Fujian and Guangdong provinces, but later it spread to the central and southern provinces such as Jiangsu, Anhui, Jiangxi, Hubei, and Sichuan. The original aims of the Society were only to promote mutual assistance and protection of its members. At the end of Emperor Qianlong's reign, it changed its aim to 'Opposing the Qing, Restoring the Ming'. The members shared the story of *The Revenge of Shaolin Temple*. It tells how Emperor Kangxi was afraid of the power of the monks in the Jiulian Mountain Shaolin Temple in Fujian to challenge the Qing government, so he gave the order to set fire to the temple one night. Only five out of the 128 monks survived, and they later created the Hongmen. However, this story is pure fabrication. It was made up to arouse anti-Qing sentiment in the people and to promote the idea that only by martial force could the Qing dynasty be overthrown.

Many members of the Heaven and Earth Society practiced quan skills. They acknowledged their membership by claiming that they learned the quan in the Shaolin Temple and put Hong Quan first. It is unclear whether or not the 'Shaolin Temple' they referred to ever actually existed. But it is certain that Hong Quan was very popular in the areas where the Society was active.

The Society of God Worshippers and popular martial arts

The Society of God Worshippers was set up by Hong Xiuquan in Hua County (now Huadu District of Guangzhou City) of Guangdong Province in 1843. It was so called because the followers regularly gathered together to worship their God. The society called upon people to worship the Huang Shangdi (God) and to annihilate the Yanluo Yao (demons, the rulers of the Qing Dynasty), so as to establish a peaceful and harmonious state. It can be seen that the Society of God Worshippers was, in effect, an anti-Qing religious organization.

In the early stages, the society preached their doctrines secretly through the practice of martial arts as other contemporary populist sects did. When Hong Xiuquan was conducting missionary work in the south-east part of Guangxi Province, he gathered people together to practice martial arts every night. Afterwards, he set up a martial arts society to promote his form of God worship.[20]

The Society of God Worshippers had encouraged the enrollment of elite martial artists since its establishment. Many of them later became prominent generals of the Taiping army or princes of the Taiping Heavenly Kingdom, for instance, Yang Xiuqing, Xiao Chaogui, Chen Yucheng, Hu Yichao, Qin Rigang, Lin Fengxiang, and others. The Prince Yi, Shi Dakai, was said to be keen on horse riding, horseback archery, the long sword, and the spear dance.[21] Shi was particularly good at quan skills and had taught hundreds of disciples in Hengyang of Hunan Province.[22]

After seven years' preparation, the Society of God Worshippers established the Taiping Heavenly Kingdom in Guangxi in 1851 and declared Nanjing the capital two years later. For 14 years, the Taiping armies were involved in an unsuccessful war with the Qing army across 18 provinces. Therefore, the newly-recruited soldiers brought new forms of martial art skills to the Taiping armies. Meanwhile, the martial arts skills of the Taiping armies had also spread to different regions.

To sum up, the popular sects and societies had utilized the practice of martial arts to preach their doctrines for the purpose of launching revolts against the

Qing government and anti-imperial campaigns, which in return had promoted the development of martial arts in the wider society. However, the mysticism inherent in the religious doctrines had played a negative role in the development of Chinese martial arts. For example, the White Lotus deceived people who practiced martial arts into believing that their god would protect them and make them invulnerable in battle, encouraging them to fight enemies who were equipped with firearms and cannons. Such deceptive principles go against the essence of Chinese martial arts.

The development of the schools of quan

Some of the schools of quan that can be seen today emerged before the Qing dynasty, but most of them took their shape during the Qing dynasty. According to documents collated between 1983 and 1986, there were more than 100 schools of quan during the Qing dynasty that have clear historical origins, principles of quan, unique styles, and independent systems. These schools of quan in the Qing dynasty mainly included: Shaolin Quan, Xinyi-Liuhe Quan, Taijiquan, Xingyiquan, Baguazhang, Baji Quan, and so on. The development of these quan schools can be broadly generalized in three ways.

Expansion of the schools of quan

Since the early Qing dynasty, some quans of the same or similar styles and characteristics were often classified into one school. In this sense, some of the schools of quans were expanded, for example, the Shaolin Quan.

At the end of the Ming dynasty, the Shaolin Temple in Mountain Song of Henan Province was destroyed. However, it was rebuilt and cherished by the Qing emperors who aimed to consolidate their rule by promoting the central plains culture, including the Buddhist culture. Therefore, the emperors' attitude towards the practice of martial arts by the Shaolin monks was one of tacit support. Consequently, the fame of Shaolin martial arts was spread further than in previous dynasties. At the same time, the practice of Shaolin martial arts spread in civil society. As a result, some quan schools with similar styles and skills claimed their origin in the Shaolin Quan. Later, there emerged a nationwide 'School of Shaolin Quan', separate from the Shaolin Quan in the Shaolin Temple. The 'Southern Shaolin Quan' was one of them, although there are no documentary records to prove the existence of the Southern Shaolin Temple.

As mentioned above, the development of the Shaolin Quan in the Qing dynasty witnessed an infusion of the practice of qigong from the *Yijinjing*, *Baduanjin*, and *Fenxing Neiwaigong*. It also demonstrates the expansion of martial art techniques within the Shaolin Quan.

Variations within the schools of quan

In the late Qing dynasty, some of the quan masters established their own schools by adapting other existing ones, for example, the Taijiquan. As mentioned above, Chen quan of Wen County in Henan Province is regarded as the originating quan of Taijiquan by some historians of martial arts. The Chen quan was only practiced and passed on within the Chen family until the years of Chen Changxing (1771–1853), of the thirteenth generation of the family, who taught Yang Luchan the Chen quan. Thereafter, a number of schools of Taijiquan emerged throughout the country. For instance, Chen Qingping (1798–1868), of the fifteenth generation of the family, invented the Zhaobao Taijiquan; He Zhaoyuan (1811–1891), disciple of Chen Qingping, later adapted the Zhaobao Taijiquan and created the He Taijiquan. Yang Luchan invented the Yang Taijiquan building on the Chen quan, while his son Yang Jianhou (1839–1917) and grandson Yang Chengfu (1883–1936) adapted the Yang Taijiquan into a martial art form which is still popular in modern-day China. Wu Yuxiang, who learned the quan both from Yang Luchan and Chen Changxing, later created the Wu Taijiquan. The Wu Taijquan was combined together with Xingyiquan and Baguazhang by Sun Lutang (1861–1933) to create the Sun Taijiquan in Republican China.

Mergers of the schools of quan

Due to the close communication between quan masters and the development of various martial arts theories within the quans, some new schools of quan were established by combining older schools during the Qing dynasty, particularly during the late Qing period. For example, the Cai-li-fo Quan was created by Chen Xiang (1805–1875) by combining the Fo Quan, Cai Quan, and Li Quan; while the Five Ancestors Quan was created by Cai Yuming (1853–1910 or 1849–1902) by merging the White Crane Quan, Hou Quan, Luohan Quan, Dazun Quan, Taizu Quan and Heyang Quan.

A selection of notable martial arts classics

Records of spear skills

Records of Spear Skills was written by Wu Shu (1611–1695), a famous martial artist of the late Ming dynasty and early Qing dynasty. He began to practice horseback archery and read *The Art of War* when he was young. In 1633, Wu began to learn spear skills from Shi Jingyan. In later years, he also practiced the Sha, Yang, and Emei spear skills, as well as the spear skills and sabre skills of *Gengyu Shengji* by Cheng Zongyou. In 1678 he wrote the *Spear Skills of Menglvtang*, which was about the spear skills he had learned from the Shaolin monk Hongzhuan. *Records of Spear Skills* runs to four volumes. Apart from Volume 3 and several sections of Volume 4, the book was mostly about the practice of spear skills. In this classic work, he detailed and theorized about the spear skills he had practiced and researched throughout his life.

Quan Classics•Compilation of Quan Skills

Yin Yinlu writes that the quan skills included in *Quan Classics•Compilation of Quan Skills* were summarized first by Xuanji, a monk of the Ming dynasty. He passed on his skills to Chen Songquan, and Chen passed on them to Zhang Minge, who finally compiled the book. During the reign of Emperor Kangxi, Zhang Kongzao added the *Quan Classics* and *Essentials of Practicing Hand Techniques* to the book. Then Cao Huandou added more notes to the book during the reign of Emperor Qianlong. The book includes two volumes, *Quan Classics* and *Compilation of Quan Skills*, covering mnemonic rhyme, recipes for the whole body, essentials for the lower body, profound essentials, essentials of practicing, quan skills and so forth.

Techniques of Internal Quan

Techniques of Internal Quan was written by Huang Baijia (1634–?) who was a scholar of the early Qing dynasty and a promoter of internal quan. Influenced by his father and other frustrated adherents of the Ming dynasty, as well as a culture during the early Qing that did not advocate practicing martial skills, Huang decided to learn internal quan from Wang Zhengnan. Seven years after Wang's death, Huang wrote *Techniques of Internal Quan* and *Biography of Wang Zhengnan*. *Techniques of Internal Quan* records the origins, hand skills, footwork, and the styles of internal quan, as well as its prohibited movements, specific movements, heart sutra, pressure points attacking skills and more. The book is an important source on the history of internal quan and its techniques.

Chang's Martial Art Skills

Chang's Martial Art Skills was written by Chang Naizhou who had learned martial arts from childhood and was adept in both literary and martial arts. He had learned sabre skills, spear skills, quan skills, and cudgels skills from various masters. Afterwards, he tried to combine different schools of martial arts, the principle of Yin and Yang, and theories of traditional Chinese Medicine, with his Chang quan skills, and finally produced *Chang's Martial Art Skills*. The original version included 131 articles on two topics, cultivating qi and military reference. In 1932, Xu Zhen reorganized the book into six volumes, comprehensively covering many aspects of the practice of qigong and martial arts.

Liuhe Quan

The surviving *Liuhe Quan* is a transcribed copy collected by Tang Hao. According to the preface, it was Ji Longfeng (1602–1680) of Shanxi Province who invented the Liuhe Quan. The skills of Liuhe Quan were derived from spear skills. Liuhe means 'six integrations' in Chinese, and these were the integration of mind and thought, qi and strength, muscle and bones, hands and feet, elbow and knee, and shoulder and hip. Liuhe Quan includes six movements, and each movement generates 12 movements, but the 12 movements are still in a sequence. This book is important in the studies of the history and tactics of Liuhe Quan.

Taijiquan

The book was authored by Li Yishe (1832–1892). Li began to learn quan from Wu Yuxiang when he was 22 years old. After ten years' practice, Li became a master of Taijiquan and compiled the *Manual of Taijiquan* during the reign of Emperor Guangxu. He also noted in the book that the first article, *Taijiquan Treatise*, was obtained from Wang Zongyue, Yandian of Wuyang County in Henan Province. But the rest of the book was the work of himself and Wu Yuxiang, or else revisions of the formulas of the Chen quan. The book has 16 articles on different aspects of Taijiquan. It is still regarded as a classic work on Taijiquan today.

Notes

1. *Manuscript of the History of Qing*. (Republic of China) Zhao Erxun. Qingshigao•Xuanju Zhi (清史稿•选举制).
2. Zhang Deze, *Investigation of the Bureaucracy of the Qing Dynasty* (Beijing: China Renmin University Press, 1981), 92–93.
3. (Republic of China) Zhao Erxun. Qingshigao•Xuanju Zhi (清史稿•选举制); (Yuan) Ma Duanlin. Wenxian Tongkao•Xuanju Kao (文献通考•选举考).
4. Green Standard Army, former armed forces of the Ming dynasty or the Han people, but incorporated into the Qing forces.
5. (Republic of China) Zhao Erxun. Qingshigao• Xuanju Zhi (清史稿•选举制).
6. (Qing) Kang Youwei. Wuxu Zougao (戊戌奏稿).
7. (Qing) Liu Jinzao. Xu Wenxian Tongkao• Xuanju Wu (续文献通考•选举五).
8. (Qing) Chang Naizhou. Chashi Wuji Shu (苌氏武技书).
9. (Ming) Wu Shu. Shoubilu•Liujia Qiangfa Shuo (手臂录•六家枪法说).
10. Gu Liuxin, *Taijiquan Skills* (Shanghai: Shanghai Education Publish House, 1982).
11. Neigong, any variety of the Chinese breathing, meditation, and spiritual disciplines associated with Taoism and martial arts.
12. (Qing) Huang Yugeng. Xuke Poxie Xiangbian (续刻破邪详辩).
13. Li Wenhai, *The History of the Qing Dynasty* (Beijing: Renmin University Press, 2000), 231.
14. Archives Department of the Palace Museum, *Historical Documents of the Yihetuan* (Beijing: Zhonghua Book Company, 1959), 69.
15. Former Heaven, the birthplace and final destination of human beings. It is equivalent to the Buddhist Pure Land or the Western Paradise. Unborn Venerable Mother refers to the Goddess of Public Religion in the Ming and Qing dynasties.

16 (Qing) Zhupidang (朱批档), 17 January 1740 (in Chinese Lunar Calendar).
17 (Qing) Qi Xuebiao. Ji Yaokou Wanglun Shimo (纪妖寇王伦始末).
18 (Qing) Junjichu Lufu Zouzhe•Nongmin Yundong (军机处录副奏折•农民运动).
19 Society for the History of Yihetuan, *Proceedings of the History of Yihetuan* (Beijing: Zhonghua Book Company, 1984), 162.
20 Investigation Group for the Literature and History of the Taiping Heavenly Kingdom of Guangxi Province, *An Investigative Report on the Revolt of the Taiping Heavenly Kingdom* (Beijing: Sanlian Publishing House, 1956).
21 (Qing) Xu Ke. Qingbai Leichao•Yixia Lei (清稗类钞•义侠类). A collection of anecdotes of the Qing dynasty.
22 (Qing) Xu Ke. Qingbai Leichao•Jiyong Lei (清稗类钞•技勇类).

Chapter 9
Martial arts in the Republic of China (1912–1949)

Overview

The Republic of China lasted for 38 years, during which it witnessed intense political unrest, clashes of different ideological trends, as well as the conflict between foreign and indigenous physical education and sports. Despite this complicated political and social environment, the development of Chinese martial arts still made some progress.

Above all, martial arts were further popularized by the formation of various societies and academies in the urban areas. The development of Chinese martial arts had continued slowly in the late Qing dynasty, but gradually gained momentum again after the Xinhai Revolution in 1911. More enlightened members of the public began to promote the idea of 'strengthening the body to strengthen the state'. The ruling classes and educationalists gathered martial arts talents and set up societies to support the development of Chinese martial arts. Many martial arts societies were set up one after another in the cities. According to incomplete statistics, there were more than 30 martial arts societies in Shanghai, including the Jingwu Athletic Association which was set up in 1910; there were 25 martial art societies in Beijing, including the Beijing Sports Research Institute which was set up in 1911; and there were more than ten martial art societies in Tianjin, including the Chinese Warrior Society which was set up in 1911. It was the same in other large and medium cities. After the foundation of the Central Guoshu Academy[1] in Nanjing in 1928, martial arts academies at provincial, municipal, and county levels were set up widely throughout China. As a result, martial arts organizations were represented in most of the urban areas of Republican China.

These urban martial arts societies and academies hired a large number of public quan masters as coaches. From then on, the teaching of Chinese martial arts broke through the familial and regional boundaries of the past. The original master-run organizational form of teaching martial arts also developed into a society-run and government-run organizational form. Since then, the orderly development of Chinese martial arts has been overseen by these organizations. For instance, the large-scale activities conducted by the Jingwu Athletic Association and Chinese

Martial Arts Association (CMAA) would determine the activities of the subordinate martial arts societies, while the overall developmental strategies of Chinese martial arts were largely decided by the Central Guoshu Academy.

Another distinguished feature in this period was that martial arts were included in the modern education system. It was a scientific and standardizing transformation of values, ways of practicing, performing, and competing, allowing these traditional cultures to accommodate modern Chinese society. Martial arts were formally included in the curriculum of physical education in schools from 1915. Since then, the practice of martial arts has transformed from a master-apprentice inheritance into a group teaching class. Meanwhile, some little-known public martial art skills that had been transmitted orally were compiled in illustrated textbooks. Furthermore, this period also saw the advent of some books introducing martial arts from a micro perspective, such as *A Brief Introduction of Chinese Martial Arts* and *Theories of Chinese Martial Arts*.

In regard to the quan skills, both practice of martial skills and qi were stressed by most schools and styles. Jiang Rongqiao simplified the qigong created by his master Zhang Zhankui into 12 sequences, which were taken as the essential movements for practicing Xingyiquan.[2] Wang Xiangzhai, building on Xingyiquan, composed the Yi Quan, which majored in the skills of health-preservation and martial techniques. In addition, there also emerged some new schools of quans combining other schools, for example, the Sun Taijiquan mentioned in the last chapter. The evolution of the quans reveals how martial arts strove to innovate to survive in modern society.

In addition, martial arts became a formal competition event of the National Games in 1933. Since then, the organization of martial arts contests followed those of sports meetings, including the selection of competing events, regulations, rules and so on. In modern China, the development of Chinese martial arts was advanced by taking into account developments in Western scientific knowledge, in areas such as physiology, anatomy, psychology, dynamics and more.

The rise and fall of the New Martial Arts of China

The compilation and promotion of the New Martial Arts of China

In the early years of the Republic of China, Ma Liang initiated the compilation and promotion of the *New Martial Arts of China*. Ma Liang (1878–1947) was born in Baoyang (now Baoding City) of Hebei Province and was a senior military official of the late Qing dynasty. Ma had composed his new style of quan skills and wrestling skills by adapting the training methods of Western military gymnastics and applying them in the armies and martial schools he was in charge of. In 1911, when Ma was serving as a military commander for the Republic of China in Shandong Province, he invited some martial arts masters to compile a new textbook named *New Martial Arts of China*. The book was revised in 1914.

With Ma Liang's great effort, his idea of promoting the book won support from the government. In 1917, the army and police systems adopted it as a compulsory training programme. In the summer of the same year, the new martial arts courses were listed as a compulsory module in physical education for all secondary schools throughout the country, and it was expanded to the higher education system later that autumn. In the autumn of 1918, the government adopted the new martial arts as the form of official physical education of the state. In the same year, Part I of Ma Liang's *New Martial Arts of China* was published by the Shanghai Commercial Press. In order to promote the *New Martial Arts of China*, Ma Liang set up a martial arts institute for the training of martial arts coaches in Ji'nan in 1914. These coaches were appointed to different regions throughout the country.

Contents of the New Martial Arts of China

The book covered four subjects: wrestling, quan-jiao (quan and footwork), cudgel skills, and sabre skills. Each subject was divided into two parts. Part I was for beginners, while Part II was for advanced learners. Part I was completed in 1918, but Part II was never finished.

The contents included in Part I were mostly about the basic movements that were easy to learn. It helped the learners to gain command of the basic martial art skills and the essential approaches to physical training. Taking quan-jiao as an example, the book contained 24 sequences. All of them were basic movements of the body, the hands, the feet, and the joints. The teaching methods of the four subjects were laid out in progressive steps, from individual gesture to group paired training.

Significance and decline of the New Martial Arts of China

Ma's work was influential in the development of Chinese martial arts. It had brought word-of-command and sectional teaching methods into Chinese martial arts teaching by learning from Western military gymnastics. Therefore, the entire teaching and learning process was further elaborated. It also contributed to the development of Chinese martial arts by causing them to be used for physical education in schools and to be further popularized by the martial arts societies and academies.

However, the promotion of the *New Martial Arts of China* came into conflict with the New Culture Movement and the May Fourth Movement in the 1910s, at a time when the Chinese people were ambivalent about the values of the old and the new. The *New Martial Arts of China* was adopted by the restorationists to spread anti-democratic ideas, while the radical democrats responded by criticizing the book. With the overt emphasis on military training, and the failure to finish the second volume, the *New Martial Arts of China* was gradually abandoned.

The thriving Jingwu Athletic Association

From Jingwu Gymnastics School to Jingwu Athletic Association

The Jingwu Athletic Association, formerly known as the Jingwu Gymnastics School, was founded by Huo Yuanjia (1869–1910). Huo was born into a family of martial artists in Jinghai (now Tianjing City) of Hebei Province. In 1909, he was invited by his friends to Shanghai and later established the Jingwu Gymnastics School in Zhabei District there. The following year, Huo agreed to restructure the Jingwu Gymnastics School into the Jingwu Gymnastics Association at the suggestion of his students, since the name and organization of a 'school' had restricted the expansion of their Jingwu martial arts. They rented the former building of the Shanghai Volunteer Corps for the association.

In July 1915, the site was destroyed by a hurricane, but a new site in the present-day Yangpu District was found in 1916 with the generous support of entrepreneurs Chen Gongzhe, Yao Chanbo, and Chen Fengyuan. The number of members increased greatly after the relocation. The founders considered that the meaning of the term 'gymnastics' was restrictive, so they changed the name again to Jingwu Athletic Association.[3] Huo Yuanjia was still honoured as the founding father of the association.

Aims and responsibilities of the Jingwu Athletic Association

The association aimed to 'strengthen the Chinese people through promoting martial arts and studying sport'.[4] Before 1915, members of the association only practiced martial arts. From 1915, however, the association brought in other forms of leisure activities and established martial arts, literary, recreation and sports, and military gymnastic departments.

The Department of Martial Arts was responsible for the promotion of martial arts. The association treated every school of martial arts coming from different regions of China equally. Martial arts taught in the association included more than 50 styles of individual quan technique, such as Tantui quan, Gongli quan, and Shizizhan quan; more than 20 styles of paired quan technique; more than ten styles of weapon technique, such as Damo Sword, Bagua Sabre, Qunyang Cudgel, and Qimen Spear; and more than 50 styles of paired weapon technique. The Department of Literary Studies was in charge of general knowledge courses, including Chinese, English, traditional Chinese painting, bookkeeping, traditional Chinese medicine, first-aid, speech, calligraphy and more. The Department of Recreation and Sports was set up to carry out recreational and sporting activities. The recreational activities included Peking music, Cantonese music, orchestral music and brass music; while sports-related activities included hunting, football, tennis, shot, discus, billiards, basketball, balance beam, skating, javelin, horizontal bar, swing, shooting and more. The Department of Military Gymnastics took charge of teaching military gymnastics. It can be seen from the divisions that the association was rooted in martial arts education, but also stressed physical, moral and intellectual education.

Expansion of the Jingwu Athletic Association

The development of the association was accelerated when it moved to its new site. More than 20 local schools, such as Nanyang Public School, Chinese Gymnastics School, and Fudan Public School; as well as some local enterprises, such as the Hengfeng Cotton Mill and the Commercial Press; and some societies, such as the Industrial Youth Inspirational Society; employed martial arts teachers from the Jingwu Athletic Association.

In order to meet the needs of the society, the association set about establishing new branches. In 1914, three branches were set up in Shanghai, in addition to one branch in Shaoxing City of Shanghai Province, the first branch outside Shanghai. The *Charter of Jingwu Athletic Association of China*, formulated in 1915, officially set the Jingwu Athletic Association of Zhejiang as the headquarters of the association in order to expand its reach. After that, branches of the Jingwu Athletic Association were set up one after another in southern China, at Hankou, Guangzhou, Foshan, Shantou, Zhaoqing, Xiamen, Nanchang, Nanning, and Tianjin. Around 1920, some Southeast Asia cities, such as Singapore and Malacca, had many Chinese inhabitants set up Jingwu branches. In some other cities of Southeast Asia, such as Hong Kong and Kuala Lumpur, they even set up women's branches or divisions. It is said that there were 42 branches and more than 400,000 members of the Jingwu Athletic Association by 1929.

The regional branches were closely coordinated by the headquarters. In relation to the teaching of martial arts, the headquarters was responsible for the appointment of the directors of the martial arts departments of the branches, as well as for sending martial arts coaches to work with the local coaches. The headquarters also issued martial arts textbooks to standardize the teaching procedures of the branches. The branches in turn sent their coaches to study in the headquarters. Regarding the association's affairs, the headquarters would send their staff to supervise and support the operation of the branches, while the branches would often report to the headquarters. In 1921, the *Central Magazine* (later renamed as *Jingwu Magazine*) was launched by the headquarters to maintain the connection with each branch, and to further popularize martial arts and the spirit of martial arts.

After the Mukden Incident in 1931, the Jingwu Athletic Association was active in anti-Japanese propaganda campaigns, which led to their being regarded as enemies by the Japanese. Therefore, the Japanese forces destroyed the headquarters of the association as soon as they conquered the Zhabei District in 1932. Although efforts were made to rebuild the association in the following years, it was attacked again during the Battle of Shanghai in 1937. Most of the collected martial arts classics and relics were destroyed by the Japanese.[5] With the victory of the Chinese in the Second Sino-Japanese War, the Jingwu Athletic Association was again reconstructed in Shanghai in late 1946. However, the Jingwu associations in Southeast Asia had continued to develop during this time.

The Central Guoshu Academy

Origin of the Central Guoshu Academy

Zhang Zhijiang, a government official of the Nanking Nationalist Government, convened 26 senior officials to support the establishment of a central guoshu academy in the second half of 1927. The proposal was approved by the central government on 15 March 1928. On 24 March, the preparatory academy was founded in Nanjing. The academy was administered and funded by the government and was mainly responsible for the training of martial arts coaches. In June 1928, the academy was formally named the Central Guoshu Academy. Zhang Zhijiang was selected as the director and Li Jinglin as the deputy director.

Improving the administrative structure of the Central Guoshu Academy

In the early period, there were two authoritative units overseeing the academy, namely, the governing and the monitoring councils. Subordinate to the two councils, the Shaolin Department and the Wudang Department were set up to take charge of the teaching affairs. The Wudang Department was responsible for Taijiquan, Baguazhang, and Xingyiquan, while the Shaolin Department was in charge of all other martial arts. This categorization was not only unscientific, it also aggravated old sectarian tensions between the different martial arts schools. Within three months of their establishment, there were fights between the departments, with even the leaders involved. Therefore, the two departments were abolished and the academy was restructured. The governing council remained the highest authority, administering three subordinate offices responsible for teaching, publishing, and general affairs. This institutionalization was formalized and written into the *Outline of the Organization of the Central Guoshu Academy* released in 1929.

In February 1929, the Nationalist Government issued an order that all provinces, cities, counties, and villages should set up martial arts academies. Meanwhile, the *Outline of the Organization of the Central Guoshu Academy* regulated that the first chairs of all local academies should be appointed by the relevant local governors or those with equivalent social prestige.

This appointment system not only guaranteed sufficient financial support from the local governments for the local martial arts academies, but also contributed to the expansion of the network of the martial arts academy system. By 1933, 25 provincial or municipal martial arts academies had been set up. There were even more academies established at the county level, for instance, 83 in Qingdao City of Shandong Province alone.

Aims and responsibilities of the Central Guoshu Academy

According to the *Outline of the Organization of the Central Guoshu Academy*, the academy aimed to promote Chinese martial arts and to improve people's health. In doing so, the academy employed a variety of scholars and practitioners to study and teach martial arts and other sports, to compile books on martial arts, and to administer routine affairs in relation to guoshu. In practice, the major responsibilities of the Central Guoshu Academy were to promote martial arts education, organize the national examinations in guoshu, and publish relevant books and periodicals.

To promote guoshu education, the Central Guoshu Academy set up different levels of classes: advanced class, teacher-training class, regular class, youth class and juvenile class. All of these classes covered both the general courses, including the 'Three Principles of the People', Chinese, geography, history, mathematics, Guoshu history, Guoshu studies, physiology, military science and music; and the technical courses, including footwork, quan skills, weapon using skills, military skills and athletics. Apart from traditional Chinese martial arts, the students also practiced foreign combat arts, such as boxing and Japanese sabre skills.

In organizing the national guoshu examination, the Central Guoshu Academy emulated the model of the old imperial martial examination and the athletic contests of that time. It followed a top-down promotion system, which included the prefectural, municipal, and provincial exams before the central exams. The guoshu examination also included the literary and martial skills exams. The central exams were initially proposed to be held annually. However, only two central exams were held before the disbanding of the Central Guoshu Academy. The first central exam was held in Nanjing in August 1928. Three hundred and thirty-three candidates from 17 provinces and municipalities and the Central Guoshu Academy attended the exam. The exam included a preliminary test and a formal test. The preliminary test examined individual skills in quan, sabre, sword, cudgel and spear, while the formal test required two candidates fight each other with different unarmed and armed martial arts. The second central exam was also held in Nanjing, in October 1933, witnessing 428 participants from 21 provinces and municipalities taking part in it. The rules of this exam were similar to the first one but this exam employed more detailed scoring methods. During the formal exam, the candidates were provided with protective clothing. Boxing was added to the exam. Women were allowed to participate in it for the first time.

From its establishment, the Central Guoshu Academy had begun compiling martial arts monographs. By 1934, 22 monographs had been published, including *Illustration of Zha Quan*, *Illustration of Qingping Sword* and *Textual Research on Shaolin and Wudang Sects*; 12 had been completed in a compilation, including *Lianbu Quan*, *Baji Quan* and *Digest of Xingyiquan*; and another 11 monographs were under way. Some of these monographs were put to use as textbooks within the Academy. In addition to monographs, the Academy also established periodicals. For example, the *Guoshu Xunkan* was published, later renamed the *Guoshu Weekly*. The local guoshu academies also founded their own periodicals. All these publications advocated the compilation of knowledge of traditional Chinese martial arts, as well as communication between martial arts organizations and practitioners from different regions.

The disbanding of the Central Guoshu Academy

With the outbreak of the Second Sino-Japanese War in the early 1930s, most of the local guoshu academies were disbanded one after another. Only those located in the areas that had not been occupied by the Japanese continued their activities, such as in Sichuan Province. On 14 August 1937, the Japanese air force bombed Nanjing and the Central Guoshu Academy was forced to move to Changsha, later to Kunming, and then to Chongqing. Without the support of the government, most of the teachers and students left during this period. When the Academy settled down in Chongqing, there were only about 20 staff and students left. In the following years, they tried to revive the importance of the Academy in Sichuan Province, but failed. In 1946, the Academy returned to Nanjing. But they did not have a building nor had they the financial resources to keep the organization running. Therefore, the organization had to announce its disbandment in 1948.

Martial arts as physical education in school

The beginning

After the Xinhai Revolution, some believed that the introduction of the firearm to China had decreased the athleticism of the Chinese people.[6] They proposed reinvigorating athleticism and a warlike ethos in the people. This vision was in accordance with the educationalists' objectives. Some schools began to put martial arts into their curricular or extracurricular activities of physical education, and used them for performance events or competitions during sports meeting. This tendency was particularly strong in the big cities, such as Beijing, Tianjin, Shanghai, and Nanjing. Therefore, some educationalists believed that martial arts were ready to play a significant part in the education system. In April 1915, the proposal to make martial arts a compulsory subject in schools was approved at the first national conference of the National Education Association.

Selection and training of the teachers

In Republican China, martial art teachers were selected in three ways. First, the schools tended to employ outstanding public martial art masters in the early stages, and this practice continued to the end of the Republican period. For example, Liu Dianchen was employed by the Beiyang Institute of Political Science and Law, Tsinghua School, Technical Institute, Yude School, and Nanyang Public School (now Shanghai Jiaotong University).

Second, the schools also employed teachers from the martial arts societies. Apart from the aforementioned case of the Shanghai Jingwu Athletic Association, martial art masters from other martial art societies such as the Beijing Sports Research Institute[7] and the Ji'nan Martial Arts School[8] were also welcomed by the local schools.

Third, the schools employed the graduates of all levels of the martial arts academies and athletic schools. On the one hand, the students of the athletic departments in normal (teacher-training) colleges and schools were required to learn martial arts skills. On the other hand, the athletic schools themselves became a reserve pool for the training of martial arts teachers. For example, the Beijing Sports College (originating from the Sports School of the Beijing Sports Research Institute), and the Sports College of the Central Guoshu Academy taught their students martial arts. So their students were eligible to teach martial arts after graduation. In addition, the Jingwu Sports Normal College, the advanced class and teacher-training class run by the Central Guoshu Academy, and the Ji'nan Martial Arts School, had also recruited students who majored in martial arts from across the nation.

The development of martial arts in schools

Since the Ministry of Education of China (MEC) had demanded all schools undertake martial arts education in 1915, voices stressing the role of martial arts in schools were continually raised at the national education conferences. Moreover, the ME had also specified the number of class hours and detailed contents for martial arts teaching in its curriculum criteria for all primary and middle schools, normal schools, and the physical education departments in colleges. However, the results were not satisfactory due to the shortage of martial arts teachers and textbooks.

According to a survey of 40 colleges and secondary schools throughout the country conducted by the Beijing Sports Research Institute in June 1924, 52.5 per cent of colleges and schools listed martial arts as a compulsory course, 22.5 per cent had carried out martial arts activities after school, and 25 per cent did not carry out martial arts activities either in school or after school.[9] In 1940, Zhang Zhijiang pointed out at the National Sporting Conference that less than 20 per cent of schools at all levels had included martial arts classes, and most of them were extracurricular.[10] It can be seen how the war with Japan had interfered with the development of martial arts in schools.

Nevertheless, the principle of teaching martial arts in schools had expanded the audience for Chinese martial arts. Collective teaching methods had also enriched the training methods of martial arts. The compilation of martial arts textbooks also proved beneficial for the compilation and theorization of traditional Chinese martial arts.

Martial arts competitions and performances

Martial arts competitions and the changing rules

In April 1923, the first National Martial Arts Meeting of China was held in Shanghai, which was the first national meeting of different martial arts in the history of sport in China. Delegates from 20 martial arts societies from Shanghai, Beijing, Tianjin, Jiangsu, and Shandong took part in the event. Rather than real competition, the participants performed their martial arts skills in individual and paired styles, while students from more than ten schools of Shanghai performed their martial arts skills in group form. The meeting did not set any evaluation criteria to rank the participants. In this sense, this event cannot be defined as an 'athletic competition'.

In 1924, martial arts were first adopted as a performance at the 3rd National Games. But it was not until the 5th National Games in 1933 that martial arts were featured as an athletic competition. Some simple rules of modern athletic competition, such as ranking the contestants in different groups by weight, were created. However, without distinguishing events by style they failed to showcase the value of martial arts contests for either the athlete or the spectator.

Building on this, the 18th North China Sports Meeting in 1934 divided the martial arts contests into individual quan skills, paired quan skills, individual weapon skills, and paired weapon skills. At the 6th National Games in 1935, the competitors were examined on their gestures, sequence, and force of the movements. Despite this, the rules were still primitive; but it showed some improvement since it included both static and dynamic posture criteria, as well as the force of the movements which is an important characteristic in martial arts.

In general, the engagement with athletic competitions accounted for some progress in the development of Chinese martial arts in Republican China. However, the Central Guoshu Academy, government-run and the highest authority administering Chinese martial arts, upheld the military values of martial arts. This can be seen in the way that the national guoshu examination was an emulation of the old feudal imperial martial examination. In this military context, Chinese martial arts could hardly be sportized, while martial arts performance could hardly transform into athletic competitions. Unfortunately, even this limited evolution ceased during the long war starting in the late 1930s.

Chinese martial arts abroad

Diffusion overseas is not a new phenomenon in the history of Chinese martial arts. Before the establishment of Republican China, martial arts were often brought abroad by Chinese emigrants or brought back to their home countries by foreign students who had studied in China. In the middle period of Republican China, martial arts masters were often sent by the headquarters of the Jingwu Athletic Association to coach in their overseas branches. Some regional martial arts societies started their own overseas performances, for instance, the Southern Fujiang Guoshu Team from Yongchun County of Fujian Province performed martial arts in many cities of Singapore and Malaysia in the autumn of 1929. Among these touring performers, the Nanyang Tour Group, jointly organized by the Central Guogshu Academy and the National Sports College, and the Chinese martial arts team, led by the China National Amateur Athletic Federation, were the most influential.

In January 1936, the Nanyang Tour Group set out with ten prominent masters led by Zhang Zhijiang. It was accompanied by a basketball team of six players. They presented 65 martial arts performances in various cities of Singapore and Malaysia. The tour lasted for three months and they returned to Shanghai on 10 April. Wherever the Nangyang Tour Group went, they received a warm welcome from both Chinese and local people.

In 1936, the 11th Olympic Games were held in Berlin, Germany. The China National Amateur Athletic Federation, acting as the Olympic organizing committee for China, decided to send a martial arts team to perform in Germany. The team was setup in May, and included nine masters, one coach, and one administrator. In late July 1936, the team held three performances in Hamburg. On the night of 11 August, they had a formal performance as part of the Olympic Games. Their performance lasted for one hour, included 20 martial arts, such as group Taiji exercises, quans, and other individual and paired weapon skills. They were warmly received by the crowd of more than 10,000 spectators. During the trip, the team was also invited to perform in Frankfurt and Munich. At each performance, the Chinese martial artists received much applause, and they were often asked to repeat parts of the performance, in particular the unarmed against spear pair, who were often asked to repeat their performance five or six times. After the performances, some of the masters were asked for their autographs. The team not only showed the world the glamour of Chinese martial arts, but also brought added honour to the Olympic delegation of China.

Reconceptualization of martial arts and notable classics

Defining martial arts in the modernizing China

After the Xinhai Revolution, Chinese society witnessed a societal and cultural conflict between Western and traditional Chinese ideologies. In the field of sport studies, this process is generally addressed by both Chinese and non-Chinese sport historians as a manifestation of the modernization or sportization of the traditional Chinese 'sporting forms'. In this sense, the sportization or athleticization mirrored the modernization and scientization in the evolution of Chinese martial arts.

On the one hand, therefore, some martial art societies began to redefine Chinese martial arts from a sporting and athletic perspective, beginning in the early years of the Republic of China. For them, martial arts were no long merely a form of fighting art, but a form of sport. For instance, the Beijing Sports (体育, Tiyu) Research Institute and Shanghai Jingwu Athletic (体育, Tiyu) Association used the term Tiyu in their names, and aimed to promote the value of martial arts as exercise. With the introduction of martial arts into physical education in schools and athletic competitions, this new conceptualization of martial arts was gradually accepted by mainstream Chinese society.

On the other hand, the promotion of athleticism had also led Chinese people to understand the nature of martial arts in a more scientific way. Chinese people, in particular in traditional society, had long been convinced that martial arts were initiated and transmitted by supernatural powers. The function of martial arts was often greatly exaggerated. Since the New Culture Movement of the 1910s, Chinese sport historians, such as Tang Hao, began to stress the value of martial arts as exercise and call for empirical research to investigate the nature and benefits of Chinese martial arts. It not only shows that Chinese people were aware of the athletic connotations of Chinese martial arts, but also demonstrates that Chinese sport historians were beginning to study Chinese martial arts from a historical materialist perspective.

Notable works on martial arts

In the Republic of China, a great number of creative works on martial arts were published. These works can be grouped into four categories. First, works on elucidating the theories of quans by drawing on the principle of Yin-yang. For instance, Chen Xin's *Illustration of Chen Taijiquan*, Sun Lutang's *The Bagua Quan* and Yu Min's *An Overview of Baguazhang* were the most remarkable productions of this category.

The second group of works was an introduction to various schools of quans. The vast majority of monographs at that time belonged to this category, which generally covered the inherent relationship, movements, formula and rhyme, essentials and style, and illustrations of extant schools of quans. For some of these monographs, the authors had tried to use their own experience to improve the skills by methods such as setting out techniques in verse. The most productive master was undoubtedly Jiang Rongqiao who authored more than 20 monographs on various martial arts, such as the Xingyiquan, Baguazhang, Taijquan, Mizong Quan, and Shaolin Quan, and various martial arts styles, such as the sabre, spear, sword, cudgel and whip. He also compiled the stories of the superb masters in the *Legend of Contemporary Martial Artists*, which introduced the schools of quans in a literary way.

The third group of works investigated the history of Chinese martial arts; these were mainly written by Tang Hao, while some were by Xu Zhen. Beginning in the late 1920s, Tang had widely collected relevant handwritten copies of public martial arts as well as conducting field research, and he later published the empirical works *The Shaolin and Wudang Sects*, *Essentials of Shaolin Quan* and *The Internal Quan*. Tang also authored *Illustrations of Chinese Martial Skills* and *Xingjianzhai Essays* which contained many records of the history of Chinese martial arts. Tang's works were quite impartial and well argued. They not only provided certain proofs to overturn long-held legends of ghosts and gods in the origins of Chinese martial arts, but also paved the way for later researchers and the establishment of the discipline of the history of Chinese martial arts.

The fourth category referred to those martial arts works learning from Western science. One form of this category included textbooks that adapted the performance of martial arts styles to a word-of-command training method by learning from the training methods of Western military gymnastics and calisthenics, such as Ma Liang's *New Martial Arts of China* and Wu Zhiqing's *Illustration of Zha Quan*. Another form consisted of works taking Western sports sciences into account, such as Xu Zhiyi's *An Elementary Introduction to Taijiquan*. It used psychology to explain the principles of driving the qi with mind and moving the body with qi in Taijiquan, and the techniques of consciousness, breathing, and movement; used physiology to explain the postural requirements of Taijiquan; and used mechanics to guide the regular pattern of using internal force in Taijiquan. The book articulated the interrelation between modern science and the practice of Taijiquan in an accessible way.

Notes

1 Guoshu was the term for martial arts adopted in the Republic of China.
2 Jiang Rongqiao, *Xinyi Muquan* (Taiyuan: Shanxi Science and Technology Press, 2002).
3 Chen Tiesheng,'The History of Jingwu-ism,' in *Biography of the Jingwu Athletic Association*, ed. Chen Tiesheng, 1919, 1–5.
4 At this stage, the sports study curriculum included physical education and Western sports.
5 China Sports History Society, *Sport in Modern China* (Beijing: Beijing Institute of Physical Education, 1989), 265–273.
6 Beijing Sports Research Institute, *Sports Periodicals* (1924).
7 Beijing Sports Research Institute, *Sports Periodicals* (1924).
8 Ma Liang, 'A Brief Overview of Martial Arts and Sports in Northern China over the Past Five Decades', *Sport and Sanitation* 3, no. 3 (1924).
9 Beijing Sports Research Institute, *Sports Periodicals* (1924).
10 The Committee of the Literature and History of Chinese Sport, 'Selected Propositions on Sport in Modern China', in *Records of Sport History (Volume 16)* (Beijing: People's Sports Press, 1991), 5–17.

Chapter 10

Martial arts in the People's Republic of China (1949–)

On 1 October 1949, the People's Republic of China (PRC) announced its establishment. Since then, the development of Chinese martial arts has achieved significant progress under a communist regime. Martial arts have not only enriched people's cultural life, but they have also invigorated their health, as well as accelerating China's cultural communication with other countries; and Chinese martial arts have earned their fame in the global community.

A new environment for the development of martial arts

Initialization (1949–mid-1960s)

The ambition of the Chinese Communist Party (CCP) in developing sport was expressed immediately when the All-China Sports Federation (ACSF) was approved to be set up in October 1949. At the preparatory meeting, Vice President Zhu De indicated the significant role of many traditional Chinese sporting forms, while Feng Wenbin, Director of the Preparatory Committee, pointed out that various kinds of Chinese martial arts should be carried out. On 10 June 1952, Chairman Mao put forward the slogan of 'Developing Sport and Strengthening People's Health' to encourage all Chinese people to participate in sports, including traditional sports such as Taijiquan, during the Second National Congress of the ACSF. After the foundation of the Ministry of Sport of China (MSC) in 1952, martial arts became regarded as a key sport to preserve and promote.

From 8–12 November 1953, the National Performance and Competition for Traditional Sports was held in Tianjin, with delegates coming from more than a dozen ethnic groups throughout China as well as the Han people. About two thirds of them were workers and peasants. Martial arts performances and contests were the major content of this event, with 145 delegates participating in 332 events. For *quan* forms alone, there were Shaolin Quan, Luohan Quan, Baji Quan, Hou Quan, Mian Quan, Zha Quan, Bagua Quan, Taijiquan, Tongbi Quan, Tanglang Quan. In addition, there were various kinds of armed martial arts performances and contests, including the sabre, the spear, the sword, the cudgel, paired fights and others. He Long, Vice Premier and Director of the MSC, spoke to journalists during the event. First, he said, there were a great many martial arts from different ethnic groups which should be classified and preserved. Second, these traditional Chinese martial arts should be easy to practice in order to better serve in strengthening people's bodies. Third, the practice of martial arts should not only retain the traditional forms, but also be open to a changing society. After this meeting, some elite delegations were invited to perform for the leaders of the central government.

With the impact of this meeting, martial arts developed rapidly throughout the country. Sport committees at all levels set up special departments and appointed cadres to administer the development of martial arts. Martial arts were warmly welcomed by the grass roots, and various martial arts organizations were rebuilt or founded. In 1954, the first national martial arts team was built through the elite martial arts masters and coaches who had been invited to perform in Beijing. From 1957, some special sports institutes and university sport departments began to add martial arts to the curriculum. With the priority given by the government, the social status of martial arts practitioners was significantly promoted. Some of them were even selected as members of the National People's Congress (NPC) or appointed to advanced positions such as professor or associate professor.

However, the unregulated administration of martial arts non-governmental organizations (NGOs) led to some issues in the development of martial arts in the mid-1950s, such as dissemination of feudalism and fraud. With the efforts of the MSC, this problem was rectified, but it's worth noting that some administrators leaned too far in the other direction and became over-conservative as a result.

After this short intermission, development continued. In 1956, the *Regulation of Sports Competitions of the People's Republic of China (Draft)* was released, which took martial arts as a performing programme to be held in a fixed term. During the12-Region Martial Arts Performances Meeting of the same year, the organizing committee set rules and ranked participants in different grades. This substantially paved the way for martial arts entering sporting competitions. Starting in 1957, the MSC conducted a nationwide forum on the study of martial arts for three consecutive years.

In September 1958, the CMAA was set up, followed shortly by the establishment of 18 provincial martial arts associations. The CMAA then invited experienced martial arts practitioners to regulate *The Rules for Martial Arts Competition*. In 1959, the National Youth Sports Meeting and the First National Games first used *The Rules* to run martial arts competitions. The implementation soon greatly facilitated the competitive level of martial arts in the provincial levels, but the rules also contained some weaknesses, such as including some gymnastic and dancing movements.

During this period, the studies of martial arts also took a step forward. Publications on different schools of martial arts merged, such as Taijiquan, Qingnian

Quan, Mian Quan, Hua Quan, Zha Quan, Quanshu Shi-er Fa, Baguazhang, Taiji Sword and Taiji Sabre. In addition, a martial arts textbook was compiled for students in university sport departments.

Impact of the Cultural Revolution (mid-1960s–mid-1970s)

China was severely damaged by ultra-conservative ideology during the Cultural Revolution. The development of martial arts was no exception. Many martial arts experts suffered persecution, and some were even imprisoned and died. Many classic martial arts works and weapons were destroyed. Training and competition were forced to shut down.

From 1972, the development of martial arts began to recover together with other sports. National performances and competitions returned. In 1974, a martial arts delegation was sent to America for mutual cultural communication. However, the development of Chinese martial arts did not completely recover until the downfall of the Gang of Four, in particular until after the 3rd Plenary Session of the 11th Central Committee.

The flowering of martial arts in post-reform China (mid-1970s to 1980s)

The 3rd Plenary Session of the 11th Central Committee, held in December 1978, was an epoch-making event which kicked off a new era in the development of Chinese martial arts. In November 1982, the MSC convened the First National Working Conference for Martial Arts in Beijing, the most important large-scale conference for martial arts in new China. More than 360 martial arts practitioners attended the conference, including the highest government officials in charge of martial arts above the provincial levels, the first chairs of sports institutes, and martial artists, professors, coaches, and participants.

The conference summarized the experiences and lessons of the development of martial arts since the founding of the PRC, and formulated the following policies and tasks in developing martial arts in post-reform China: to popularize martial arts at grass-roots level; to classfify, preserve and pass down martial arts; to develop martial arts in a scientific way; to strengthen the building of martial arts teams and organizations; to obtain support from NGOs in developing martial arts; to enhance the development of martial arts performances and competitions; to unit all martial arts practitioners and eliminate sectarianism between different schools; to reinforce moral education in the development of martial arts; to further develop the study of martial arts; and to promote Chinese martial arts overseas.

In August 1987, the MSC issued the *Decision to Intensify the Development of Martial Arts*. This decree again underlined the policies and tasks in developing martial arts of the 1982 conference. Additionally, the decree stressed developing martial arts in the education system. In December 1992, the Second

National Working Conference for Martial Arts was held in Sichuan Province with the participation of nearly 400 practitioners. The conference acknowledged the progress achieved in the past ten years and planned to give priority to the development of athletic martial arts, with the aim of making martial arts an Olympic sport. The conference also put forward the marketing of martial arts for the first time, with the implementation of a market economy in China.

Reformation was the key theme of this conference. In addition to routine affairs, the conference put the following two issues in the agenda: to set up the Research Institute of Martial Arts (RIMA) under the MSC and its provincial subordinates; and to set up an International Fund for the Development of Martial Arts. Moreover, the conference restructured the board of the CMAA and amended the *Statute of the Chinese Martial Arts Association* and the *Statute of Membership of the Chinese Martial Arts Association*, as well as giving 35 cities or counties the moniker of 'Hometown of Chinese Martial Arts'.

In sum, Chinese martial arts achieved remarkable progress and entered a period of prosperity after the 3rd Plenary Session of the 11th Central Committee.

Development of governing authorities

National level

When the MSC was founded, a special board was constituted to manage the development of traditional Chinese sports, including martial arts. In 1955, a unit under the Athletic Department of the MSC was set up to manage the development of martial arts. With its establishment in 1958, the CMAA took charge of the development of Chinese martial arts, defined as a nationwide non-governmental sports organization with independent juridical qualification and a non-profit association. The first board of the committee had 25 members. Between 1964 and 1984, the board was reconstituted five times, and was chaired consecutively by Li Menghua, Dong Shouyi, Zheng Huaixian, Huang Zhong, and Xu Cai. The sixth board of the CMAA, with 115 members, was assembled during the Second National Working Conference for Martial Arts in 1992, with Zhang Yaoting as Chairman.

In 1986, the RIMA was set up under the MSC, with Xu Cai as the first Director and later Zhang Yaoting as the second Director. In 1987, the RIMA took over the Athletic Department of the MSC to administer Chinese martial arts training and competition. In 1994, the MSC set up the Martial Arts Management Center (MAMC). Since then, the CMAA, RIMA and MAMC have been the premier authorities overseeing Chinese martial arts, with the decision-making positions of these governmental or NGOs all occupied by the same group of officials.[1]

Other levels

Since the establishment of the CMAA, a great number of martial arts associations of all levels have been set up, in particular after the First National Working Conference for Martial Arts in 1982. The provincial and municipal martial arts associations were first set up under the instruction of the MSC. The provincial associations are supervised by the CMAA, while the municipal associations are coordinated by the provincial associations. As with the CMAA, decision-making positions were taken by government officials, even though these associations were registered as NGOs.

Following the establishment of provincial and municipal martial arts associations, there emerged many lower levels of associations, such as township and district. The structure of these lower associations is roughly the same as in the provincial and municipal associations. However, the decision-makers are not compulsorily restricted to government officials. The major objective of these associations is to popularize martial arts. According to the statistics, there were more than 700 martial arts associations in 20 provincial administrative regions in 1989. An umbrella of all levels of martial arts associations from the top to the bottom had clearly formed.

Apart from the martial arts associations, martial arts clubs and academies have also been contributing since the 1950s, but it was not until the early 1980s that they came to play a significant role in developing martial arts, when the provincial clubs and academies were set up. These organizations were supervised and funded by the provincial sport committees to take charge of the development of martial arts of the provincial administrative regions jointly with the corresponding provincial martial arts associations. After the establishment of the RIMA in 1986, most provincial martial arts clubs and academies were renamed as martial arts institutes.

Martial arts in the educational system

Primary and secondary schools

Since the establishment of the PRC, the Chinese government has concerned itself with the health of the younger generations, and regarded physical education as an important means to develop full-grown men. Martial arts were also given importance as a programme of physical education in school. Martial arts were included in the *Teaching Program for Primary and Secondary Schools* issued by the MEC in 1956, the PRC's first national teaching programme. In 1961, the *National Teaching Program for Higher, Primary, and Secondary Schools* regulated that martial arts should take up six periods in primary school and eight periods in secondary schools each semester; primary school students above third grade learned basic movements and quan forms, while secondary school students learned youth and basic paired quan forms.

In the early 1990s, Member of the State Council Li Tieying repeatedly stressed that martial arts should be included in school education from primary level up, and that advocated assessment criteria should be introduced. Therefore, officials from sport and education authorities jointly made the effort to add martial arts to the *Assessment Methods of Physical Education of China* in 1993. A number of primary and secondary schools in Beijing and the suburbs of Shijiazhuang in Hebei Province were pilot schools for the formulation of detailed assessment criteria.

Additionally, some primary and secondary schools have built martial arts associations, clubs, and squads alongside regular curricular activities. Some schools are given priority and supported in developing martial arts by local sport authorities. In summary, the development of martial arts in primary and secondary schools has steadily progressed over the past three decades.

Colleges and universities

The development of martial arts in colleges and universities has also been remarkable in the PRC, which can be attributed to the superior conditions, such as well-trained teachers and playgrounds, since the 1980s when a large number of graduates of martial arts studies were allocated to colleges and universities. Their arrival not only satisfied the curricular martial arts requirement, but also set off martial arts mania on-campus.

In 1979, the First Shanghai College Martial Arts Competition was held by the Administration of Higher Education of Shanghai. In 1982, Tongji University and Peking University set up martial arts associations. Other colleges and universities throughout the country followed suit. In 1985, the General Administration of Chinese Medicine (GACM) organized the First National Martial Arts Competition for Chinese Medicine Colleges in Shenyang Chinese Medicine College of Liaoning Province, with representatives of 27 colleges competing. The second and third competitions were held in Heilongjiang Chinese Medicine College in 1987 and Shanxi Chinese Medicine College in 1990. The GACM also conducted training camps for college and university martial arts teachers. In 1992, martial arts were included in the Fourth National College Sports Meeting. In 1994, the First National Higher Education Martial Arts Meeting, organized by the MEC, was held in Peking Medical Sciences University, and from then on held annually.

Sports institutes

The development of martial arts in the sports institutes features the compilation of textbooks and the recruitment of graduate and postgraduate students for a martial arts major. In August 1958, the MSC assembled the deans of the sports institutes and for the first time proposed setting up a martial arts major. After the forum, the Beijing Institute of Physical Education and the Shanghai

Institute of Physical Education both set up martial arts departments, while other sports added martial arts as an optional course. This enhanced the role of martial arts in the sports institutes and facilitated the cultivation of teaching, training, and research talent.

In 1961, the MSC called for a number of martial arts experts to compile a general textbook, *Martial Arts (1961)*, for undergraduate students of the sports institutes, drawing on their existing teaching materials. Contributors included Chang Zhenfang, Li Tianji, Zhang Wenguang, Liu Yuhua, Cai Longyun, Xi Yuntai, Chen Changmian, Zheng Xueming, Zhai Jinsheng and so forth. In 1963, the Beijing Institute of Physical Education began to recruit postgraduate students, and over time it has produced a great number of talented martial artists. After the low point of the Cultural Revolution, from 1972 education in sports institutes began to recover, including martial arts, in particular after the restoration of the national college entrance examination in 1977.

In 1978, the MSC called for martial arts experts to revise *Martial Arts (1961)*. *Martial Arts (1978)* was a four-volume handbook with a brief history of martial arts as well as many martial arts forms and illustrated martial arts skills. In 1983, however, this large textbook was cut down into the two-volume *Martial Arts (1983)*. The first volume concerns general knowledge of martial arts and training of basic movements, while the second volume covers the training of traditional Chinese quan forms and attacking and defending techniques. The textbook was revised again in 1991, adding an introduction to martial arts classics, and martial arts terminology as an appendix.

Recruitment of master students also resumed in 1978. Postgraduate education indicated that martial arts education had become a modern, scientific discipline to foster advanced martial arts specialists. Martial arts education has been expanding in the sports institutes since the 1980s as well. In 1983, Beijing Institute of Physical Education set up a martial arts faculty (later a martial arts department). Soon afterwards, Shanghai Institute of Physical Education, Wuhan Institute of Physical Education, and Chengdu Institute of Physical Education all set up martial arts institutes. Different levels of education have also been introduced – junior college students, correspondence students, advanced classes for coaches, and training camps. These students are taught not only martial arts theories and techniques, but also general knowledge, including philosophy, plutonomy, anatomy of sport, and psychology of sport. To fulfil the requirements, undergraduate students must achieve certain standards of athletic skill and refereeing as well as be capable of leading martial arts training, teaching, and competition.

As for martial arts competition in the sports institutes, the First and Second National Martial Arts Tournament for Sports Institutes were held in Chengdu Institute of Physical Education in 1987 and Tianjin Institute of Physical Education in 1992 respectively, with all 13 sports institutes taking part. The six sports institutes under the MSC umbrella are eligible to send a delegate to participate in the annual National Martial Arts Tournament. They are Beijing Institute of

Physical Education, Shanghai Institute of Physical Education, Wuhan Institute of Physical Education, Chengdu Institute of Physical Education, Shenyang Institute of Physical Education, and Xi'an Institute of Physical Education. In addition, martial arts teachers and experts in sports institutes have contributed greatly to the study of martial arts and have published many high-quality papers and books.

Elite martial arts teams

Establishment of elite martial arts teams

The assembly of elite martial arts teams in the PRC began in the 1960s and developed rapidly from the 1980s on. In November 1953, a squad of elite martial artists was selected by the MSC during the National Performance and Competition for Traditional Sports held in Tianjin as aforementioned, and trained in the Central Sports Academy (later the Beijing Institute of Physical Education) in 1954. This was the PRC's first elite martial arts team. However, the team was disbanded in 1955.

From 1956, the National Martial Arts Performances Meeting was held annually to prepare for the First National Games in 1959. In order to achieve success in the National Games, each provincial administrative region formed a martial arts team. The players and coaches were gathered for training for weeks or even months, greatly advancing the development of elite martial arts teams in China.

In 1979, the MSC revised and issued *The Rules of Martial Arts Competition*, first regulated in 1959. According to the *Rules*, competitors had to take part in extra traditional martial arts during national competition. The expansion of the martial arts involved resulted in the further popularization of martial arts, as well as interest in participating in martial arts competitions. Consequently, more and more martial arts teams of all levels were established.

Training conditions and standards have also continued to improve since then. According to a survey of 14 provincial administrative regions in 1992, there were 49 coaches and 262 competitors in the first tier (provincial level); 218 competitors in the second tier (municipal level); 2,742 competitors in the third tier (lower than municipal level); and 43 martial-art-characteristic schools. The training system covers elite martial arts teams, specialized sports schools, amateur sports schools, and martial-art-characteristic schools.

Training of elite martial arts teams

In the 1960s, the chief training principle of martial arts was to seek for perfect structure and sequences in performing martial arts forms; increasing more exercise load or stress; stable in touching down the ground when doing jumping or floating as guided by the MSC. Outstanding martial artists in this period included Chen Daoyun of Anhui Province and Xu Qicheng of Liaoning

Province. In May 1972, the National Invitational Tournament of Martial Arts was held in Hefei in Anhui Province. In November of the same year, the National Martial Arts Performances Meeting, after a six-year hiatus, were held in Ji'nan in Shandong Province, with 21 provincial delegates attending.

Martial arts were added to the 3rd National Games in Beijing in 1975, inspiring provincial sport administrators to develop competitive martial arts. By 1978, most provincial administrative regions had built elite martial arts teams, except in remote areas such as Tibet, Inner Mongolia, and Xinjiang. In general, competitors were required to compete in an appointed set of martial arts forms, an optional set of martial arts forms, and a traditional martial art during national competition. Competitiveness was significantly promoted, in particular in Chang Quan, which added many challenging movements. Outstanding martial artists of this period included Li Lianjie and Li Xia (a woman) of Beijing, and Wang Donglian of Shanxi Province.

In the 1970s and 1980s, a great many traditional martial arts were brought to competition arenas, including quan forms such as Xingyiquan, Baguazhang, Tongbei Quan, Baji Quan, Pigua Zhang, Fanzi Quan, Zui Quan, Hou Quan, Yingzhua Quan, She Quan and Ditang Quan; weapon skills such Double Sabres, Double Spears, Double Swords, Double Hook, Changsui Double Swords, Double Daggers, Emei Ci, Bagua Sabre, Yexing Sabre, Zui Sword, Hou Cudgel, Double Whips, Jiujic Whip and Rope-dart. Paired martial arts also made progress in this period. In the past, these martial arts performances generally entailed two competitors, but now it often involved as many as five. Some martial artists unduly stressed speed and aesthetics but neglected essential skills. Therefore, the MSC regulated that basic skills would also be scored, and successfully redressed this tendency.

In the early 1990s, the MSC put forward the *Sport for all Plan* and *Olympic Strategies*. From 10–16 December 1994, the MAMC organized the National Martial Arts Training Conference in Tianjin. In response to state sport policies seeking victory, it was decided to emphasize athleticism in martial arts training in future.

The rise of public martial arts

From the early 1950s, martial arts were welcomed by workers, peasants and students. Many forms of martial arts squad were set up in villages, factories, mines, schools and government sectors, arousing mass fervour throughout the country. Although public martial arts fell out of favour in the mid-1950s and during the Cultural Revolution, they began to once more develop moderately in the pre-reform era.

After the First National Working Conference for Martial Arts in 1982, the public was allowed to set up martial arts organizations, leading to a growing number of public martial arts clubs, schools, stations and societies. A great number of public martial arts competitions of various forms and scales, as well as seminars and forums, were held.

This was unprecedented in the history of Chinese martial arts; there may have been more than 10,000 public martial arts organizations and millions of students in public martial arts schools after the 1982 Conference. In order to further popularize martial arts and honour the meritorious, the MSC organized the 'Thousand Excellent Martial Arts Instructors' campaign in 1984.

The selection of the 'Hometown of Chinese Martial Arts' was also launched in response to the rapid expansion of martial arts in the public. It was first put forward by the RIMA during a conference in Zhuzhou in Hunan Province. The official document in 1991 declared that the 'Hometown of Chinese Martial Arts' selection would take place every three years from 1992. Within seven months of the announcement, 36 cities, counties or districts had submitted applications, with 35 selected. In 1993, the MSC introduced two stipulations – the conducting of random inspections every year and a general inspection every three years, and the organization of inter-town competitions.

Martial arts competitions

Martial arts forms

The performance of martial arts forms plays a leading role in all martial arts competitions in the PRC. The following table provides a brief overview of national level martial arts forms competitions (see Table 10.1).

Sanshou

In the PRC, the term Sanshou generally refers to Jiaodi and unarmed combat of the previous ages. People tried to make these forms of martial arts into a sport event in the Republic of China era, but it was not until the establishment of the PRC that this happened. In 1978, the Athletic Department of the MSC set up an investigating group to develop Sanshou. Taking advice from veteran martial arts practitioners, the group later drafted a *Report on the Promotion of Sanshou*. In March 1979, the MSC decided to make the Sport Committee of Zhejiang Province, Beijing Institute of Physical Education, and Wuhan Institute of Physical Education pilot units. Their delegates performed Sanshou at the National Exhibition and Exchange Meeting for Martial Arts held in Nanning in Guangxi Province in May of the same year. In September, they were sent to Shijiazhuang to compete with the Hebei Province Sanshou team during the Fourth National Games. Based on these efforts, preliminary competition rules for Sanshou were drawn up.

During the National Martial Arts Performances in May 1980, the MSC brought the pilot units to Taiyuan in Shanxi Province to draft the *Competition Rules for Sanshou of China*. In May 1981, the delegations of Beijing Institute of Physical Education and Wuhan Institute of Physical Education organized an open Sanshou competition during the National Exhibition and Exchange

Meeting for Martial Arts in Shenyang, Liaoning Province. In January 1982, the MSC convened representatives from provincial sport committees and the six MSC sports institutes in Beijing and issued the *Competition Rules for Sanshou of China*. Accordingly, a nine-level weight rating system was created. From 1982, the National Athletic Martial Arts Performance was held annually with this system in place. From 1988, performances were carried out in the form of challenges. A growing number of national Sanshou invitation events were also held throughout the country.

In 1988, the CMAA, the RIMA, the Sport Committee of Zhejiang Province, and the Sport Committee of Shenzhen City jointly organized an international martial arts festival. Sixty competitors from 15 countries or regions competed in the Sanshou challenge, which lasted for three days. The foreign delegates were stunned by the superb performance of the Chinese Sanshou masters, and also began to recognize the competition rules for Sanshou.

In 1989, *Competition Rules for Sanshou* was formally published. The First National Sanshou Challenge using these rules was held in Yichun, Jiangxi Province. This was a remarkable event in the development of Sanshou. To facilitate training, the CMAA compiled *Chinese Sanshou*, a textbook published by the People's Sports Press in 1990. In February 1991, Chinese delegates won six events during the International Sanshou Invitation held in Beijing. Generally speaking, the Sanshou athletic system has taken shape in post-reform China, as noted in *The Development of Athletic Sanshou and the Building of Sanshou Teams*, a report put forward at the National Conference on the Training and Competition of Sanshou in May 1991.

Taijiquan, Taiji Sword and Taiji Tuishou competition

The quan, sword, and Tuishou of Taiji are generally categorized in the PRC as quan forms. They have been popular since the mid-1980s and have become the only quan forms with individual competition at the national level. Taijiquan often entails the 42 Sequences, the Yang, the Wu, the Chen, and the Sun forms, while Taiji sword often involves certain swordplay forms, and Taiji Tuishou often involves more paired hand skills. Taijiquan is a compulsory component of Taiji sword and Tuishou competitions.

In the mid-1980s, Taijiquan was expanding in some overseas countries. However, since Taijiquan was a popular quan form with a long history and developed theories and training methods, some Chinese sport administrators realized that the development of Taijiquan should be given priority. In so doing, the MSC required a fixed quantity of players to participate in Taijiquan competitions, to ensure the development of a reserve pool. From 22–25 April 1984, the Wuhan International Taijiquan and Sword Invitational Tournament was held, with the participation of more than 100 men and women from 18 countries and regions, including the US, Japan, Guatemala, France, Singapore, and Hong Kong.

Table 10.1 Competitions of martial arts forms at the national level between 1953 and 1997

Date	Event	Place	No. of delegates	Martial arts	Significance
8–12/11/1953	National Performance and Competition for Traditional Sports	Tianjin	145	332 martial arts performances	Elite players invited to Beijing to perform for state leaders
3/11/1956	12-Region Martial Arts Performances Meeting	Beijing	92	All martial arts categorized into quans and weapons	Trial of the preliminary competition rules for martial arts; trying to demonstrate the exercise value of martial arts with the knowledge of sports medicine
1957					The MSC accepts martial arts as a form of athletic competition
16–21/6/1957	National Martial Arts Performance Evaluation Meeting	Beijing	183 from 27 delegations		30 players win first prize, gaining 8 points out of 10
7–16/9/1958	National Martial Arts Meeting	Beijing	260 from 27 delegations	Competitors required to add one optional traditional martial art; many innovative martial arts forms emerged	
9–22/9/1958					After the National Martial Arts Meeting, the CMAA set up; *Competition Rules for Martial Arts* preliminarily drafted, allowing composition of self-invented martial arts forms
1959					*Competition Rules for Martial Arts* with specific scoring criteria officially released – a landmark in the recognition of martial arts as a form of athletic competition

Date	Event	Location	Participants	Notes	Rules
22–27/3/1959	National Youth Martial Arts Meeting	Beijing	197 from 25 delegations		Rules first adopted
22–26/9/1959	First National Games	Beijing	172 from 25 delegations	978 competitions; many innovative martial arts forms emerge	
18–25/9/1960	National Martial Arts Meeting	Zhengzhou	192 from 23 delegations	Competitions in Chang Quan, Taijiquan, long weapons, short weapons, with individual and group rankings; performances only to pick the elite and ranked in three grades	Emergence of many stunning movements
15–19/10/1963	15-region Martial Arts and Archery Championship	Shanghai	83 from 15 delegations	Ranked by group, individual (in one martial art), and individual all-round (multiple martial arts)	
12–16/9/1964	19-region Martial Arts and Archery Championship	Ji'nan	135 from 19 delegations	Various schools of traditional martial arts enrolled	
20–24/9/1965	Second National Games	Beijing	78 from 17 delegations	Various schools of traditional martial arts enrolled	
1966–1971				More than 260 performances	Not restricted to former rules
					Martial arts performances and competitions all cancelled during the Cultural Revolution
1–15/11/1972	National Martial Arts Performances Meeting	Ji'nan	360 from 21 delegations	Emergence of many innovative self-invented martial arts forms and performances of group basic skills	
23–30/8/1974	National Martial Arts Meeting	Xi'an	More than 300 from 25 delegations		

continued

Table 10.1 Continued

Date	Event	Place	No. of delegates	Martial arts	Significance
13–25/9/1975	3rd National Games	Beijing	380 from 20 delegations		Certain tendencies of dancing movements in martial arts performance
8–12/8/1977	National Martial Arts Competition	Bayannur	378 from 27 delegations	1,485 performances	
15–29/10/1978	National Martial Arts Competition	Xiangtan	More than 430 from 29 delegations		
17–28/9/1979	Fourth National Games	Shijiazhuang	336 from 28 delegations		Implementation of revised Competition Rules for Martial Arts
12–23/10/1980	National Martial Arts Performances	Kunming	21 delegations		
18–29/10/1981	National Martial Arts Performances	Fuzhou	24 delegations		Delegations allowed to choose martial arts with regional characteristics
19–27/9/1983	Fifth National Games	Shanghai	189 from 29 delegations		
1984					The term 'performance' removed, replaced by 'competition' for national martial arts competitions
27–11/5/10/1984	National Martial Arts Competition	Wuhan	296 from 27 delegations		
1985					MSC regulates the ranking system for martial arts, with five levels
21–30/5/1985	National Martial Arts Competition	Yinchuan	305 from 28 delegations		
20–25/6/1986	National Martial Arts Competition	Ji'nan	327 from 21 delegations		

22–25/9/1986	National Martial Arts Elite Competition	Nanjing	124 from 19 delegations	
1987				Martial arts accepted by Sixth National Games with 16 gold medals
3–10/6/1987	Preliminary Martial Arts Competitions of Sixth National Games	Hangzhou	376 from 35 delegations	
3–10/6/1988	National Martial Arts Competition	Changsha	330 from 31 delegations	
1989				A great number of young talents stand out MSC changes name of National Martial Arts Competition to National Martial Arts Championship; promotion and relegation system adopted for group martial arts forms competitions
1990				Martial arts accepted by Asian Games as competition sport
1991				MSC revises *Competition Rules for Martial Arts* again
1993	Seventh National Games	Chengdu		7 gold medals for martial arts
1997	Eighth National Games	Shanghai		Of 28 sports, martial arts the only one not in the Olympics; 15 gold medals designated for martial arts

In September of the same year, the National Taijiquan and Sword Invitation was held in Harbin. Afterwards, the MSC formally approved Taijiquan and sword as individual annual national competitions. After 1987, the CMAA and the RIMA often gathered together veteran Taijiquan masters and practitioners to figure out competition rules for Taijiquan and sword, and organized training camps for instructors. In 1991, the MSC formally issued *Competition Rules of Taijiquan and Sword*.

Taiji Tuishou entails strong athleticism, compared to Taijiquan and Taiji sword. At first only men were allowed to take part in competition, divided into nine weight groups. It was not until 1994 that women were allowed to compete. As early as 1979, Tuishou had been included in the National Exhibition and Exchange Meeting for Martial Arts held in Nanning, Guangxi Province. Tuishou grew as a form of sporting competition after that. In 1989, the MSC drafted the competition rules for Tuishou, then in 1991 *Competition Rules for Tuishou* was officially released. The rules were revised during the First and Second National Exhibition and Exchange Meeting for Tuishou, held in Ji'nan, Shandong Province in 1992 and Hangzhou, Zhejiang Province in 1993 respectively. The 1993 Meeting also summarized the achievement and lessons of the development of Tuishou in the past decade and assigned tasks of improving refereeing, compiling textbooks and more.

National Exhibition and Exchange Meeting for Martial Arts

The National Exhibition and Exchange Meeting for Martial Arts dates back to the late 1970s and is now one of the five major national martial arts competitions administrated by the MAMC. The meetings respond to the MSC's policy on classifying and preserving Chinese martial arts and aim to showcase the rich variety of traditional Chinese martial arts in the public society. They contain the aged group (over 60 years old), the adult group (18–59 years old), and the youth group (12–17 years old). Excellent martial arts individuals or teams are rewarded.

The First National Exhibition and Exchange Meeting for Martial Arts was held in Nanning in January 1979 and attracted 284 men and women from 29 provincial administrative regions throughout the country, as well as Hong Kong and Macau. More than 500 forms of martial arts were performed. This greatly contributed to the classification and preservation of traditional Chinese martial arts.

From 1980, the National Exhibition and Exchange Meeting for Martial Arts was held annually, but the Meetings declined due to a shortage of financial support and rigorous selection in some regions, and to inferior performances by some delegations. Therefore, the meeting began to be held only every two years from 1986. There were National Exhibition and Exchange Meetings for Martial Arts in 1988, 1991, and 1993. However, the event was still shrinking. Apart from the reasons mentioned above, there are also some inherent deficiencies in the competition system, and further reformation was necessary.

Warrior Cup

The Warrior Cup is one of the five major national martial arts competitions administered by the MAMC, in the aim of expanding the reserve pool of elite martial artists. Martial arts students in amateur sports schools overseen by the provincial sport committee, or in sports institutes, and young athletes under 15 in elite martial arts teams, are eligible to compete for the Warrior Cup.

The Warrior Cup originates from the National Martial Arts Competition for Amateur Sports Schools in 1984. In 1986, it changed its name to the National Youth Warrior Cup Martial Arts Competition. The 1986 Warrior Cup in Changchun had 142 young martial artists from 17 delegations, and the 1987 Warrior Cup in Zhengzhou attracted 189 young martial artists from 24 delegations. Between 1984 and 1993, ten Warrior Cups stimulated the development of elite martial arts at youth level. In addition, the CMAA and the RIMA compiled the Shaolin Guiding Quan in 1988 to serve the training and competition of youth martial arts.

China and the rise of the Asian and world martial arts champions

Taking the lead in organizing international and continental martial arts competitions was a major approach to the internationalization of Chinese martial arts from the early 1980s. From 22–25 April 1984, the Wuhan International Taijiquan Invitation was held, the first international competition for an individual martial art in China. More than 100 competitors from 18 countries and regions participated. In August 1985, 89 competitors from 12 countries and regions gathered in Xi'an for the First International Martial Arts Invitation, during which the preparatory committee of the International Martial Arts Federation was set up. The Second International Martial Arts Invitation was held in Tianjin in 1986, with 145 competitors from 20 countries and regions. In the 3rd International Martial Arts Invitation held in Hangzhou in 1988, the number of participants jumped to 202, from 31 countries and regions, with 531 events. This scale was unprecedented in the history of martial arts.

Meanwhile, most of the countries involved accepted the proposal of the RIMA to add Chang Quan, Nan Quan, Taijiquan, Sabre Skill, Spear Skill, Sword Skill, Cudgel Skill as major programs for the martial arts competitions in the 11th Asian Games. Moreover, the First World Martial Arts Championship was held in Beijing in October 1991, with more than 500 competitors from 40 countries and regions. Sanshou was included in the Second World Martial Arts Championship, held in Malaysia in October 1993. The International Martial Arts Federation was accepted as a member of the International Sports Federation in 1994.

Chinese martial arts have also had an active role in Asian competition since the 1980s. For instance, Chinese martial arts delegations had great achievements in the First Asian Martial Arts Championship in Japan in 1989 and the Second Championship in Hong Kong in 1989. After seven martial arts were accepted by the 11th Asian Games in 1991, martial arts were part of the First East Asian Games held in Shanghai in 1993, due to the efforts of the CMAA.

Public martial arts competitions

With the explosion of public martial arts in the 1980s, a great number of public martial arts competitions were organized throughout the country, often during regional martial arts festivals, in three major forms.

First, martial arts competitions in the revolutionary base regions – The first competition of this kind was held in Jinggangshan, Jiangxi Province in November 1990, with nine delegations from eight provinces and a total of 64 participants. Only amateurs with a *hukou* (home registration) in a revolutionary region could take part. The event was also concerned with the material and spiritual role of martial arts in constructing society in the revolutionary base regions, and the further arrangement of martial arts competitions in these areas. The second competition was held in Shanwei, Guangdong Province in December 1992, with the number of participants expanding to 295 from 32 delegations, and the addition of Sanshou.

Second, martial arts competitions in the 'Hometowns of Chinese Martial Arts' – from 26–30 August 1993; the first competition of this kind was held in Wen County in Henan Province. Delegations were sent by 34 of the 35 hometowns, bringing the overall number of delegates to over 400, consisting of amateur players of all ages and well-trained competitors. Both martial arts forms and Sanshou were included.

Third, competitions between public martial arts organizations – For instance, the First National Martial Arts Invitation for Public Organizations was held in Qionghai in Hainan Province, with 21 delegations from 18 martial arts organizations competing in martial arts forms and Sanshou for seven days. Six organizations took first prizes, while Taizhou Martial Arts Club of Zhejiang Province was group Sanshou champion.

Classification of martial arts legacies

The classification of martial arts was put on the MSC agenda in 1955. However, it was not put into practice, due to the influence of ultra-conservative ideology. In January 1979, the MSC issued *An Announcement of Classifying the Martial Arts*. Soon afterwards, a panel was set up and carried out a survey of 13 provincial administrative regions. In May of the same year, a National Exhibition and Exchange Meeting for Martial Arts of unprecedented size was held in Nanning, Guangxi Province.

Some sporting administrations and martial arts societies also began to perform regional surveys of martial arts. For instance, the Hebei Province Sport Committee and Martial Arts Society surveyed 32 counties between July 1980 and August 1982, visiting 234 martial arts masters from 77 quan schools or local martial arts societies. They also took photos of 50 masters and made detailed records of 19 types of quan, including Chuojiao Quan, Tongbei Quan, Baji Quan, Liuhe Quan and Yanqing Quan. The sport committees of Chongqing and Jiangbei County funded Master Zhao Ziqiu's martial skills. The research institute of the Sport Committee of Guangdong Province classified more than 300 types of quan from five big schools – Hong, Liu, Cai, Li and Mo. A monograph was also published. The Henan Province Sport Committee also founded a special panel for the classification of martial arts. In general, however, most regions throughout the country had not yet begun this work.

A turning point came when the MSC called for further classification and preservation of martial arts during the First National Working Conference for Martial Arts in 1982. In response, the MSC set up a special panel. In May 1983, the panel gathered representatives from provincial sport committees and the six MSC sports institutes in Nanchang. The conference requested that all units set up a special panel for the classification and preservation of martial arts, and came up with a detailed working schedule.

In 1983 and 1986, panels at all levels employed more than 8,000 staff and volunteers and spent more than one million RMB to carry out a large-scale nationwide campaign of classifying and preserving martial arts, unprecedented in history. It succeeded in identifying 129 schools of quan; collecting more than 6.5 million words on Chinese martial arts from various historical sources; and recording nearly 400 hours of martial arts from masters over 70 years old. In addition, the campaign received donations of 482 martial arts classics and 392 weapons. This campaign also stimulated the patriotism of practitioners who later played a significant role in leading the development of Chinese martial arts.

In order to showcase the achievements, national exhibitions were held in Chengde, Hebei Province in 1984 and in Beijing in 1986. A rich variety of weapons, classics, and other precious historical records were exhibited. Hundreds of relevant martial arts practitioners, even state leaders, participated. During the events, meritorious sport committees and individuals were praised and rewarded.

The study of martial arts

On 25 June 1987, the Martial Arts Society (MAS), a branch of the China Sports Science Society, was set up in Beijing, under the oversight of the RIMA. The first board had 91 members and 17 executive members, with Xu Cai as Commissioner and Zhang Shan as Secretary-General. In 1990, Xia Bohua succeeded Zhang Shan. The second board in 1992 had 80 members and 11 executive members, with Zhang Yaoting as Commissioner and Wang Yulong as Secretary-General.

The MAS is a non-governmental academic organization aiming to promote the study of martial arts. Academic martial arts societies at provincial or lower level now began to be set up. Since 1987, the RIMA and the MAS have jointly organized 11 large-scale academic activities, such as national conferences or international congresses on the study of martial arts. A total of 809 articles have been submitted and 221 accepted for these events, with more than 1,300 scholars participating. The articles have been edited and published as symposia.

Meanwhile, local martial arts societies have also organized many academic activities on the study of martial arts. For instance, the Martial Arts Society of Gansu Province and the Research Institute of the Sport Committee of Gansu Province jointly organized four national or international conferences between 1990 and 1993 and published a few symposia, including *Chinese Martial Arts and Traditional Culture* and *The Study of Martial Arts Science*. These activities have broadened the field, and research into the concepts, philosophical foundations, physiological mechanisms, technical principles, and health sciences of martial arts has also been advanced.

Furthermore, a considerable number of periodicals and monographs have emerged since the 1980s. The influential *Chinese Martial Arts* is published monthly by the CMAA; *Martial Arts and Fitness* was published bi-monthly by the New Sports Periodical Office, which folded in 1994; *Martial Arts Circles* is published monthly by the Martial Arts Society of Guangdong Province and is the most influential local periodical; *Martial Arts Soul* is published monthly by the Beijing Martial Arts Academy; *Jingwu* is published monthly by the Martial Arts Society of Heilongjiang Province; *Shaolin* and *Taiji* are published bi-monthly by the Sport Committee of Henan Province. As for monographs, there are a great number, notably including *Simplified Taijiquan*, *Youth Quans*, *Mian Quan*, *Hua Quan*, and *Notable Masters of Chinese Martial Arts*.

Internationalization

International communication of Chinese martial arts

Sport has often been used as an initial approach to diplomacy in the PRC. As early as 1960, a youth martial arts team accompanying the China sports delegation was sent to Czechoslovakia to perform at a friendship party during the Second Czechoslovakia National Athletic Meeting. This was the start of 'martial arts diplomacy' in China. At the end of the same year, a goodwill delegation led by Zhou Enlai that included a martial arts team was sent to Myanmar, with the team's performances warmly welcomed by the local people.

The Sino-US relationship was rebuilt in the early 1970s. US Secretary of State Henry Kissinger suggested that Zhou Enlai send a martial arts team to the US during ice-breaking visits. In June 1974, a Chinese martial arts delegation was invited to tour the US and Mexico, and was received by President Nixon in the White House. This visit drew extensive global attention. In September of the same year, a youth martial arts team was invited to Japan, enhancing mutual trust and friendship between China and Japan. Since then, the international communication of Chinese martial arts has become more frequent. It has not only promoted Chinese martial arts throughout the world, but has also satisfied the political needs of the Chinese government.

From the 1980s, the MSC began to internationalize Chinese martial arts in a more organized way, as suggested by the MSC during the national working conference in 1982. The CMAA sent a number of elite coaches abroad to teach martial arts, including to Mexico, Canada, the UK, Singapore, the Philippines, Australia, Italy, Thailand, Malaysia, and Nepal, and trained a great number of local martial arts instructors. Based on incomplete statistics, about 160 coaches and 71 delegates were sent out from 13 provincial administrative regions.

The CMAA and the RIMA also conducted training camps to satisfy the growing number of incoming foreign martial arts learners in China. These camps now cover a variety of cities, including Shanghai, Hangzhou, Ji'nan, Qingdao, Guangzhou, Shenzhen, and Beijing. According to a survey conducted in 11 provincial administrative regions, more than 4,000 people and 280 delegations have been received since 1982. The Beijing Institute of Physical Education has trained more than 30,000 foreign martial arts students in the past decade.

China and international martial arts organizations

In order to further promote Chinese martial arts globally, in October 1984 the CMAA invited the leaders in charge of martial arts in 12 countries and regions to Wuhan to discuss the establishment of an international martial arts organization. These included France, Italy, Japan, Mexico, the Philippines, Singapore, Sweden, the US, Thailand, and Hong Kong. The representatives signed a memo to found an international martial arts organization and agreed that China would take the lead.

During the First International Martial Arts Invitation held in Xi'an in August 1985, representatives from 17 countries and regions gathered to further discuss the issues of founding an international martial arts organization. The preparatory committee of the International Martial Arts Federation was set up in Xi'an on 26 August 1985, with its five members hailing from China, the UK, Italy, Japan, and Singapore. Xu Cai, Vice President of the CMAA, was nominated to be Director of the preparatory committee, and the secretariat was set up in Beijing. On 3 October 1990, the International Martial Arts Federation was officially established in Beijing with 38 member states, later increasing to 45. Li Menghua, former director of the MSC, was the first president.

Following the International Martial Arts Federation, continental martial arts organizations began to be formed. The European Martial Arts Society, with eight member states, was set up in Italy in November 1985; the South American Martial Arts Federation, with nine member states, was set up in Argentina in November 1986; Zaire founded the African Martial Arts Federation, with seven member states, in 1989.

In November 1986, the preparatory committee of the Asian Martial Arts Federation was set up in Tianjin, with representatives of eight countries and regions attending. The Asian Martial Arts Federation was officially founded in Yokohama, Japan on 25 September 1987, with 11 countries and regions as the first member states. Xu Cai was the first president. It was also decided that the Asian Martial Arts Championship would be held every two years. By 1994, the number of member states had grown to 25. In 1994, Yuan Weimin, director of the MSC, was selected as the second president of the Asian Martial Arts Federation.

Note

1 This composition of governing authority is also evident in the development of other sports in China under the Juguo Tizhi (whole-country support for the elite sport system) and the Olympic Strategies. It is expedient despite the overlap of politics and governance, since the officials are able to develop Chinese sports with government support, and are simultaneously qualified to participate in international sport affairs as non-government staff. For further information about centralized sport governance in China, please refer to our chapter: 'Fan Hong and Fuhua Huang', in Ian O'Boyle and Trish Bradbury (eds) (2014) *Sport Governance: An International Perspective*, London: Routledge; or a journal article focusing on the case of Chinese basketball: Fuhua Huang and Fan Hong (2015) 'Globalisation and the Governance of Chinese Sports: The Case of Chinese Basketball', *The International Journal of the History of Sport* 32(8): 1020–1043.

Index

Page numbers in **bold** denote tables, those in *italics* denote figures.

Accounts of Marvels 3, 70
Administration of Higher Education of Shanghai 194
African Martial Arts Federation 210
All-China Sports Federation (ACSF) 189
Ancient Warfare of China, The 60
An Lushan Rebellion 94
Analects 163
Analects of Confucium 31
Anecdotes of the Sui and Tang 74, 99
animal fights 49
Annals of Master Lv 2, 9, 26, 30
Announcement of Classifying the Martial Arts, An 206
Archery Silver Cup 73, 78
Archery Society 119
Armour of the Golden Bell 169
Arowasna Apocrypha 3
Array of Discipline 139, 143, 156
array-oriented battle 21, 25, 160
Art of War, The 32–33, 77, 110, 164, 172
Asian Martial Arts Championship 210; the first in Japan 206
Asian Martial Arts Federation 210
Assessment Methods of Physical Education of China 194

Ba Man Holding a Spear, The 100
Baduanjin 167, 171
Bagua: Baguazhang 34, 43n121, 166–167, 171–172, 181, 187, 191, 197; Quan 32, 168–169, 187; Sect 160, 168
Bagua Quan, The 187
Bai Juyi 83, 102
Baida 132; in Wuzazu 145; in Yongzhuang Xiapin 155

Ban Gu 47
Bao 109, 123n13
Baopuzi 76
Barchah 136
bar-lifting 52
barracks 108–109, 111, 116, 118
Batur Tengriqut 46
Bayu Dance 19, 36, 72
Beijing Martial Arts Academy 208
Beijing Sports College 184; the Sports School of the Beijing Sports Research Institute 184
Beijing Sports Research Institute 176, 184, 187
Beimeng Suoyan 99
Bian Zhuangzi 30
Bianliang 107, 121, 123
Biographical History of Eastern Han, A 56
Biographies of Eminent Monks 74
Biographies of the Eminent Generals 163
Bodhidharma 75
bodhisattva Vajrapani 74
Book of Changes 34–35
Book of Documents 5, 24
Book of Han 25, 47, 49, 52, 54, 58, 60
Book of Jin 57, 68, 70, 77–78
Book of Northern Wei 69–70, 75, 77–78
Book of Origins 3, 5, 8
Book of Rites 15–17, 19, 30
Book of Song 69
Book of Southern Qi 71, 76
Book of Sui 78, 85–87, 93, 95–96
Book of the Later Han 54, 59–60
Book of the Southern Man 40
Boshi 118
Bow, The 110

Breaking the Battle Array 100
Brief Introduction of Chinese Martial Arts and Theories of Chinese Martial Arts, A 177
Broadsword 6
bronze weapons 9, 12, 15; armour 14; arrows 16; dagger-axes 10–11, 36; halberd 11–12; sword 13, 39, 46, 56–57, 63; spear 9, 11, 63
Buddhabhadra 74–75
Buddhism 66, 73–74, 168; Zen 75

Cai-li-fo Quan 172
Cangyuan 3–4
Cao Bingren 144
Cao Mo 25
Cao Zhang 49
Cefu Yuangui 97
Central Guoshu Academy 176–178, 181–185; *Outline of the Organization of the* 181; Sports College of 184
Chai Shao 85
Chancellor on the mountain 76
Chang Naizhou 160, 165, 167, 173
Chang's Martial Art Skills 173
Chao Cuo 46–48, 59–60
Chaohua Temple 73
Chariot 9, 11–12, 15, 20–22, 24, 32, 35, 46
chariot battle 9, 12, 20–22, 24, 35
Chen Changxing 172, 187
Chen Fengyuan 179
Chen Gongzhe 179
Chen Qingping 166, 172
Chen Sheng 45
Chen Xiang 172
Chen Zhaogun 132
Cheng Zongyou 146, 148–149, 151, 156, 172
Chenqiao Mutiny 107
China Martial Arts Association (CMAA) 177, 190, 192, 199–**200**, 204–206, 208–209
China National Amateur Athletic Federation 186
China Sports Science Society 207
Chinese Communist Party (CCP) 189
Chinese Gymnastics School 180
Chinese Martial Arts and Traditional Culture 208
Chinese Warrior Society 176
Chiyou 2–3, 34, 70
Classic of Filial Piety 163

Classic of Mountains and Seas 1, 3
Classic of Poetry 9, 15, 17–19
Classic Thesis 47–49, 52
Cold Food Festival 87
Collection of Books in the Qing Dynasty, A 157
Collection of Li Bai's Works, A 86
Collection of Military Martial Arts, A 139, 145, 154
Collections of Tangut Script 135
Commentary of Zuo 15, 19, 77
Commercial Press 180
Competition Rules for Sanshou of China 199
Competition Rules for Tuishou 204
Competition Rules of Taijiquan and Sword 204
Complete Essentials for the Military Classics 134, 155–156; crossbow 111; other weapons 115–116; sabre 112; spear 114
Complete Library in Four Branches of Literature 154–155
Comprehensive Illustrated Manual of Martial Arts 154
Comprehensive Mirror in Aid of Governance 72, 88, 117
Comprehensive Statutes 95
Comprehensive Studies in Administration 100
Confucianism 31, 142, 163
Confucius 18–19, 22, 30, 31, 33
cudgel skills: in Ming 143–144, 146–148, 155–156, 167, 178; in Song 121; in Sui, Tang, Five Dynasties and Ten Kingdom 95
Cudgel Treatise 146, 148
Cuju 47, 63n9, 87
Cultural Revolution 191, 195, 197, **201**

Dafu 17–18, 41n55
dagger skills 99
dagger-axe 3–4, 6, 9–12, 19, 22, 24, 26, 36–36, 46, 100, 145
Dai people 5
Dandao Sabre Skill 151
Da-nuo-tu 48
Daoyin 75, 80n40
Dare-to-Die Society (Meiming She) 120
Decision to Intensify the Development of Martial Arts 191
Deng Zhan 52
Developing Sport and Strengthening People's Health 189, 196, **200**
Development of Athletic Sanshou and the Building of Sanshou Teams, The 199

Di 66, 77
Dian 39–40
Dian Wei 62
ding-lifting 52
Discourse of the States 21
Dong Haichuan 162, 166
Dong Shouyi 192
Dong Zhongshu 58
Dong Zhuo 54
Dongbatiao 5
Dongfang Shuo 58
Dou Fu 54
Dou Jiande 94
Double Ninth Festival 131, 138n16
Double Third Festival 131
Dragon Boat Festival 87
Dream Pool Essays 109, 135
Du Fu 90, 92
Duan Chengshi 93, 101
Duan Lun 85
duck-shooting 92
Duke Huan of Qi 25
Duke Min of Song 28
Duke Wen of Jin 15
Duke Wen of Teng 22
Duke Zhuang of Lu 15, 17
Duke Zhuang of Zheng 15
Dream Tour of Lin'an, A 122–123
Dynastic Records 100

Eight Trigrams 34, 75, 166
Eighteen Martial Skills 110, 123, 132, 140, 145–147, 155
Elementary Introduction to Taijiquan, An 188
Eleventh Olympic Games 186
Emperor Daoguang of Qing 169
Emperor Daowu 70
Emperor Duzong of Song 117
Emperor Gaozong of Song 119
Emperor Gaozu of Han 36, 47, 54, 56–58
Emperor Gaozu of Tang 86, 89, 94
Emperor Guangxu of Qing 165, 174
Emperor Houzhu of Southern Tang 87
Emperor Huhai 54
Emperor Huizong of Song 118, 120
Emperor Jiajing of Ming 147, 154
Emperor Jianwen of Ming 142
Emperor Jianwen of Southern Liang 68
Emperor Jingzong of Tang 87–88
Emperor Kangxi of Qing 169–170, 173
Emperor Liezu of Southern Tang 87
Emperor Ling of Han 58

Emperor Longqing of Ming
Emperor Qianlong of Qing 167–168, 169, 173
Emperor Qinzong of Song 135
Emperor Renzong of Song 108, 117–120
Emperor Shengzong of Liao 132
Emperor Shenzong of Song 108–111, 120
Emperor Shun of Han 54
Emperor Shunzhi of Qing 163
Emperor Taizu of Jin 128; Aguda 128–129
Emperor Taiwu of Northern Wei 74
Emperor Taizong of Tang 83–85, 89, 92, 94, 96; Li Shimin 85–86, 89
Emperor Taizong of Yuan 133
Emperor Tianqi of Ming
Emperor Wanli of Ming 141
Emperor Wen of Han 58
Emperor Wen of Sui 82, 87
Emperor Wen of Tang 87, 93
Emperor Wen of Wei 46; Cao Pi 47, 52, 60, 68
Emperor Wen of Western Wei 79
Emperor Wencheng of Northern Wei 74
Emperor Wu of Han 47, 49, 54, 60, 68–70
Emperor Wu of Jin 70
Emperor Wu of Southern Liang 73, 76
Emperor Wu of Wei 49, 68; Cao Cao 49, 62, 68, 79n1
Emperor Wuzong of Yuan 133
Emperor Xianfeng of Qing 162
Emperor Xiaohui of Western Jin 76
Emperor Xiaowen of Norther Wei 69, 73–74, 78
Emperor Xizong of Tang 88
Emperor Xuanwu of Norther Wei 77, 89
Emperor Xuanzong of Tang 87–88, 91
Emperor Yang of Sui 84
Emperor Yingzong of Song 117
Emperor Yingzong of Yuan 133
Emperor Yongle of Ming 142
Emperor Yongzheng of Qing 169
Emperor Yuanzong of Southern Tang 87
Emperor Zhangzong of Jin 128, 130
Emperor Zhengde of Ming 150
Empress Wu Zetian 84, 86, 99
Epitaph for Wang Zhengnan, The 144
Esoteric Scripture of Huangdi 33
Essential Treatise of Quan 151
Essentials of Shaolin Quan 188
European Martial Arts Society 209
Everlasting 90
Experience and Methods of Using Crossbow 146, 156

Explaining Graphs and Analyzing Characters 4
Explaining the Ancient Characters 11
Extensive Records of the Taiping Era 89
external quan 144

Fan Kuai 56–57
Fan Zeng 57
fangs 120
Feng Keshan 168
Feng Wenbin 189
Fenxing Neiwaigong 167, 171
First National Martial Arts Competition for Chinese Medicine Colleges 194
First Shanghai College Martial Arts Competition 194
Five Archeries 20, 42n71
Five Dynasties and Song 92
Five Elements 33–34, 75, 166–167
Five Ridings 20, 42n72
Five Weapons 3, 11
Five Wisdoms 21
Flail 108, 115–116
Flying Sabre to the Arrow, A 123
Former Heaven, Unborn Venerable Mother 168
Four Books 156, 163
Four Noblemen of the Warring States 25
Fu Jian 78
Fu Sheng 78
Fu Xuan 72
Fubing System 82–83, 88
Fudan Public School 180
Fujian tangshou 152
Fuxi 34

Gan Ning 62
Ganqi Dance 3, 39–40
Ge Hong 76, 96
General Administration of Chinese Medicine (GACM) 194
Geng Gong 60
Geng Ju 147
Genghis Khan 126–127, 129, 133–134
Gengyu Shengji 156
Ghost Festival 89
Good Words of Sui and Tang 72
Goulan 107, 120–122, 123n2
Green Standard Army 164, 174n4
Guan Fu 54
Guan Sheng 113
Guan Yu 60, 137

Guan Yu Attending the Banquet Alone with only A Sabre 137
Guan Zhong 21; see also Guanzi
Guanzi 15, 21
Guo Mo 70
Guo Moruo 20
Guo Yunshen 166

halberd skills 95
hand-fighting 69
Hanfeizi 1, 22, 28
Han-Jin 79, 81n61
Hanlin Academy 141
He Liangchen 139, 143, 146, 156
He Zhaoyuan 172
Heaven and Earth Society, The 169–170
Hemudu ruins 6
Hengfeng Cotton Mill 180
History of Chinese Weapons, The 136
History of Jiaodi 72, 87–88, 122
History of Ming 142, 145, 147, 156
History of Song 109–111
History of the Northern Dynasties 79
History of Yuan 128, 133
Holism 165
Hongmen 169–170; Hongjia 169; Hongbang 169
Hongmen Banquet 48, 56
Hongyang Sect 168
horseback archery: in Jin and Southern and Northern dynasties 73, 76–77, 79; in Liao, Jin, Western Xia, and Yuan 127–132, 135; in Pre-Qin 35, 69; in Sui, Tang, Five Dynasties and Ten Kingdoms 84, 86, 89, 108; in Qing 160, 163–164, 170, 172
Houyi 8
Hu Zhiyu 132
Hua Quan 208
Huainanzi 1, 3, 30, 37
Huang Baijia 156, 173
Huang Shangdi 169
Huang Zhong 192
Huang Zongxi 144
Huangdi 1–3, 5, 8, 18
Huiguang 74
Huishang Temple 73
Hundred Skills 52, 54, 64n25, 72, 86–88, 116
Hunyuan Sect 168
Huo Qubing 60
Huo Yuanjia 179

Illustrated Codes for Military Training 108
Illustration of Chen Taijiquan 166, 187
Illustration of Neigong 167
Illustration of Zha Quan 188
Illustrations of Chinese Martial Skills 188
Imperial Martial Examination 182, 185; in Sui, Tang, and Five Dynasties and Ten Kingdoms 82, 84–85; in Song 110, 117–118; in Ming 140–142; in Qing 160, 163–165
Industrial Youth Inspirational Society 180
Inquiring Balance 48
Institute of Physical Education: Beijing 194–196, 198, 209; Chengdu 195–196; Shanghai 195; Shenyang 196; Tianjin 195; Wuhan 196, 198; Xi'an 196
internal quan 32, 43n120, 144–145, 156, 167, 173, 188; Neijia Quan 167
Internal Quan, The 188
International Martial Arts Federation 205
International Taijiquan Invitation 205
iron claw 99
iron sword 8, 56, 135

Japan 82, 113, 140; early spread of Chinese martials into 62–63; the exchange of martial arts between China and 151–152; Japanese Woko 139, 143, 147–148; *New Treaties on Military Efficiency* 154; sumo 87; Tangshou was diffused in 159n80; *see also* Sino-Japanese War
Japanese Karate Originates from Fujian 152
Japanese Sports Information Chronology 63
Japanese Weapon Prevue 63
Ji Jike 166
Ji'nan Martial Arts School 184
Jia Lanpo 6
Jian Dance 100
Jiang Rongqiao 177, 187
Jiang Ziya 32
Jiangnan Military Defense Strategies and Plans 139
Jianqi dance 100
Jiaoshou 118
Jie 66, 77
Jili 115
Jingke 25, 26, 29
Jingli 141
Jingwu: *Charter of Jingwu Athletic Association of China* 180; *jingwu* 208; Jingwu Athletic Association 176, 179–181, 184, 186–187; Jingwu Gymnastics School 179; *Jingwu Magazine* 180; Jingwu Sports Normal College 184; Shanghai Jingwu Athletic 184, 187
Jingyin Mingwen 20
Jiyou 28
Jottings of Tang, The 88
Journey to Mountain Song 147, 150
judo 140, 151–152
Jurchen people 119, 126–127, 132–133, 135

Kang Youwei 165
Karate 151–152, 159n80
Khitan 35, 99, 126–127, 130–133, 135
King Cheng of Chu 15
King Jie of Xia 15
King Tang of Shang 9
King Wen of Zhao 22
King Wen of Zhou 19, 34; Ji Chang 19
King Wu of Western Zhou 18–19, 24, 32
King Wuling of Zhao 35
King Xuan 20
King Yi of Zhou 19
King Zhou of Shang 15, 18–19, 24, 72
Kok Turks people 35, 86, 89, 100
Kublai Khan 126, 134
Kunlun slave 99

Lai Dagan 77
Lan Caihe 137
lance 3, 9, 11–12, *14*, 115, 135, 145, 156
Lantern Festival 87–88
Lao-Zhuang philosophy 75
Legend of Contemporary Martial Artists 188
Legend, The 99
Li Bai 86, 96–97
Li Chengfen 146
Li Chongrun 96
Li Chuo 96
Li Cunxian 87
Li Cunxu 87
Li Feiyu 166
Li Guang 59–60
Li Guangbi 94
Li Hongzhang 163
Li Jinglin 181
Li Kaigu 99
Li Menghua 192
Li Qingzhou 87, 89
Li Shentong 85
Li Siye 95
Li Te 78

Li Teiying
Li Yuan 89; Emperor Gaozu of Tang 86, 89, 94
Li Yuanji 85, 94
Liezi 23, 30
lion dance 100, 102–103
Lishi Dance 70
Literatures of Tang 92
Liu Bang 48, 57
Liu Chong 77
Liu Dianchen 184
Liu Hongji 85
Liu Kun 68
Liu Quan 85
Liu Sheng 56
Liu Wuzhou 100
Liu Xu 49
Liu Yao 77
Liu Yuanhai 77
Liuhe Quan 174, 207; *Liuhe Quan* 174; Xinyi-Liuhe Quan 166, 171
Loyalty Society 119
Lu Su 58
Luo Sect 168
Luozu Sect 168
Luxuriant Dew of the Spring and Autumn Annals 58
Lv Bu 54
Lv Bu against with Three Men 137
Lv Qian 68

Ma Liang 177–178, 188
Ma Spear 144, 165
Maiden of the Southern Forest 29, 32
Major Events in the Ming Dynasty 150
Manual of White Crane Quan 152
Mao Yuanyi 156
Making of Emperor Gaozu of Tang, The 89
Marco Polo 136; see also *Travels of Marco Polo, The*
martial academy: in Ming 140–144; in Qing 163; in Song 117, 118–119
Martial Arts and Fitness 208
Martial Arts Circles 208
martial arts diplomacy 208
Martial Arts Management Center (MAMC) 192, 197, 204–205
Martial Arts Society (MAS) 207–208: of Guangdong Province 208; of Heilongjiang Province 208
Martial Arts Soul 208
Martial Arts 195
martial dance 82; of Jin and the Southern and Northern dynasties 72; of Pre-Qin 3–5, 18–20, 30, 36, 38 (see also Dian); of Qin and Han 48; of Sui, Tang, Five Dynasties and Ten Kingdoms 100, 102; war dance
May Fourth Movement 178
Meihua Quan 168–169
melee weapon skills: in Song 110, 117; in Sui and Tang 94
Mencius 22, 163
Meng Can 168
Meng Wanying 88–89
Meng Yuanlao 116
meteor hammer 99, 147
Methods of Sima, The 24, 32–33, 164
Mian Quan 208
military strategies 32, 110, 117–118, 128, 141, 163
Min Xin 113
Minggong 73
Ministry of Education of China (MEC) 184, 193–194
Ministry of Sport of China (MSC) 189–194
Miscellaneous History of the State of Yue and Wu 8, 26
Miscellaneous Morsels from Youyang 93, 101
Mogao Grottoes 71, 87–88
Mohism 31
Mongolian 126–128, 130–137
Mozi 22, 26, 30–31
Mubing System 107
Mukden Incident 180
Mulian Saves His Mother 123
Murong Han 77
Murong Ke 78

Nadam Fair 132, 134
Naha-Te 152
Nakhi 5
Nanyang Public School 180, 184
Nanyang Tour Group 186
National Education Association 183
National Exhibition and Exchange Meeting for Martial Arts 198, 204, 206
National Games: first 190, 196, **201**; second **201**; third 197, **202**; fourth 198; fifth **202**; sixth **203**; seventh **203**; eighth **203**
National Martial Arts Elite Competition **203**
National Martial Arts Invitation for Public Organizations 206

National Martial Arts Meeting of China 185, **200–201**
National Martial Arts Performances Meeting 196–197, **201**
National Martial Arts Tournament 195
National People's Congress (NPC) 190
National Performance and Competition for Traditional Sports 189, 196, **200**
National Sporting Conference 184
National Sports College 186
National Teaching Program for Higher, Primary, and Secondary Schools 193
National Working Conference for Martial Arts: the first 191–193, 197; the second 192
National Youth Martial Arts Meeting **201**
neishe 118–119
Neolithic Age 6–8, 36
New Book of Tang 84–85, 88, 92–97, 102
New Culture Movement 178, 187
New Martial Arts of China 177–179, 188
New Treatise on Military Efficiency 139, 152–156; archery theory and other shooting technology 146; Japanese sabre skills 151
Nie Zheng 25
Nine-rank Official System 84
North China Sports Meeting 185
Notable Masters of Chinese Martial Arts 208
Notes on the Jingchu Areas 70

Ode to Gallantry 86
Ode to Sword Dance 147
Ode to the Quan by a Taoist in Mount Emei 148
Old Book of Tang 85
Old History of the Five Dynasties 87, 99
Old Man Huang of the Eastern Sea 72
On Archery Techniques 146
On Bronze Swords and Bronze Spears 63
On Short Weapons 72
'On the Sword' 22–23
Oneness of Heaven and Men 32, 165
Opposing the Qing, Restoring the Ming 168–169
Oracle 14, 16, 18, 20, 35–36
Origin of Words and Phrase, The 71
Ouyang Yuqian 49
Overlord Society 120
Overview of Baguazhang, An 187
Overview of the Capital of Western Han 52
Overview of the State of Wu 52, 54

paired fights 48–49, 52
paizhang 71–72
Palace, The
Paleolithic Age 2
Pao Quan 166–167
Past of Lin'an, The 121
Pei Min 102
People's Republic of China (PRC) 189
Poem for Li Zhao, A 96
Poem for Zhuangyuan, A Yi 96
Prefectural Annals of Ningbo 144
Preliminary Martial Arts Competitions of Sixth National Games **203**
Prince Liu An 49
Prince of Lanling 72
Prince Wanyan Ang 133
projectile 8, 60, 93
Pu Yuan 59
Pucha Shijie 132–133, 135

Qi 32, 43n118
Qi Jiguang 33, 139, 142–143, 146, 148, 151–152, 154
Qian Liu 87; Emperor of Wu-Yue 87
Qiang 66, 77–78, 137n1
Qianshi
Qigong 167, 171, 173
Qihuda 136
Qingshui Sect 160, 168
Qiu He 85
Qiu Mu 28
Qiu Xinggong 85
Qu Yuan 22
Quan Classics: Essentials of Practicing Hand Techniques 173
Quan of Emei Taoist and Japanese Sword 154
quan-jiao (quan and footwork) 178
Questions and Replies between Emperor Taizong of Tang and Li Weigong 110

Ranqiu 31
Readings of the Taiping Era 77
Record of Biyan 75
Record of Linji 75
Record of Military Training 139, 154
Record of the Buddhist Monasteries of Luoyang, The 74
Record of The Three Kingdoms 62
Records of Armaments and Military Provisions 85, 146, 154, 156
Records of Capital Lin'an 117, 122
Records of Entertainment in Lin'an 120, 122

Records of Jiangbiao 54
Records of Origin on Things and Affairs, The 94
Records of Spear and Sabre Skills 97
Records of Spear Skills 147–148, 172
Records of the Ancient and Contemporary Sabers and Swords 76
Records of the Grand Historian 2, 5, 9, 15, 18, 22, 29–30, 35, 45, 52, 54, 56
Records of the Music Bureaus 72, 100
Records of the Odds 101
Records of the Three Kingdom 47, 54, 58, 60, 62
Records of Wuxing 87, 89
Reformation of the Military System 109
Region Martial Arts Performances Meeting 190–199
Regulation of Sports Competitions of the People's Republic of China (Draft) 190
Regulations of Assembling the Secondary Bao Supervisors for Military Training in the Capital 109
Regulations of Military Skills Test in the Capital 108
Report on the Promotion of Sanshou 198
Research Institute of Martial Arts (RIMA) 192–193
Research Institute of the Sport Committee of Guangdong Province 207; of Gansu Province 208
Revenge of Shaolin Temple, The 170
rice-ball-shooting 92
Righteousness Hall Military Martial Arts Compilation 139, 147
Rites of Zhou 5, 12, 14, 16, 26
rock painting 3–4, 37–39
rope lasso 99
Ruins of Yin 9, 16
Rules of Martial Arts Competition, The 190, 196

sabre skills; in Ming 143–144, 148, 151, 153, 155–156; in Qing 164, 172–173; in Republic of China 178, 182; in Sui and Tang 97–98
Sancai Tuhui 154–155
Sanmiao 2–3
Sanshou 198–199, 205
Sanyang Sect 168
Sengchou 74
Sequel of Biographies of Eminent Monks 73
Sequel of Comprehensive Studies in Administration 87, 155

Seven Military Classics 110, 117–118, 163–165
Shangshe 118–119
Shaolin and Taiji 208
Shaolin and Wudang Sects, The 188
Shaolin Temple Stone Tablet 86
Shaolin: cudgel skills 143; Department 181; Fujian Temple 170; martial arts in Jin and Southern and Northern dynasties 73–77; in Ming 147–148, 150, 155–156; monks 172; neigong 167; quan 144, 162, 169, 171, 187, 189, 205; Sect 140; spear 146; temple in Sui and Tang 85–86
Shaozi Cudgel 169
Sharp Sword 96
She (社) 88
She (射) 17
Shen Kuo 109, 135
Shi 41n55, 84
Shi Jilong 78
Shi Jingyan 147, 172
Shi Le 78
Shi Min 78
Shi Yanneng 87, 89
Shield Dance 39–40
Shoubei
Shu Han 58, 60
Shundi 1, 3, 18
Shuri-Te 152
Sima Xiangru 58, 60
Simafa 110
Simplified Taijiquan 208
Sinanthropus 1–2, 6
Sino-Japanese War: the first 160, 169, 181; the second 183
Six Arts 20, 30, 140
Six Codes of Tang 92, 96–97
Six Dynasties Dance 18
Six Secret Teaching 32, 110
Society of God Worshippers, The 170
Society of the Heaven and the Earth 167
Song Cunbiao 147
Song Mountain 74
Songs of Chu 9
Sorrows on the Qu River 90, 92
South American Martial Arts Federation 210
Southern Fujiang Guoshu Team 186
Southern Shaolin Quan 171
Spear of Yang Jiaoshi 154
Sport for all Plan and Olympic Strategies 197
Spring and Autumn Annals 28

Spring and Autumn Annals of the Sixteen Kingdoms 95
Spring and Autumn Annals of Wu and Yue 8, 29
Spring Autumn Annals of the Sixteen States 69
state of Cheng Han 78
State of Dai 77
State of Eastern Wu 58
State of Han 25
State of Lu 25, 28, 30
State of Song 26
State of Wu 25
State of Wu and Yue 26
State of Zheng 26
Statute of Membership of the Chinese Martial Arts Association 192
Statute of the Chinese Martial Arts Association 192
stone axe 7, 8, 36
straw-dog shooting 130–131
Strength contests 52
Study of Martial Arts Science, The 208
Su Shi 119
Suantou 115, 147
Sumo 63, 87
Sun Bin 32
Sun Bin's Art of War 32
Sun Ce 62
Sun Lutang 172
Sun Quan 58, 59, 62
Supplementary Biography of Zhuge Liang, A 59
sword dance: in Jin and the Southern and Northern dynasties 72; in Ming 147; in Qin and Han 48–49, 57; in Song 117; in Sui, Tang, Five Dynasties and Ten Kingdoms 100–102
Sword of Goujian 26
Sword of the Western Xia 135
sword-fighting 22–23, 29
swordplay 49–50
swordsmanship 14, 22–23, 26–27, 29–32, 39, 47–49, 58, 63, 76–77, 86, 96–97, 143–144, 147

Tachi 63
tactical fighting 1–2, 8, 32
Taibai Yinjing 97
Taihe Music Scores 137
Taiji Illustrated 166
Taiji Sword 191, 199, 204
Taiji Tuishou 199, 204

Taijiquan Treaties 166
Taijiquan 31–32, 162, 166, 171–172, 174, 177, 181, 188–190, 199, **201**, 204–205, 208
Taiping army 170
Taiping Heavenly Kingdom 160, 170
Taishi Ci 59
Taixi Village 11–12
Tang Hao 174, 187–188
Tang Shunzhi 139, 146, 154
Tangut 126–127, 130, 135, 137n1
Tao 32; Taoism 31–32, 54, 66, 73, 75–76, 77; Taoist 76, 96, 148, 157n35, 174n11
Tao Te Ching 32
Tao Yuanming 3
Taoan Mengyi 150
Teaching Program for Primary and Secondary Schools 193
Techniques of Internal Quan 156, 173
Temür Khan 129; Emperor Chengzong of Yuan 129
Terracotta Warriors 46, 56–57, 60, 62
Thesis of Mr Fu Ting 147
Third Plenary Session of the 11th Central Committee 191–192
Thirteen Poems on the Classic of Mountains and Seas 3
Thirty-two Forms of Quan Treatise 153
'Thousand Excellent Martial Arts Instructors' campaign 198
Three Strategies of Huang Shigong 110
three-bladed thrown spear 136
Tianli Sect 160, 168
Tiger Tail Whip 169
totemism 4–5
Toubi Futan 156
Travels of Marco Polo, The 129, 133
Treaties on Armament Technology 60
trebuchet 93–94
Tumupu Crisis 139
Turban Rebellion 147
Two Poems of Xiangpu 132

unarmed combat 27–28, 47, 49, 108, 150, 156, 198; in Liao, Jin Western Xia, and Yuan dyansties 132–134; in Pre-Qin 15–16; in Qin and Han 52–56; in Southern and Northern dynasties 70–72, 74; in Sui, Tang and Five dynasties 99–100
unshared housing and unshared farming 119
Upheaval of the Eight Princes 66

waishe 118–119
Wang Anshi 109
Wang Jingze 71
Wang Kui 85
Wang Lan 69
Wang Lun 168
Wang Mang 58
Wang Qiyao 90
Wang Renze 86
Wang Shichong 85
Wang Siyi 155
Wang Xiang 69
Wang Xin 155
Wang Yanzhang 95
Wang Yulong 208
Wang Yuzi 89
Wang Zhang 52
Wang Zongyue 166, 174
Wanyan Gouying 135
Wanyan Talan 135
warlike: ethos 49, 58–73, 183; manner 5; spirit 18, 20–21, 24, 35–36, 85–86, 127, 130, 132
Warrior Cup 205
warrior-like 19–20, 25
Washe 107, 120–122, 123n2, 133
Water Margin, The 123, 145, 150
Wei Academy 142
Wei Dao'er 89
Wei-Jin 68, 76, 79n3
Weiliaozi 32
Weisuo 142
Western Ways of Military Training, The 163
Western Wei and Northern Zhou 82
Western Zhou 5, 9–13, 15, 17–18, 32, 40n19, 78
White Crane Quan 152
White Lotus 160, 168–169, 171
willow-shooting 79, 130–131
Wokou 139, 143, 147, 152–154; *Wokou Incidents* 148
World Martial Arts Championship 205
Wu Daozi 102
Wu Guang 45
Wu Shu 147, 151, 165, 172
Wu Yuxiang 160, 166, 172, 174
Wu Zhiqing 188
Wuhua Sabre Skill 151
Wuji Sect 168
Wujinshi 164
Wujuren 164
Wusong Jiayi Wobianzhi 148
Wutanhua 164

Wuxiang Liaodong Langsi Ge 97
Wuxing-Xiangke Quan 166
Wuxing-Xiangsheng Quan 166
Wuyi 47
Wuzazu 145, 155
Wuzhuangyuan 141, 164
Wuzi 32, 77, 110, 164

Xia people 9
Xiahou Ying 57
Xialei 25
Xianbei 35, 66, 68, 77–79, 130, 137n9
Xiang Bo 57
Xiang Dance 19
Xiang Yu 57–58
Xiang Zhuang 48, 56–57
Xiang-pu-peng 88
Xiangshe 107–120, 123n3
Xiao Yan 67
Xiao-er-yuan 88
Xie Zhaozhi 145, 155
Xin Dynasty 58
Xingjianzhai Essays 188
Xingtian 3
Xingyiquan 166–167, 171–172, 177, 181, 183, 187, 197
Xinhai Revolution 176, 183, 186
Xiongnu 45–47, 56, 59–60
Xisuijing 75
Xu Cai 192
Xu Zhen 173, 188
Xu Zhiyi 188
Xue Rengui 90
Xue Zhu 26
Xueyu 118
Xunzi 18

Yamatai-koku 63
Yandi 1–3
Yang Chengfu 31, 172
Yang Luchan 162, 166, 172
Yang Xuanzhi 74
Yang Yuhuan
Yangtze River 36, 66, 75, 158n56
Yanluo Yao 169
Yao Chanbo 179
Yao Ji'er 89
Yaodi 1, 18
Yihetuan Movement 160
Yijian Shuangdiao 90
Yijinjing 75, 167, 171
Yin and Yang 29, 33–34, 47, 75, 167, 173

Index

Yin Yinlu 172
Yingzheng 25–26, 45–46, 54, 58
Yinqi Cuibian 20
Yongle Encyclopedia 123
Yongzhuang Xiaopin 155
Youruo 31
Youth Quans 208
Yu Chan 70
Yu Dayou 139, 146–148, 153, 155
Yu Jian 70
Yu Lidi 77
Yu Lu 168
Yuan Tingdong 60
Yuanhuaji 99
Yuchi Jingde 94, 132, 137
Yuchi Jingde Used a Long Whip against with the Spear 137
Yudi 2, 18
Yue 36–37
Yunjian Jottings 148
Yunnan 3–5, 39
Yuyao City 6

Zeng Congzi 26
Zhang Anguo 89
Zhang Bailu 168
Zhang Songxi 144
Zhang Yaoting 208
Zhang Zhankui 177
Zhang Zhijiang 181, 184, 186
Zhang Zhuo 74
Zhangsun Sheng 93
Zhao Kuangyin 107; Emperor Taizu of Song 107–108
Zhapu 100
Zhenfu 141
Zheng Huaixian 192
Zheng Ruozeng 139, 143, 155
Zhishi 141
Zhou Dunyi 166
Zhou Wei 97, 134, 136
Zhuangyuan Zhang Xie, The 123
Zhu De 89
Zhu Guozhen 145, 155
Zhu Shi 110
Zhu Yuanzhang 139; Emperor Hongwu of Yuan 139–140, 42
Zhuang Zhou 32
Zhuangzi 22, 23, 25, 27, 29, 32, 80n39
Zhuanzhang 166; Turning Palms 166
Zilu 22, 31
Zong Lin 70
Zongqi 141
Zou Yan 33
Zu Ti 70
Zuo Si 52, 54

Printed in the United States
By Bookmasters